Copyright © 2017 by Greg Williams. All rights res
may be used or reproduced by any means, graphi
including photocopying, recording, taping, or by a..., ... storage retrieval
system without the written permission of the author, Greg Williams, except for brief
quotations in critical articles or reviews.

~Sailors' Prayer Against Perils~

Lighten our darkness, we beseech thee, O Lord; and by thy great mercy defend us from all perils and dangers of this night; for the love of thy only Son, our Savior, Jesus Christ. Amen.

Dedication

This book is dedicated to *"The Eleven"*

My true friends and crewmates who gave their lives aboard the *Deepwater Horizon*, April 20, 2010:

Jason Anderson	**Toolpusher**
Dale Burkeen	**Crane Operator**
Don Clark	**Assistant Driller**
Steve Curtis	**Assistant Driller**
Roy Kemp	**Derrickhand**
Karl Kleppinger	**Floorhand**
Dewey Revette	**Driller**
Shane Roshto	**Floorhand**
Adam Weise	**Floorhand**
Gordon Jones	**Mud Engineer**
Blair Manuel	**Mud Engineer**

And, to those heroes who fought that fateful night to help others survive:

Chad Murray	Chief Electrician
Stan Carden	Electrical Supervisor
Randy Ezell	Senior Toolpusher
Nick Wilson	Logistics Coordinator
Karl Rhodes	Floorhand
Curt Kutcha	Master
Andrea Fleytas	Dynamic Positioning Operator
Doug Brown	Chief Mechanic
Dave Young	Dynamic Positioning Operator
Bill Francis	Rig Medic
Troy Hadaway	Rig Training Safety Coordinator
Crew of the Damon B. Bankston	Support
The NaKika Team	Support
United States Coast Guard	Support

Finally, to the many others not listed here, whose brave actions will never be forgotten.

Table of Contents

Acknowledgments iv
Preface v
Introduction 1
That Night 3
    The Cadillac El Dorado 4
Commuting! 5
    Oops! (Part I) 12
Going Off the Deep End 13
    Dale 17
Comin' & Goin' 19
    Peter 25
Constructing a Game-Changer 26
    Seasick 37
King of the Gulf: 38
    Deepwater Horizon's Star-Spangled Operations in the Gulf of Mexico 38
    Jed 45
Gettin' to the Office 46
    Sisterhood 52
Precursors: 53
    A Brief Summary of the Contractual History of the Companies & Entities Involved in the Macondo Well 53
    Rumors 59
Getting in the Seat 60
Another Day at the Office 68
    Don 79
Workin' Nights 80
    Hearing Loss 88
Cramming: It's Not Just for School 89
    Oops! (Part II) 96
Going with My Gut: No, Thank You 97
    DPOs 104
Drillers Drill—That's What We Do 105
We Live for This! 112
    Oops! (Part III) 121

Little Roughneck *122*
    Jimmy 130
The Project: *131*
  CAPM™—Continuous Annular Pressure Management **131**
    Gordon, Karl, & Greg Meche 144
Loss *145*
    Karl 150
O Fateful Night—The Incident *151*
  Views from the Rig **151**
Injustice, the American Way *166*
    Chris 173
The Aftermath *174*
    Blue Eyes 182
Memorials: Our Horizon! *184*
    Mike 187
Deepwater Horizon, The "Movie" *188*
    Adam 190
Conclusion *191*
Appreciation *192*
Glossary of Terms *194*

Table of Figures

Figure 1 RBS8D (Deepwater Horizon) in HHI Fabrication **28**
Figure 2 RSB8D in HHI Shipbuilding Yard **29**
Figure 3 Deepwater Horizon 3 Main Subassemblies in Yard **30**
Figure 4 Deepwater Horizon Deck Jacked-up Ready for Pontoon Skid **31**
Figure 5 Deepwater Horizon Subassemblies Mated **32**
Figure 6 Illustration of Deepwater Horizon Dimensions **33**
Figure 7 One (of 8) Deepwater Horizon Propulsion Thrusters **35**
Figure 8 U.S. Petroleum and Other Liquids, Consumption, Production, and Net Imports (1949-2014) **41**
Figure 9 Total Energy Production and Consumption in the Reference Case. (1980-2040) **42**
Figure 10 US Oil Production and Imports **43**

Acknowledgments

To my family:

Thank you for never giving up on me, even when I sometimes came up short. Without your help, love, kindness, and support, I would have never overcome the hardships. Without you, this tribute to *Deepwater Horizon* and her crew would never have been possible.

To the families of the lost:

My heart and the hearts of the entire oil and gas industry extend to you and your families. You have experienced the ultimate sacrifice and I pray that your losses will never be in vain. I hope this book lives up to your expectations. Within these pages will be memories and accounts of your loved ones that you haven't yet heard. I hope they will be a consolation to you. Thank you for your time, emails, phone calls, Facebook postings, and other messages you have sent to me. It has been a treasure to have learned more about your lives and the lives of my friends.

To the survivors:

None of you asked to have your lives put on television for the entire world to see. None of you asked to have your homes raided by media, your stories twisted and mutilated and turned into a spectacle. None of you asked to have a motion picture produced that portrayed your friends in their final hours, forcing you to endure their deaths over and over again; but, most of all, no one asked you to accept this reinvented story as the truth. Within the pages of this book, you will finally be able to claim the *real* story of that rig and the people who worked it. My heart goes out to each and every one of you who still to this day may be struggling with survivor's guilt, the thought that you could have possibly done something to change the tragic outcome and the events that followed. I have been blessed to call you friends, and I thank you for your contributions to this project and for your kind words of inspiration.

Preface

I still enjoy telling Deepwater Horizon family stories. Any chance I catch someone saying something about "The 11", I say, "Hold on a minute." Then I tell them a little quick story about one or two of the guys. Each time, I pick a different one. When I'm finished, I look them in the eye and say, "Now, it can't be 'the 11' anymore. Now you know something personal about 'so-n-so'. When you hear someone say, 'the 11', you'll know in your heart that it's now personal to you, too." Today, it was Karl Kleppinger.
~~Mitch Gill, BP HSE Rep, Deepwater Horizon

Throughout this book are anecdotes contributed by members of the *Deepwater Horizon* family. These were lifted almost verbatim from our *Deepwater Horizon* Family Facebook page, a place where we shared stories from the rig during the long healing process.

These vignettes add humor, reality, depth, color, pain . . . really, they allow readers to glimpse the humanity of many of the characters who worked the decks, some still with us, others passed on.

The contributor's name follows the vignette.

Introduction

"I arrived onboard in October of 2008, and worked on the Horizon until the fateful night of April 20th, 2010. The Deepwater Horizon was one of those special places that happens only once in a lifetime. This is what made it different, and special to me: There has never been a drilling rig like it, and there will probably never be. I don't know if my words can ever do it justice, but it was always like family there, and it was the best place I could think of for anyone to bust-out on."
~~Mike Glendenning, Mechanic, *Deepwater Horizon*

Nearly everybody has heard of the *Deepwater Horizon*, a remarkable drilling rig tragically lost in the U.S. Gulf of Mexico on April 20, 2010. The explosion onboard that rig took eleven lives, eight of whom were my crew and close friends, my second family.

People have formulated their own ideas about the accident, the offshore oil and gas industry, and the rig itself. Many of those notions may have been influenced by televised images, "talking heads" on various media offering opinion and conjecture, and the movie, *Deepwater Horizon*, a movie held in derision as "distorted fabrications" by those who worked and walked those decks for *Horizon's* ten years of operation.

I have undertaken this book project to tell readers the *real* story. It is a story of an industrious team of people who routinely made the impossible possible, by pushing boundaries and the limits of their equipment, never turning away from a challenge. In the 1990s-2000s, oil and gas exploration companies were making huge "plays" in the Gulf of Mexico, especially in deepwater, and the *Deepwater Horizon* and her crews were right in the thick of these discoveries.

From the construction of the rig in Ulsan, South Korea, this book chronicles the *Deepwater Horizon's* amazing discoveries and records that spanned the course of a decade. The *Horizon* crew pushed limits reaching depths the world had never before seen; depths people didn't even think possible only five years before they punched through! With advances in technology and skilled personnel, the *Deepwater Horizon* led the field in performance for the Transocean fleet, so much so that Transocean Rig Managers sent people to see what we were doing on the *Horizon* that made us so good.

In this book, I provide a historical perspective of oil, the evolution of offshore drilling, and the shaping forces behind exploration, discovery, and development that have pushed offshore drilling into deeper waters in its quest for energy beneath the seabed. I also examine the economics of the gas and oil industry, and the shortage of trained personnel needed to fill positions on these drilling units which cost more than one-half billion dollars each.

Lastly, I take readers on a whirlwind tour of the companies, mergers, and oversight organizations that created the multi-faceted dynamic at the time of the incident in 2010.

Learning hands-on at the coal face, from Floorhand to Driller, I not only try to explain offshore drilling in lay terms, I also share stories of the people and the rig we operated. These stories are where I hope the reader sees those who worked this rig as real people, the humor, fears, the dangers, the mundane, the thrills, the joys, the conditions, and eventually, the pain experienced by the survivors and the families, indeed the collective heartache of the entire *Deepwater Horizon* family. One chapter provides a unique perspective of the incident—first-hand accounts from those aboard the rig that night and others who provided direct support.

These are their words. Their stories. All heroes.

Right after a major discovery, I left *Deepwater Horizon* as a Driller in 2008, after over seven years aboard. It was my final time as part of the *Horizon* crew as Transocean reassigned me to a special project that would have aided deepwater Drillers everywhere. This new technology was eventually test-proven and targeted to be implemented on the *Deepwater Horizon*, one year before the rig moved to the fateful Macondo well. Because the industry had so over-expanded to where every offshore producer was suffering for more drilling rigs, the business decision was made not to implement this innovative technology that might have prevented the accident.

I want the truth to be known that the events that unfolded in April 2010 were one hundred percent avoidable. Notwithstanding the new technology, if the tools already in place—proper planning, in-depth engineering completed and reviewed by multiple people, and disciplined processes and approvals—were utilized, this tragedy at sea could have been avoided.

To those left behind, peace be with you. To "The Eleven", rest easy my friends.

That Night

"Some days punch us in the gut so hard it seems we can feel the whole universe gasp with despair."
~~Curtis Tyrone Jones

"Hello?" I said as I answered my cell phone, excusing myself from the table. When the phone rings that late at night, especially from a U.S. number, it's usually not good news.

I was in Halifax, Nova Scotia, on April 20th, 2010. I was having a few drinks with one of my vendors, set to start BST-Cold Water Survival Training in the morning, a requirement I had to complete to board the *Henry Goodrich* just southeast of St. Johns, Newfoundland, Canada. I was on the project team to fly out to the rig and ride it into the Cow Head shipyard facility to begin the 25-year Out-of-Service (OOS) Repairs and Upgrade in Marystown, Newfoundland.

"Greg!" It was John Carroll. "The rig is on fire, man!" He was calling me while driving his normal crew change trip from Many, Louisiana, to Port Fourchon—the same trip we used to make together. He was supposed to meet his relief, Dewey Revette, the following morning.

"What?" I asked in disbelief. "What do ya mean, the 'rig is on fire!'?"

"It's all over the news, Greg. It's bad, man." I could hear it in his voice. I looked at my watch. 11:40 p.m. U.S. Central Time. I was standing outside and it was freezing. My heart raced, my skin was burning, and I was breaking out in a sweat.

I hung up with John and called as many people as I could, to try find out what was going on. I had kept up with all my guys from the *Deepwater Horizon*. When I left the rig in March of 2008, it was like leaving my family. *How bad was the fire? Who had been rescued? Was everyone accounted for? Did anyone know anything about what happened?* All I found out was what little I gathered from the crew scheduled to shift-change the following day. And they didn't know much at all.

I ran back to the hotel, and when I got to my room, I just sat on the end of my bed watching the news, in shock. I just couldn't believe what I was seeing. There she was, my home away from home for nearly eight years of my life, engulfed in a flaming inferno lighting up the darkness of the Gulf of Mexico.

I booted up my computer and pulled up the GRS reporting system and quickly scanned the last IADC Report to see who was working night shift. A feeling in the bottom of my stomach started to rise through my chest and turned into a burning sensation in my throat. Tears streamed. I could barely breathe. That had been *my* crew that had been on tour...

The Cadillac El Dorado

I also remember going to a mandatory DWOP [Deepwater Operations] meeting in Cypress Bend, Louisiana. A good time, don't get me wrong. But, I flew from Portland, Maine, to Detroit, Michigan, and Mike Marzolf flew from Bangor to Detroit where we met up with Kenneth-Peter Hildre, and we all flew to Lafayette on the same airplane—the Captain, the Chief Mate, and the First Engineer. We each had a reserved rental car. So, I asked the Hertz lady if we could trade in our three Ford Tauruses for one Cadillac. She said, "No problem," and we all went to Cypress Bend in the same car—a brand new Cadillac El Dorado. We parked right next to the Rig Manager's, John Keeton's, truck.

He was like, "How is it you got a rental Cadillac?"

At first, I just said, "You paid for it, Keeton." Later, I was like, "Just saving the company money. One Caddy is cheaper than three Fords."

I remember that someone did put a bumper sticker on the back of the rented Cadillac. I think it was a gay pride sticker for the Captain, Chief Mate and First Engineer to ride around with! I returned that car with the sticker still on it.

Peter Cyr

Commuting!

"Myself and Billy Lawhorn were riding an S-61 to the rig when, with no warning, the gyro went out midflight. When one of those gyros goes out midflight like that, the most violent bull in the rodeo circuit cannot jerk and twist as fast as that helicopter did. I just knew we were going to crash."
~~Owen McWhorter, Subsea Engineer, *Deepwater Horizon*

On March 15th, 2008, in the wee hours of the morning, I was headed for the *Deepwater Horizon* for what I thought was a normal 14-day hitch. For me, this crew change was like any other, a long, five-hour commute to Houma, Louisiana. At the time, I lived with my wife and kids in Many, a small town in Northwest Louisiana and was lucky enough to be living near a couple of the guys (John Carroll and Mike Sepulvado), so we rotated the driving responsibilities.

My routine before each hitch was always the same. The afternoon before, while my wife was working, I'd grab a quick nap, then pack up my things and wait for the kids to get home from school. During the summers, I'd take them to baseball or softball practice, or whatever sport they were playing. After practice, we'd drive to my mom's to see her and my sister.

During those years I worked offshore, I made sure to spend time with my mom. Around 2005, she had been diagnosed with colon cancer. She made it through the treatments with a lot of love and prayer, and was now in remission. The Sundays before I left for the rig, she made it a family tradition to cook up a big, Sunday dinner. In fact, she would start preparing the meal the entire week beforehand. She always made my favorites—beef tips and gravy or fried chicken—with all the traditional sides, like cornbread, and mashed potatoes. Being from the south, there was never a meal without two things: Dr. Pepper and sweet tea. It just didn't happen. It was Biblical.

After dinner, I drove my family home and we would watch TV and wait for the guys to show up. My kids never went to sleep early on the days I left. It didn't matter if it was 10:00 p.m. or 2:00 a.m. It was just our routine. They wanted to make sure that they were still awake to get a hug and a kiss before I left. As we would drive away, they would each get an "I love you" honk.

I used those drive times to and from the heliports to do most of my thinking, about my life and about what I needed to do better as a person. Call it introspection, meditation, or "drive therapy", I have clocked thousands of thinking and driving hours while working offshore. (Later in my career, those commutes have turned into 24-hour one-way trips to international locations.)

Along the way, we always made sure to gas up somewhere, especially during hurricane season when it's especially prudent to have a full tank of gas and a little bit of cash tucked away. When there is no power, gas and are cash precious. I've heard horror stories of guys not filling up, departing the rig, and getting stranded.

No one brings any highly-valued vehicles, either. Take for instance that Porsche 911 Turbo Coupe that's parked in the driveway—don't bring that to a heliport! The dust swirling from the choppers taking off and landing all day, every day will sandblast vehicles parked in the lot all day, *every* day. Offshore commuters chose vehicles that are comfortable for long drives, easy on gas, and vehicles they're not too worried about their appearance.

Years back, I worked for Delton Kennedy, a Driller on the *Horizon* from Franklinton, Mississippi. He drove an old Chevy S-10 pick-up to and from the heliport, a small truck, but the perfect vehicle for him. It got like 35 miles a gallon and was cheap to keep running. One year, we had a hurricane coming and the Rig Manager hired trucks to transport all our vehicles from the heliport to New Orleans for safe-keeping. The vehicles were locked behind a gate and our keys left in a hotel lock box. When we ended our hitch, we took the bus to the hotel. I distinctly remember the look on Delton's face when the guys asked him, "Hey, you drive the blue S-10, right?"

"Yeah, Ole Blue, she's still runnin'."

"Can we use her for a minute when we get to town?"

"What are you talking about?"

"If no one's there to unlock the gate, we need to use Ole Blue to knock it down."

Delton's eyes got as big as saucers. "Why you want to tear my little truck up for?"

"Delton, you have the shittiest truck out of all of us," they laughed, "so we all agreed to use yours."

"And where was I for this discussion?" We arrived at the hotel, they unlocked the gate, and Delton's fine 1985, faded blue S-10 was spared any gate-ramming duties.

I locked my truck. Our hitch was about to begin, but I had actually been "at work" from the time I left the house. Every time I walked into the heliport, I felt like I was back at my old high school. The heliport was dimly lit with several television monitors broadcasting the news in the background. Rows of shelving lined the rooms, each shelf marked with a rig tag so the ground crew could easily identify which bags needed to be loaded onto which chopper. This heliport happened to be one of the "fancy" ones. At some of the others, we used our bags as pillows or foot rests.

The routine was always the same. First, I'd check-in with the Dispatcher with my body and baggage weight. Next, I'd grab a cup of coffee, and sit in one of the non-padded, hard, plastic-backed chairs to wait for the helicopter briefing.

More of the crew would straggle in before 5:30 a.m. check-in. Those that didn't live within driving distance flew into New Orleans the night before and rode the bus to

Houma. Those guys came in well-rested with a full night's sleep. Our Rig Manager, John, was good about giving folks that drove the option of staying in a hotel the night before heliport check-in. I chose not to take advantage of the hotel option for a good night's sleep. If I chose the hotel option, I would miss seeing the kids when they came home from school and enjoying that last ball practice or last hug. Spending those last few hours with my family instead of getting a good night's sleep in a hotel was an easy decision for me. I'd been doing this for my kids' entire lives. In essence, my family only had half of me. The other half was committed to the rig and my crewmates—people I considered as my second family.

When the PHI (Petroleum Helicopters, Inc.) ground staff finally called us for the helicopter briefing, everybody on that bird headed into a small room to watch a flight safety briefing on DVD. (I remember back when they had VCR tapes, and before that, when pilots gave it from the cockpit!) The briefing covered what to do in the event of a helicopter crash and basically, how to survive it if you made an intact water landing. Most helicopters crashes aren't intact water landings, but they can't train for a worst-case scenario because, well, we all know what the worst-case scenario is. We had been flying with PHI for a long time, ever since I had started on the *Horizon* in 2001. We knew most of the pilots by first name. Some fellas had flown in Vietnam, and I could tell those guys by the way they took off and landed—amazing to watch from the outside, but shitty to ride with them as a passenger.

The video usually lasted 10-15 minutes, and depending upon the tone of the person giving the briefing, it was almost a sure bet someone was going to fall asleep. Years ago, no one cared much about someone dozing off. But more recently, a PHI safety officer would step in and wake the person up and start the video over again—from the beginning! So, anyone dozing off didn't last long. The guys wanting to squeeze in that last cigarette or hit the head before getting on the helicopter would have something to say about anyone sleeping and risking a restart of the safety briefing!

After the briefing was finished, people rushed to the smoking area or the bathroom. Some of the helicopter flights were more than an hour depending on how far the rig was offshore, not a real comfortable place to be when a bathroom is needed. I have ridden in just about every type of helicopter—from the small, five-seat Bell 407s to the larger 19-seat S92s—and none of them had a bathroom. But, they did have bags in case you felt inclined!

Heading out the door, we grabbed foam ear plugs from a bin and the guys outside handed us our noise-breakers (ear muffs) for double protection. Sometimes, we donned our survival vest at the heliport door, and other times, out on the tarmac just before boarding the helo. I always tried to stay close to the end of the line so I would be one of the last on and one of the first off. I might have to sacrifice a better seat, but to me, closest to the door was the best seat in the house, even in an emergency.

The bird was full, with two pilots and eighteen others plus me, all seated, buckled up, and finally preparing to lift off. With the sun just starting to peek into the edge of the sky, the pilots started up the engines. The smell of jet fuel crept into the air once the burners ignited. Each time at this point of departure, as the blades started to rotate, my mind always took me back to the first time I ever flew in a helo.

It was the summer of 1997. I had been working on land rigs for a few years when I made the decision to go offshore to try to make a bit more money. I was flying out of Houma in a PHI chopper. In those days, the only flight safety gear available were life jackets and ear muffs, and the flight safety briefing was given by the pilots onboard from the cockpit *while* they were doing the helo pre-check. Being my first time offshore, I had no idea what to expect, so I packed everything except the kitchen sink for my seven days away from home. I was working for Hercules Offshore and heading for Rig 11 as a Floorhand.

Rig 11 was a Bethlehem jack-up built in 1969, the smallest offshore rig I have ever been on to this day, with tiny living spaces and an even a tinier rig floor. As a Floorhand, I found myself in some very tight places like the redFox Wastewater Treatment units, or the horsehead under the rig floor. Most "normal-sized" folks would have trouble getting into these places, but for a six-two guy dressing about two-fifty, it was almost impossible. Somehow, though, I managed to make it happen.

As the helo blades started turning, I was amazed that other guys on the crew were already dozing off or laying their heads down. I remember thinking that the worst times for these pilots were takeoff and landing, so I knew I wasn't going to be asleep during either! But *these* guys who had been commuting back and forth for a while seemed comfortable sleeping anywhere, anytime.

As we lifted off into the morning air, it was a cool mid-40s onshore. But as we got further out, it started to warm up, causing the fog to lay in thick. I could see the pilots chatting back and forth about 20 minutes into the flight. Other than me and the pilots, everyone else was still asleep except Danny, the Senior Toolpusher, and also the OIM (Offshore Installation Manager). Years later, I leaned that his bottom-bearing MODU (Mobile Offshore Drilling Unit) or a MODU Unlimited license was the epitome of an OIM as this was a license to be an OIM on ships or bottom-bearing rigs. Very, very few people carry that license these days, and it is becoming even rarer with the new licensing regulations.

As the chopper started to slowdown, I could hear the sound of the blades and the engine change as if we were altering the route. There is a particular sound when the air is pitched one way or the other under the blades, and I could hear and feel it inside the cabin. The pilots were chatting as the sound changed again, as if we were heading back on our original course. Only a few minutes passed and I was hoping they knew where they were going because all I saw ahead was thick, grey fog. Suddenly, the chopper jerked and halted mid-air, as if they had pulled all the way back on the controls! The fog blew clear in front of the bird and I could see through the cockpit windows in big, black, bold letters the name H E R C U L E S-11 on the side of the hull. I was thinking, *Man, I'm sure glad they didn't just plow into the rig on my first day!* All of a sudden, nobody inside the cabin was asleep!

The chopper hovered in place while the pilots chattered back and forth for a minute. Then, the chopper leaned a little to the left, then to the right, and then began easing forward closer to the rig another 20 or 30 feet. As they started to slowly bring the chopper up looking out of their windows for the helipad, we suddenly stopped and the bird sort of dropped when they realized we were under the damn thing! Had they continued climbing a few more feet, the rotors and blades would have crashed into the support structure of the bottom of the helipad. I can only imagine what would have happened if the rotor blades collided with the overhanging structure 60 feet above the ocean! It most certainly would not have been pretty!

The pilots quickly maneuvered out from underneath the helipad, then circled around and above the rig. We then could clearly see the helipad sticking out just above the fog as they brought it in for a clean landing. I still think back to that flight and hairy landing because it reminds me that we don't have control of *anything* on these flights except for our own bodily functions.

Today's chopper ride only took about 40 minutes, but they all seem like a lifetime when I wake up groggy, bleary-eyed, with a cotton mouth. The *Deepwater Horizon* was stationed in an area of the Gulf of Mexico denoted as "Mississippi Canyon Block 771", some 153 miles south of New Orleans. All I wanted to do was get off the chopper, meet my relief, get something to drink, and unpack my things before going on tour at noon.

As the chopper approached the helideck, they throttled back the engine, and one of the pilots opened his small side window. Not only were these helicopters state-of-the-art, they also had air conditioning and heating, something older birds don't have. Still, flights always seemed warm to me, and the fresh air on my face from the open window was refreshing, cooling off the cabin a bit before landing.

On approach, I could see the *Horizon* Fire Team mustered around their stations: one on the forward foam cannon and one on the aft foam cannon, ready for any emergency. The HLO (Helicopter Landing Officer) stood just below the helideck at the bottom of the stairs with sack lunches and paperwork for the pilots. The pilots brought the helicopter in, touched down, and brought the engines down. As the blades continued to turn, two Roustabouts ran out with wheel chocks and chocked the helicopter. The pilots brought the blades and engine to a full stop, and waved the HLO to approach. He opened the doors, and seat belts started unclicking.

As we all sat quietly, I could feel the rocking of the rig and hear the wind blowing outside. The S92 had an airplane-like fold-down door, so boarding and egressing were much easier than on some of the other helos. Egressing some models meant crawling out onto the sponson and risking a slip or damage to the inflatable buoyancy system mounted along the sides.

Steve, the Bosun, folded down the door and motioned us to offload. Roustabouts carried our bags to the luggage handler. BP had requested the luggage handler as a safety enhancement some years before. It kept us from having to carry our bags down the stairs, risking a trip or misstep and causing a domino crash with a line of people in front. As I walked across the helideck, Roustabouts drug over the fuel hose, connected the ground, and began fueling the chopper.

As we reached the bulkhead door, I was greeted by my relief, Mike Kibodeaux (28) from Gueydan, Louisiana. As he stepped out, the rest of the crew poured around him to meet their reliefs. Years before, Mike had joined the *Horizon* as a Floorhand just before I came onboard. We had both worked our way up to Driller and were proud of the *Horizon* team's accomplishments and how well our crews worked together. Handing over was a quick one- or two-liner before the HLO called from the helideck to start boarding. We wished each other a safe trip and a safe hitch. I went through the bulkhead door and shook hands with some of the other departing crew as I made my way down to the radio room to sign in.

At his desk in the radio room, Carl Taylor (59) from Jackson, Mississippi, processed in the new crew that had just landed. If there was anything anyone needed to know about their stateroom, Carl would tell them when they signed in. The guys piled by his door signing into the ship's logbook, the first thing *every* person who comes aboard does and the last thing done before leaving. This process is mandatory to always maintain an accurate and current POB (Persons On-Board roster).

I signed in and headed back down the hallway, turned right past the hospital doors, and scrambled down the stairway to the lower accommodations. My room had been freshly stripped down with new linens and fresh towels on the bed. I dropped my bag to the floor, opened my locker, and put away my things. During the first week of our two-week hitch, we had the top bunk. Once our tour relief departed, we moved into the bottom bunk knowing that we were almost home-free—just seven days left to go. After I showered, I put on my blue, button-up company shirt and a pair of blue jeans, and headed upstairs to speak with the Senior Toolpusher.

I walked to the galley, refilled my coffee, and headed to the OIM's office. I stuck my head through the door and knocked. Van Williams (54) from Waynesboro, Mississippi, had his feet propped up on his desk watching the Outdoor Channel. With the remote in his right hand and his left hand inside the bib of his overalls, he leaned his head to the side and looked at me, "Come on in here and sit-down boy. We need to talk."

On normal conversations starting my hitch, he would just say, "Sit-down and tell me about your days off," or "How's the family, son?" But, this wasn't starting out like one of *those* conversations.

He said, "Look here, HR has called out here and is telling me they want to transfer you to one of those new rigs coming out."

I sat there with a glazed-over look and didn't say a word.

"James Penny said that you need to be ready to fly out in a couple of weeks and pick the rig up in Korea," he continued. "You got a passport?"

Still sitting there motionless, "No sir," I answered.

"Well, looks like you need to be working on that."

Oops! (Part I)

We were drilling. I was asleep and felt the rig move. It was 3 a.m., and my phone rang. It was the bridge, and they said, "Pete, you better get up here! The is a barge stuck under the rig."

It was a tugboat that was towing a barge and the Captain had gone down to fix an air compressor. The DWH just happened to be in the middle of the track line on his auto pilot. There was nothing within 12 miles of us and we were stationary! The bridge guys had finally gotten ahold of the tug, but instead of turning downweather, he turned upweather and his barge loaded with anchor chain ended up around the rig and poked a hole in the side. It was on the inside, and because we had the canted legs, the hole was above the waterline.

It pissed me off after the Macondo disaster that the DWH's safety record was criticized because it had previously been involved in a collision with a barge. WTF?

Peter Cyr

Yeah, I knew a Chief Mate [Peter Cyr] that shut off my air pressure to my steady-flow bin on the very first job on the Horizon. The cement had 85gals pre-100 sacks of Cal-Chloride. I had 6 barrels of mixing water left and my cement head went wide open looking for cement. The Foam guy was Jeff Langly (who got killed on the helicopter going to the Spirit a few weeks later—we lost 10 good men that day), and I shouted to Jeff, "I don't have any air to my Steady Flow!" Right at that time, the Chief Mate turned the air back on to me. When the cement hit the CAL 2, it was over. It cemented the unit up. I was so pissed-off at the Chief Mate, I could have choked the man. We had to chip the unit out, and it took a few days of hard work to do it.

Randy Harris

I had made a few hitches on the Horizon when this happened. We had done a cement job and cleaned-up. As we left the Cement Unit, one of us hit the drill water valve. It opened up and the drain lines were closed. So, a lot of water ran over and went down the drains and they backed up into the Storeroom.

I think it was Petrobras that had just come out to tour the rig. Well, they went to the Storeroom or Warehouse, and when they opened the door, water ran out. A lot of water. Yep, it was a bad day. A lot of Computer Equipment got a little water in them. The floor got a good washing, too. Fun times. I caught hell for a long time for that one.

Randy Harris

Going Off the Deep End

"Man cannot discover new oceans unless he has the courage to lose sight of the shore."
~~Andre Gide

I am not a professional historian, but I can say that the offshore oil and gas industry has come a long, long way from its humble beginnings more than 100 years ago. Oil itself has evolved from an oddity to the "black gold" of today's world economies.

The Chinese were first reported to actually *drill* for oil back in 347 A.D., using bits attached to bamboo shafts. The Chinese purportedly used oil to burn off brine and produce salt.[1] The first "offshore" well was reported in 1803 in Bibi-Heybat Bay on the Caspian Sea, near present day Azerbaijan, made from hand-dug wells 18-30 meters from shore.[2] 1818 saw the first recorded U. S. commercial export of oil from a Kentucky well. In 1857, a process to distill kerosene from petroleum was developed that very quickly created new markets for oil—kerosene being preferred over whale oil for illumination and heating—and spurred oil exploration and development. While exploration for and development of oil in the U.S. and internationally began slowly, it later expanded very rapidly, especially driven by the proliferation of internal combustion engines, and later, natural gas for heating, electrical power generation, and cooking.

Even the use of the term "offshore drilling" in reference to early oil mining is debatable. While the earliest "offshore" wells were technically offshore, they were either still attached to or within sight of the shore and were built in shallow depths. The first production oil wells in waters were developed in 1891 on Grand Lake St. Marys in Ohio. Eight years later, the first rigs in sea waters were established off the coast of California connected to land by piers.[3] These early "drilling rigs" looked much like their land-based counterparts which were constructed of wood and simply drove pipe into the lake- or sea-floors up to depths of less than 400 feet.

Twenty years later, in 1911, the Gulf Refining Company created the first "off-shore" rig when it used barges to drill wells on Caddo Lake in Louisiana. But it wasn't until 1937 that the first offshore platform was built. Still, this platform was only one mile offshore and stood in 14 feet of water. The first well drilled beyond sight of land—10.5 miles off the Louisiana coast by the Kerr-McGee Oil Company—stood in water depths of only 18 feet.

---

[1] "Oil Well: History." *Wikipedia*. <https://en.wikipedia.org/wiki/Oil_well>.
[2] Mir-Babayev, Mir Yusif. "Azerbaijan's Oil History: A Chronology Leading up to the Soviet Era." *Azerbaijan International*. 2002. (10.2): 34-40. <http://azer.com/aiweb/categories/magazine/ai102_folder/102_articles/102_oil_chronology.html>.
[3] "Offshore Petroleum History." *American Oil & Gas Historical Society*. <http://aoghs.org/offshore-history/offshore-oil-history/>.

Knowledge of this early history is relevant to understanding offshore oil and gas exploration today. This is because many of the same forces that were at work in the early quest to find and develop new sources of oil and gas continue to evolve, shape, and direct that quest in the 21st century:

Technology, if not *the* critical force, is certainly one of the top determinants that helps us explore new sources of oil and gas. In the past, technological advances allowed exploration at increasingly greater depths, and, as oil and gas finds in deeper waters proved more profitable, technological advances both enabled, directed, and drove offshore exploration. Advances in structures (both marine and drilling), drilling tools and techniques, geology and seismology, drilling muds, robotics, positioning (ships, rigs, drilling tools), data processing and exchange all promoted the move for exploration further offshore.

Strong economic forces fuel technological advances that enable offshore oil and gas exploration. In fact, without economic forces, few, if any, technological advances in the industry would or could have happened. Rather than attempt to give a dissertation on offshore economics, it is important to understand that throughout the evolution of oil and gas exploration, there are a number of people who benefit, or have stood to benefit, from the economics of offshore oil and gas exploration and development. Of course, those who directly and indirectly risk, explore, and develop are economically driven. Similarly, community, state, and national economies are intrinsically linked to a healthy domestic production of oil and gas. But it's important to know, too, that huge state and federal tax revenues come from offshore oil and gas, beginning with the sales of exploration leasing rights to royalties on finds to taxes collected from consumers on products like gasoline and diesel fuels.

While not on the same rung as technology and economics, **political forces** have also shaped the direction and even the speed of the development of the gas and oil industry, oftentimes in a negative way. When President Truman asserted exclusive Federal jurisdiction over the entire U.S. continental shelf in 1946—and after three Supreme Court rulings upholding presidential power and Congress' inability to develop a solution—offshore leasing came to a complete halt by 1950. Because control of offshore drilling became a presidential campaign issue, when President Dwight Eisenhower was elected, Congress passed two key Acts in 1953: the Submerged Lands Act and the Outer Continental Shelf Lands Act (OCSLA). Leasing by state and federal governments was allowed, and offshore exploration and development began again. However, political forces shaped and continue to shape the industry.

Social or societal forces also drive the industry. Social concerns—some valid and others misguided—for the environment are huge shapers for the industry. Perhaps no event in history has affected the offshore industry more that the infamous Santa Barbara spill. In January 1969, an offshore rig suffered a blowout that resulted in a spill estimated at 80-100,000 barrels of oil that sullied southern California beaches and impacted waterfowl and other marine life. There have been spills before and since; however, the Santa Barbara spill was the first to be televised and incessantly reported on in the newspapers, with images of the clean-up efforts etched on the social consciousness of the country. The spill not only precipitated an immediate ban on California drilling and production, but also resulted in President Nixon's creation of the Environmental Quality Council. President Nixon's own words became a harbinger of Federal environmental policy largely hostile to offshore exploration and production:

> *"The deterioration of the environment is in large measure the result of our inability to keep pace with progress. We have become victims of our own technological genius."*
> ~President Richard M. Nixon[4]

I should note, however, that social forces don't always negatively affect the industry. For example, the "oil embargo" by the Organization of Arab Petroleum Exporting Countries (OPEC) in 1973-74 sharply heightened public demand for increased domestic production, including offshore, to reduce American dependence on foreign oil.

Another consideration in studying the evolution of offshore oil and gas exploration are **regulatory** forces. Certainly, the regulatory environment is interrelated with social and political forces, but then again, all of the forces driving offshore exploration and production—technical, economic, social, political, and regulatory—are interrelated. A big difference is that those charged with developing and enforcing governmental regulations don't answer to voters and operate with virtual impunity from judicial limitation. Because various regulatory governmental agencies regulate so many aspects of the offshore industry, they have a huge influence on when, where, and how the industry explores and develops oil and gas. Their enforcement "hammers" range from shut-downs to huge fines or bans from exploratory leases.

Finally, another very important driving force in offshore drilling is **geology**. In the Gulf of Mexico, shallow waters are more gas prone making development more difficult. As seismologists began to understand the physics of turbidite sands, 3-D seismic modeling and rig technologies converged to take advantage of high-rate wells in deep waters. Starting in about 1991, 13 years of continuous increased production from deepwater wells followed. In fact, the era of moving to deep- and even ultra-deepwater was a rare phenomenon in American petroleum history due to its rapid growth in a short amount of time. The number of deepwater rigs in the Gulf of Mexico increased from just three in 1992 to 36 in 2008. The deepwater geology created many technical difficulties to overcome, but when a deepwater well came into production, the *geology* is what created the huge increase in its

---

[4] All Presidential statements can be found at John T. Woolley and Gerhard Peters', *The American Presidency Project*™. <http://www.presidency.ucsb.edu/>.

productivity, with flowrates several times more productive than that of their shallower offshore counterparts. Oftentimes, deepwater wells averaged 10,000 barrels a day (including natural gas). The tremendous geological pressures created phenomenal deepwater well production, but also carried risks of loss-of-well control and blowouts.

I should also mention the creation of the International Association of Drilling Contractors (IADC)—a group of people with vested interests in the viability of a healthy oil and gas exploration and development. The IADC was created in the 1940s as a solution to generate more oil and gas through the sharing of technology and best practices between oil and gas drilling companies. The thirst for oil was growing exponentially during World War II. As many oil and gas economists have said, "Nothing drives the need for oil like a war!" This association grew into an industry oversight and guidance group, and offered certifications for certain key roles, such as Offshore Installation Managers, or OIMs, and offshore Drillers. While some have compared the IADC to the Bar for the legal profession or the AMA for the medical profession, it has also been compared to the patients overseeing the asylum as the IADC Board is made up of drilling contractor CEOs and other board executives. In other words, the IADC has financial interests in everything it oversees.

I've described the early beginnings of offshore oil and gas exploration, and how technological advances, economic forces, political forces, social movements, regulatory forces, deepwater geology, and even professional associations have all directed and shaped offshore and deepwater oil and gas exploration and development. It is a very summary level to be sure; however, understanding the history of offshore oil and gas and the forces that have directed and shaped the movement towards deeper waters is an important starting point to understanding the story of *Deepwater Horizon*.

Dale

I was only 23 and I had just got a job on the Deepwater Horizon. It was my first night on the rig. It was me, Tiny, Karl, Russ, and maybe one or two more I'm missing. It was late December, and at that time, I didn't know how cold it could get in the Gulf, so I didn't pack much in the way of warm clothes. We got out on the decks the wind was blowing and man, was it cold. I was freezing and Dale, my crane operator, clearly saw that I was uncomfortably cold when he was about to get in the crane, and offered me his jacket. At first, I declined, but then he insisted and I accepted it. I asked him if he was gonna get cold, and he said, "I'll be fine. I have another in my locker."

Right then, I knew Dale was a great person and someone I'm not gonna mind working my tail off for. You always hear the stories that someone would give the shirt off their back, but he really did give me the jacket off his. He never wanted the jacket back. He told me to keep it, and to this day I still have that jacket. Every time I see it hanging in the closet, it reminds me of Dale and all the rest of the crew on the Deepwater Horizon I had the pleasure of working beside.

Dustin Brown

One of my favorite and funniest memories came from when Dale Burkeen was telling one of his stories to Van Williams in the galley. We were all sitting down at the table fixing to have lunch with Dale sitting on my right and Van sitting directly in front of him.

Dale was like, "Van, did you hear about the poor baby that was born without any eyelids?"

Van was like, "No. I haven't heard anything about it."

So, Dale, with the most serious face he could make, continued telling Van the story. Dale said the doctors wanted to do a surgery on the baby that has never been tried before. It consisted of them taking some of the baby's foreskin and making the baby some eyelids. The doctors were very successful in doing this procedure, Dale said, but there was only one problem.

And Van was like, "What was the problem, Dale?"

Dale kind of hesitated and shook his head, finishing his story by saying, "Well Van, you know that poor ole baby grew up cockeyed!"

Van, not thinking it was a funny story at all, got up with his plate not saying a word, dumped his food and walked out of the galley. Dale just kept on laughing and laughing because it was absolutely our best laugh of the day! I sure miss my ole buddy, Dale Burkeen. Hope you're up there grinning at that story again!

Dennis Martinez

Ole Dale always had a good story to tell. I remember we were standing in the BOP house when Dale began a story about one time he was working as a part-time security guard at the Neshoba County Fair. They gave him a blue shirt that was two sizes too small and the front buttons where pushed out. And the pants they gave him were about six too short. He said his white socks where sticking out, and he started pulling up his coveralls to show us how high his pants were. He was just going on and on with his animated stances and imitating his own voice from the event about the encounters that he had with people, threatening to hit them with a stick and all. Just all kinds of funny stuff.

Mitch Gill

Comin' & Goin'

"So, Dale obediently came back and sat down, and Van started a hunting story so epic it should have been covered by National Geographic. It was so animated, we got totally caught up and we all almost missed pre-tour."

Sitting in my OIM's, Van Williams', office, I could feel the sweat forming on the back of my head. I had been onboard for less than an hour into what I did not yet know would be my last hitch aboard *Deepwater Horizon*. Van explained that while I was back home enjoying my days off, he'd received a phone call from Transocean HR that they intended to transfer me to the new, enhanced E-class *Clear Leader* as their Forward Driller. The *Clear Leader* was just coming out of fabrication in South Korea. At the time, given the tremendous growth in work going on within Transocean, refusing a move wasn't really an option.

"Van, do I have a say-so in this?" I felt like I'd been blindsided.

He looked over the top of his glasses, his camouflage baseball cap with a picture of the *Deepwater Horizon* embroidered on the front pointing straight at me. "Well, there is this other thing they also called me about. What do you know about this CAPM stuff?"

My movements hadn't changed much, but I could feel my skin starting to warm up. I wasn't sure at the time if it was nerves or excitement, but I sure wasn't happy about this mandatory transfer. "Well sir, I don't have a clue what that is."

Van rocked back a little. He had a seriousness to him. "Ole Thom Keeton and a French fella by the name, JP, called out here and wanted to talk with you *yesterday*. I told them you were coming out today and we would get back with them. But they went ahead and filled me in on what they were wanting to discuss."

"Well?" I asked. "What is it?"

"It's some newfangled system they are working on in corporate and they need a Driller that has experience with the equipment to help them finish developing it."

I looked down at my watch. By this time, it was around 10:30 a.m. "Van, let me grab some lunch before pre-tour, and I will come back and set down with you after pre-tour to talk more about this."

Van smiled. "Son, don't worry about any of this stuff. You get ready to go on tour, and we'll talk when we have time. We have a business to run."

"Thanks, Van," I said, trying to smile back.

I left Van's office, and stopped to throw my coffee cup away in the Senior Toolpusher's office. James "Bo" Votaw (53) from Sour Lake, Texas, was already back at his desk getting ready to eat lunch and go to pre-tour. "Hey biggun," he said. "How was your days off?"

"Hey, Big Daddy," I answered. "All's well. Kids all good and healthy. I'm ready to come back so I can pay some bills."

"I hear that," he grinned.

"I put some stuff from the IADC in that folder," I added.

Ever since I'd started as an Assistant Driller (AD), I made it my habit to study the IADC reports from the previous 14 days I was off—each day- and night-tour's report. I would look for things to make our reports better, cleaner, more understandable, and most importantly, to make any necessary corrections so we could maximize the record of the rig's performance to secure interest in the vessel and our current operations for potential clients in the future. We wanted to be the best. We wanted to set the bar for others to follow. Once I finished looking over the reports, I had put these marked-up copies into a folder on the Senior Toolpusher's desk.

"Yeah," he said. "I looked through it already and I agree. We'll make those changes and get it squared away."

"Good deal." I gave him a thumbs-up. He responded with a big grin, and I headed out of his office to grab something to eat in the galley.

The galley on the *Deepwater Horizon* contained four long tables, which sat 14 people. The tables were cream-colored frames covered with imitation wood, surrounded by a small ledge that kept plates and items from sliding off the table during rough weather. The chairs were silver frames with blue-padded backs and seats. On the far-left wall hung a 50-inch flat-screen TV that played safety clips and informational pieces about upcoming events onboard the rig. The TV was positioned between two port windows that had their covers lifted and the drapes pulled open so the sun could shine in. I have stood there many times drinking coffee before the serving windows opened, looking out across the reflective Gulf of Mexico with the morning sun warming my face.

Along the wall was a stainless-steel stand with a large pot of the soup of the day and a microwave. We'd get our main dish from one of two serving windows onboard. The noon meal always offered a decent selection of meats. There was plenty of gravy, rice, macaroni and cheese, mashed potatoes, peas, and beans available as sides. Transocean was pushing to have healthier options available for all the hands, so there was a salad bar along the wall with plenty of healthy stuff to choose.

There was a standup, glass door fridge that housed the soft drinks, juices, and perishable commodities. And right next to that was "death with doors": *the desert cooler*. Cakes, pies and numerous chocolate creations lie inside, depending on who our baker was. This thing would be loaded up with sweets, and then there was just enough room to stack the plates on tiny area on the end. It was obvious at first glance what was the more important part of this arrangement! Past the desert box and serving window 2 were the food disposal area and segregated areas for trash.

To the left was the doorway that led out into the hall. A left in the hall led to the Transocean senior offices on one side, their rooms on the other—Maintenance, Senior Toolpusher and OIM. A right in the hall led to the service partner and BP offices. The visitor staterooms and galley crew rooms were sort of in the center.

Back in the galley, past that door, there was a stand-up water cooler next to a long stainless table that held the coffee pots, milk and drink dispenser, cereals, breads, and a toaster. Beyond this and around the last table, there was a smaller table next to another galley entry door. This table held the sweets that didn't need to be refrigerated—doughnuts, cookies, cakes. There was a panel on the wall next to the table that had the status lights for the power system and a rig phone hung just next to the panel. On the other side of the doorway was another shelf that held all additional items, such as condiments that didn't need refrigeration, individual boxes of cereal, Vienna sausages, and other takeaways. Every year, we would put up our rig Christmas tree just in front of this shelf.

I grabbed some lunch and sat down at the table just in front of the salad bar. Most of my crew was already seated, talking about what they had done on their days off. Their clothes smelled like a 14-day locker with a bottle of Febreze thrown into it for good measure.

My guys from all over country all made it back for crew change: Karl Kleppinger (36) from Natchez Mississippi, was our Shakerhand; Don Clark (47) from Newellton, Louisiana, was one AD; John Carroll (30) from Florien, Louisiana, was our other AD; Ron Trenum (33) from Bogalusa, Louisiana, was our Pumphand; Roy Kemp (25) from Jonesville, Louisiana, was one of four Floorhands; Keith Ray (29) from Andalusia, Alabama was also a Floorhand. The only ones not at the table were Shane Roshto (20) from Liberty, Mississippi, and Alvin Champ from Lafayette, Louisiana, both Floorhands, and Patrick Morgan (39) from Louisville, Mississippi, our Derrickhand. Patrick, Alvin, and Shane had eaten earlier, as they always did, and were mingling about the living quarters, chatting or starting rumors about what they did on their days off. At lunch, we all talked briefly about what was going on that day, and what everybody did while we were away. I could vaguely hear Patrick laughing somewhere in the distance. He was down at the Radio Operator's office visiting with Carl.

After lunch, I headed toward the coffee shop for a quick cigarette before pre-tour. Heading down the hallway toward the coffee shop, I could hear phones ringing and people chattering in the offices just ahead. The door to the rig hospital was open and I looked in to see Matt Keller (35) from Missoula, Montana, our Medic, sitting at a desk that was too tall for him in a chair too short for the desk. I smiled whenever I saw Matt at his desk, recalling the first time we met some years back.

Matt arrived when our Medic at the time had been promoted to the RSTC (Rig Safety Training Coordinator) position. I was working my last week as an AD on the B-Tour Drill Crew for Audy "Jed" Williamson (51) from Glenwood, Arkansas. I was up checking on the work permits to see what was going on before heading to pre-tour when I passed the Radio Operator's office just as the new guys were coming down from the helipad. I stopped to chat with some of them and noticed a short fella at the back of the line. Curiosity got the best of me and I had to ask, "Hey buddy, what are you headed out here to do? Drill Quip or working the rig floor?"

In the back of my mind I was already thinking about what I was going to need do to make sure he was going to be able to work up there—ladders, extension ladders, smaller tools, things that smaller fellas need on the rig floor.

"No. I'm the new Medic," he responded.

As we shook hands, I looked behind him and around the room and asked, "Well, where's the rest of ya?" Matt and I have been friends ever since.

As I rounded the corner of the hallway, I walked in front of the Permit-to-Work desk. Don was there already looking at the open permits and filling out the ones we needed before going on tour so they could get straight to work when we relieved. I could smell fresh coffee brewing. Dale Burkeen (35) from Philadelphia, Mississippi, one of our Crane Operators, was halfway through his hitch, standing in front of the coffee pot.

"Hey Greg, whatcha know good?"

"Hell if I know, Dale. Let's have a coffee."

"Yeah, let's just do that," he quipped with his signature grin.

Dale and I had worked together for many years. I first met Dale when he was hired as a Roustabout on the *DF96*, before Transocean sold it to Noble Drilling in 2001. I was his Lead Roustabout tasked with showing him around the rig and watching after him his first few hitches until he got his bearings. We were friends from the first day we met.

At that time, I had four years of land rig and offshore experience before joining Transocean. I loved drilling and that's where my heart was, so I knew that I was headed back into the drilling department as soon as a position opened. As a newbie on my first helicopter ride out to the rig, I remember being told I needed to "go subsea". I was so green, I had to ask, "What's subsea?" A few months after Dale started, I was moved into the drilling department and Dale took my position as Lead Roustabout. Dale would come up on the drill floor and relieve us for lunch or help us out if we needed an extra hand.

One day, we were tripping pipe filled with Zinc Bromide—nasty brown-colored material that's used in drilling mud. We were fully suited-out in PPE (personal protective equipment): Tyvek suits, rubber boots, legs duct taped-up around the tops of the boots. Over that we wore slicker suits (rain jackets and pants) and a full face-shield snapped onto the brim of our hardhats, two sets of gloves—one set of thin nitrile gloves and elbow-length chemical gloves that were as tough as a turtle's back. Just bending your fingers in these took work. It was in the middle of summer and the sun was beating down. We had large fan mounted in the derrick just above the rig floor to blow down on us while we worked. But, in this kind of heat, all it did was blow the hot air around while we were all decked out in full PPE gear. I was working lead tongs (a large set of pipe wrenches), and it was my turn to go eat. Dale came up to relieve me. He had on nice, clean, sparkly new PPE and hadn't dropped a bit of sweat . . . yet.

"I gotcha Big Daddy," Dale yelled smiling, after tapping me on the shoulder.

"Alright, here ya go," I yelled back, handing him the tongs. I watched him as he jumped right in there, putting those tongs on like he had been doing it forever. I stripped off my slicker suit and headed down for lunch. When I came back, Dale was ringing wet with sweat and covered in Zinc from head-to-toe.

"You still got it, partner?" I hollered, as I got some water from the cooler.

"Hell yeah, I do!"

Dale was promoted up to the rig floor, and I was moved up to Derrickhand before we both transferred over to the *Horizon* in 2001.

Dale followed me into the coffee shop and Van was in there already having a smoke himself.

"Damn, came in at the wrong time," Dale said, poking at the boss.

"What are you talking about, son?" Van asked.

"Well, it ain't normal for me to set down and smoke with the OIM in here," Dale continued his poking.

"Why? What's wrong with me?" asked Van as he tilted his newspaper and looked over at Dale.

"Oh hell. Nothing is wrong with you. I was just mentioning that I don't normally do this," Dale went on.

"Well, obviously, there is nothing important going on, or you wouldn't be in here," Van poked back.

Dale knew that Van wasn't going to give up that easy, so he just sat down and lit his cigarette.

Then suddenly, "What are you doing?" Van asked sternly.

"Hell, Van. I'm going to have this here cigarette."

Van folded up his paper and said in a dead serious tone, "Well, when you get done, I need you to come down to my office."

Dale's face turned blood red, and he said, "Yes sir."

I knew Van was pulling his leg, but Dale didn't know at the time. Dale finished up his cigarette and headed for the door.

"Where you goin'?" asked Van.

"To your office to wait on you. Or, I can go pack my bags. Whatever you want me to do."

Van gave out a big laugh. "Boy, you get your ass back in here." So, Dale obediently came back and sat down, and Van started a hunting story so epic it should have been covered by National Geographic. It was so animated, we got totally caught up and we all almost missed pre-tour.

Peter

I don't remember what I was doing when the general alarm went off, but I hustled up to the bridge and met Pete Cyr (Chief Mate at the time). The alarm was in the port forward pontoon where the sea chest was located, and looking on the camera, we could see that the room was filled with 'smoke'. Knowing that there wasn't really anything that would burn in that space, Pete and I headed down the port forward spiral stairs at lightning speed. And of course, I was dizzy as hell and out of breath from smoking! Pete opens the watertight door and notices that all of the paint has burned off the pipe coming from the sea chest valve and immediately announces, "Holy crap! We're in trouble now! The water in the pipe must have caught fire!"

Of course, it wasn't the water on fire; just that someone had left the sea water pump on with the sea chest closed, and it heated the water up until it cooked the paint off the pipe and melted the seal, thus filling the room with steam and not smoke. Pete could always come up with a funny comment on the fly!

Tyson Cullum

I was Chief Mate and my desk was on the bridge. Pat Lawler was Sr. DPO and back then, he chewed tobacco. He had a habit of spitting in my trashcan. It drove me nuts and he knew it. One day I was rummaging around my desk looking for some paperwork. I remembered that I had tossed it and reached into the trashcan, and put my hand right into tobacco spit. I was disgusted and mad at the same time. I looked at Pat and said, "PAT! Stop spitting in my trashcan!!"

He looked back at me and without missing a beat, calmly said, "Stop throwing away shit you need."

Best comeback ever.

Peter Cyr

Constructing a Game-Changer

"I started out on that rig in Ulsan, Korea. I wouldn't take nothing for where I have been and what I have done. That was the best rig I had ever worked on in my life.... I've been on quite a few rigs, but that was the only rig I had ever been on where people listened to their boss, pulled together, and got the job done."
~~Jerry Isaac, Mechanical Supervisor, *Deepwater Horizon*

Surrounded by lush, green mountains, Ulsan, with its strategic port access to neighboring Japan, was once a quiet little fishing town. Known for its whaling and fishing industry, the city is fed by the Taehwa River, which flows into the Sea of Japan via the East Bay. However, no one would have ever suspected that during the 17th century Ulsan had been known for its primitive ship-making. According to city records, in 1642, the inhabitants of Ulsan constructed seaworthy fighting boats to defend against a formidable Japanese naval force.[5] But it wasn't until 300 years later that Ulsan returned to its shipbuilding roots. Modern shipbuilding began in the 1970s, and along with development of automotive and petrochemical industries, Ulsan experienced a 551% surge in population growth![6] Today, Ulsan is now South Korea's seventh largest city with 1.1 million people, and the largest GDP per capita at $79,623.[7]

Nothing short of amazing, Ulsan-based Hyundai Heavy Industries (HHI) landed its first shipbuilding contracts in 1972 without any shipyard infrastructure, technology, capital, or shipbuilding know-how in place. Yet, they built their facility and two tanker ships in parallel, commissioning both oil tankers and their shipyards at the same time, only two years after breaking first ground. In its first four decades, HHI delivered 2,981 vessels to 268 shipowners in 48 countries, making HHI the largest shipbuilding company in the world.[8] In 2011 alone, a total of 82 vessels were built in the shipyard with an aggregate of 10.1 million deadweight tonnage (DWT). HHI surpassed 100 million gross tonnage (GT) in ship deliveries by 2012.[9] And in 2015, HHI was selected for "World's Best Ships" for the 32nd *consecutive* year.[10]

Houston-based R&B Falcon Drilling Inc., LLC, had already developed a successful design and build relationship with HHI, with delivery of the *Deepwater Pathfinder* as well as two sister ships of the same class. In the U.S., R&B was also developing a successful relationship with another Houston company, Vastar Resources, Inc., "one

---

[5] "Ulsan History, South Korea." Travelgrove.com. http://www.travelgrove.com/travel-guides/South-Korea/Ulsan-History-c1097304.html.
[6] "History in Ulsan." World 66.com. http://www.world66.com/asia/northeastasia/southkorea/ulsan/history.
[7] "About HHI History." http://english.hhi.co.kr/about/history.
[8] "About HHI History." http://english.hhi.co.kr/about/history.
[9] "Hyundai Heavy Industries, Ulsan Shipyard, South Korea." Ship-technology.com. http://www.ship-technology.com/projects/hyundai-heavy-industries-ulsan-korea/.
[10] "About HHI History." http://english.hhi.co.kr/about/history.

of the largest independent oil and natural gas exploration and production companies in the U.S."[11] to provide drilling services and a semi-submersible drilling unit to Vastar, contractually identified as RBS8D.

The R&B Falcon design team was onsite in Ulsan from nearly the beginning of the RBS8D Project in a collaborative design and development effort. The RBS8D was HHI's first 5th generation dynamically positioned semi-submersible, a mobile offshore drilling unit (MODU). When the *Deepwater Horizon* was commissioned for acceptance testing, it was a state-of-the-art drilling rig that used GPS-aided dynamic positioning to keep the ship in place within a tight tolerance for drilling operations.

First steel was cut in August 1999. For the next 17 months, the RBS8D area of the HHI shipyard was a bustle of 24 hour-a-day activity. From the design and planning offices to the fabrication floors out to the yard, there was constant activity. Conceptual design progressed to detailed design, including not only the design of the rig itself, but the design of the plans and processes, machines and personnel required to fabricate, assemble, inspect and test, and move the completed rig to sea. And, finally, to get it to the Gulf of Mexico. Steel was forged, rolled, shaped, cut, welded, smoothed, and painted. Long-lead components were ordered, designed, fabricated, and delivered from around the globe.

The rig was fabricated and assembled into subassemblies inside the HHI fabrication facility.

---

[11] "Vastar Resources, Inc. History." Fundinguniverse.com. http://www.fundinguniverse.com/company-histories/vastar-resources-inc-history/.

Figure 1. RBS8D (Deepwater Horizon) in HHI Fabrication

These subassemblies were then moved out to the yard and assembled into larger subassemblies. The photograph above shows a pontoon end connected with another section to the right.

Figure 2. RSB8D in HHI Shipbuilding Yard

The HHI Team assembled the rig into three large subassemblies in the construction yard: the decks with the derrick, starboard pontoon, and port pontoon. The port and starboard pontoons were fabricated and assembled with their "legs" on the port and starboard sides of the deck assembly. The deck assembly was then jacked up to 26 meters primarily with four super jacks, which took three days. Finally, the pontoon assemblies were skidded underneath one at a time and attached to the deck assembly.

This photo illustrates the three major subassemblies (with the yellow super-lift jacks attached to the deck) before the pontoons were skidded into place. The track-like lines visible between the pontoons and deck are actually skids for the port and starboard pontoons.

Figure 3. Deepwater Horizon 3 Main Subassemblies in Yard

This photo illustrates the main deck assembly at its 26-meter jack-up height to begin skidding the pontoons into place.

Figure 4. Deepwater Horizon Deck Jacked-up Ready for Pontoon Skid

This final picture shows the pontoons in place. The date of the picture was August 9, 2000, the rig now starting to look like the *Deepwater Horizon*.

Figure 5. Deepwater Horizon Subassemblies Mated

Over the next few months, the cranes, the drill package, and helideck were added. Piping was connected, and power, communications and control wiring were installed. Quarters and facilities were completed. The fore and aft lifeboat platforms were erected and four lifeboats added. Six electrical power engines and generators were installed with the auxiliary power generator along with their exhaust arrestors topside. Alarms and monitors were fixed and mounted throughout the rig, as were control systems and emergency equipment. Blowout preventer (BOP) structure and BOP were installed, along with the risers, mud tank equipment, cement mixing, and pipe conveyor systems. Of course, painting was going on nearly from day one and continued close to final hand-over. Work was continuous and inspection and system checkouts and verifications were constantly progressing over major milestones.

Deepwater Horizon's final "skid-off" onto the heavy lift ship *Black Marlin* was completed on December 22, 2000. *Horizon* was then taken to sea and outfitted with the eight thrusters, four on the hull of each pontoon. The vessel underwent sea trials before final assumption of ownership by Transocean.

Upon completion, the *Deepwater Horizon* was 396 feet long and 256 feet wide. The main deck sat 61 feet above the water's surface during active drilling, with the drill floor another 15 feet higher. The derrick was 244 feet tall, towering a total of 320 feet above the ocean when lowered for drilling operations.

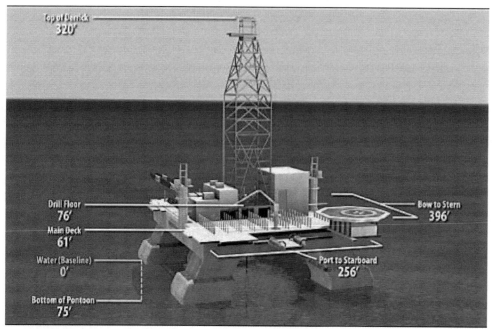

Figure 6. Illustration of Deepwater Horizon Dimensions

The *Deepwater Horizon* had a max speed of eight knots, and a cruising speed of six. Transocean—the new owner of the *Deepwater Horizon*—brokered a Chinese tug (*De Hong*) to assist getting the *Deepwater Horizon* to the Gulf of Mexico. However, after the *De Hong*, began towing out of Singapore with the *Deepwater Horizon's* propulsion assisting, the team realized that both ships were consuming too much fuel and wouldn't be able to make it the next port in tandem. So, the team, being ever resourceful at making the impossible possible, discontinued the tow and released the *De Hong* to ferry fuel. And so, that's how the two-month trip to the Gulf went, the *Deepwater Horizon* under her own power and the *De Hong* serving as a mobile fuel station . . . for 15,488 nautical miles (or 17,823 statute miles)! Because the rig was too large for either the Panama or Suez Canals, it had to sail through Indonesia, the Indian Ocean, around the Cape of Good Hope, South Africa into the Atlantic, past the Caribbean, and across the Gulf of Mexico.

The time it took for the *De Hong* to return to the nearest port, get reloaded, and return before the *Deepwater Horizon* needed fuel was a continual logistics challenge. The fuel consumption of the rig was a whopping 275 gallons per mile, according to Peter Cyr, Chief Mate during the trip from South Korea to the U.S. Cyr dryly quipped, "It was a big rig." That was putting it mildly. The trip required something like 4.3 million gallons of diesel fuel—enough to operate nearly 451 semi-trucks for a year in the U.S.[12] Every time the *De Hong* arrived with a load of fuel, the DWH had to lower into the water to get close enough for the fuel lines to reach. It took four hours to lower the rig, and after refueling, it took another six hours to pump out the pontoons to get back to transit draft.

According to Cyr, when the *Deepwater Horizon* was leaving Cape Town, South Africa, a tanker ship called on the radio, saying, "the rig with the bowed-out legs", and asked if they needed assistance, thinking the *Deepwater Horizon* had lost their tow and might be adrift at sea. "We said we were self-propelled and we're okay," Cyr replied. When asked where they were headed, Cyr answered rather coolly, "Why, the Gulf of Mexico."

"At five knots?" the caller from the tanker gasped.

"Yup."

The *Deepwater Horizon*, however, was far from underpowered. With eight 360-degree 5,500 KW Kamewa Aquamaster thrusters, capable of producing up to 100 tons of thrust per thruster for propulsion and station-keeping, the *Deepwater Horizon's* First Mate remained continually amazed. "That rig was a dream to drive. Very maneuverable. I remember during the turning test getting the rig up to 120-degrees per minute. I mean, this is a 56,000-ton oil rig as tall as a 40-story building, and you can turn it 360 degrees in three minutes?"

To illustrate, the photograph below, taken during construction, shows the size of the thrusters relative to personnel. *Deepwater Horizon* was fitted with eight of these thrusters, four for each pontoon, and they swiveled 360 degrees to provide thrust in any direction.

---

[12] Based upon U.S. DOT 62,000-mile average for semi-trucks in 2015 at an average of 6.5 mpg, 2016 Vehicle Technologies Market Report, pp. 126-127. http://cta.ornl.gov/vtmarketreport/pdf/chapter_4_heavy_trucks.pdf.

Figure 7. One (of 8) Deepwater Horizon Propulsion Thrusters

Of course, the trip from South Korea to the Gulf of Mexico was long and monotonous, but the guys still tried to have fun. One morning around 3:00 a.m., as the rig was sailing in the mid-Atlantic, Cyr recalled being passed by a lone sailboat.

"I remember it was a trimaran and a lady with a British accent was on the radio. We asked her if she had any beer onboard. She replied, 'Yes,' and kept right on going."

Finally, on February 23, 2001, *Deepwater Horizon* arrived in the Gulf of Mexico off the Texas coast for its final delivery, accoutrements, and crew-up. Less than a month later, she was drilling her first well.[13]

When the rig was first being designed, when first steel was cut, as smaller pieces were assembled into the bigger and bigger ones, I am sure that none of the shipbuilders in Ulsan had any idea they were building a future record-breaker. A single rig that would contribute *significantly* to the future oil and gas independence of the United States of America because of the *Horizon's* huge oil and gas reserve discoveries in the Gulf of Mexico. No one knew this rig would be manned by a crew who routinely *made the impossible possible*, as if it were an unwritten credo that seemed to go with the rig, and with being on this rig, the *Deepwater Horizon*. And while the crew who sailed and operated the *Horizon* on some of the most demanding and challenging deepwater drilling operations got the glory, in a way, much of this *spirit* of the rig—*making the impossible possible*—began with the shipbuilding team in Ulsan, South Korea. Perhaps a bit of that shipbuilding spirit still lingered from Ulsan's shipbuilding ancestors, who, against impossible odds, built fighting boats in the mid-1600s to oppose the formidable Japanese war boats of that time. Regardless, the crew who built the *Deepwater Horizon* deserve credit for making the impossible possible.

---

[13] 17 March 2001.

Seasick

There was a safety guy from BP, Jake "the Snake" Duhon, and all you had to do was stand in front of him and ever so slightly sway side-to-side and he would start turning green! I really felt bad for him at times, but he never let it keep him from working! Good times!

Tyson Cullum

I remember the rig rolling like two degrees and he'd be clutching the handrail and be like, "When is this rig going to stop rolling?" I couldn't even feel it.

I also remember us all sitting across from Jake in the mess room and just slowly swaying back and forth in unison until he turned green. Jake the snake!

Peter Cyr

One of my fun memories of the Horizon was Chuck Lott on the hurricane video putting the band aid on the broken derrick. I sure had some fun on that rig.

Mitch Gill

King of the Gulf:
Deepwater Horizon's Star-Spangled Operations in the Gulf of Mexico

"We realized I had made an additional seven feet of hole when the [980,000lbs.] casing hit bottom at terminal velocity.... From that day on, I was known as the Driller that ran the fastest string of 13-5/8-inch casing...ever!"
~~Greg Williams' 1st Day as Driller, *Deepwater Horizon,* Kaskida Field, 2006

When the *Deepwater Horizon* arrived on station in the Gulf of Mexico, or GoM, the rig and crew began a storied drilling career that significantly contributed, in terms of viable finds, to American energy independence by 2020.

> March 17, 2001. Blues Image, exploratory well (*Deepwater Horizon's* first well)

Throughout most of 2003, the *Deepwater Horizon* crew was busy drilling 18 development wells in the Atlantis Field. The Atlantis Field is currently the third largest field in the Gulf of Mexico, 130 miles off the coast of Louisiana,[14] with an estimated 15-years of life and reserves of 635 million barrels of oil equivalent (MMBOE).[15]

> November 3, 2003. Tubular Bells Project: Measured well depth 31,131 feet, water depth 4,300 feet. **Find:** Approximately 190 feet hydrocarbon-bearing sands *(Deepwater Horizon's* first deepwater hydrocarbons—oil and gas)

This well is now owned by Hess Corporation and is still producing today.

September 15, 2004. The *Deepwater Horizon* crew rode out Hurricane Ivan—a Category 4 storm when it hit them—still attached to the bottom! Before the storm hit, they'd sent all non-essential personnel ashore, so there were only 44 aboard, including the BP rep who refused to leave "his guys". That required some balls because everybody knew this wasn't going to be a day on Walden Pond. They'd been watching Ivan for a while after it hit the tip of Cuba as a Category 5 storm. Still, Ivan's path was difficult to predict. After making landfall in Florida and then Alabama, both well east of the *Horizon*, it actually headed east back into the Atlantic off the Carolinas, reformed, and then circled back around Florida and into the Gulf before making a second pass towards its eventual landfall in Louisiana.[16] As the storm strengthened in the Gulf of Mexico, the rig was right in Ivan's path.

---

[14] "Atlantis Oil Field." Wikipedia. <https://en.wikipedia.org/wiki/Atlantis_Oil_Field>.
[15] "Atlantis Deepwater Oil and Gas Platform, Gulf of Mexico, United States of America." Offshore Technology.com. <http://www.offshore-technology.com/projects/atlantisplatform/>.
[16] "Hurricane Ivan." *Wikipedia.* <https://en.wikipedia.org/wiki/Hurricane_Ivan>.

But because the path defied prediction, BP waited too long to make the call to allow time to displace the riser so the *Horizon* could unlatch and safely get off the well. The Transocean OIM probably should have made the call himself and not have waited on the client for the safety of the rig, the crew, and the well. But, regardless of who decided what and why, the bottom line was that the crew was forced to ride out the storm and do the best they could.

That was a night no one who was there would ever forget—although they'd like to. Lunch apparently didn't hold too well. I was told one of the guys actually said it was too rough for supper, and it reminded me of a line from the song, "The Wreck of the Edmund Fitzgerald". On the upside, the rig suffered minimal damage. Once the storm passed, the *Horizon* was the first rig back to work in the Gulf of Mexico. While all the other vessels were still motoring back to their locations, the *Deepwater Horizon* was already drilling. It was yet another "feather in the cap" of a rig that was gaining a reputation as a "charmed ship".

> March 10, 2005. Stones Field: Well depth 28,560 feet, water depth 9,576 feet.[17] **Find:** Estimated >2 billion barrels of oil equivalent (BBOE) in place[18]

Beginning December 31, 2004, the crews of the *Deepwater Horizon* deployed the subsea BOP into 9,576 feet of Gulf of Mexico waters on the Stones Project. This achievement could not have been possible if not for the teamwork and operation of the *Deepwater Horizon*. This came to be known as a world record of "The Deepest Water Depth of a Dynamically Positioned Semi-Submersible".[19] This record still stands today.

This project was later developed by Shell. In 2013, Shell designed the GOM's first FPSO (Floating Production Storage and Offloading), the *Turritella*, to begin production of the Stones Field.

> June 1, 2006. Kaskida Field: Well depth 32,500 feet, water depth 5,860 feet. **Find:** 800 feet of hydrocarbon-bearing sands

The Kaskida Field was a tremendous find, and a record for deepwater drilling! To give an idea of the significance of what 800 feet of hydrocarbon-bearing sands means, most people in the oil drilling business might only get a glimpse of a reservoir of this magnitude, maybe a find of 80-100 feet. Eight hundred feet of oil sands means, in essence, that the reservoir was at least 800 feet deep at the well. Subsea geologists who specialize in oil and gas exploration and production

---

[17] Rigzone Article, "Shell Confirms Presence of Hydrocarbons at Stones Prospect." Rigzone.com. 23 May 2005. <http://www.rigzone.com/news/oil_gas/a/22685/Shell_Confirms_Presence_of_Hydrocarbons_at_Stones_Prospect>.
[18] "Stones Field, Gulf of Mexico. United States of America." Offshore technology.com.< http://www.offshore-technology.com/projects/stones-field-gulf-mexico/>.
[19] "Transocean: World's Largest Offshore Drilling Company." NYJobSource.com. Updated 18 Mar 2014. <http://nyjobsource.com/transocean.html>.

estimated the recoverable oil to be three BBOE, making this one of the largest finds in the Paleogene (or Lower Tertiary) rock formations.[20]

> March 27, 2008. Kodiak Field: Well depth 31,150 feet, water depth 5,000 feet. **Find:** 500 feet of oil-bearing sands

Yet another huge find in the Middle and Lower Miocene Reservoirs, the Kodiak Field is still being developed. At the time of this writing, it is producing oil at a controlled flowrate (because of the high pressures and temperatures) of around 20,000 barrels of oil per day!

I began the "King of the Gulf" chapter asserting that the *Deepwater Horizon's* viable finds of oil and gas contributed significantly to America's quest for "energy independence". I think most people understand that American "energy independence" means that the United States produces as much or more sources of energy than we consume. In other words, we produce enough energy not to require energy imports. Oil and natural gas represent a huge part of the energy equation and the finds of the *Deepwater Horizon* are benefitting the U.S. today and will be for decades to come. Increased domestic production reduces our reliance on foreign oil and the potentially negative impacts to the American economy that foreign reliance brings. As we all know, some of the Mideast oil suppliers are not always looking out for American interests. In fact, it was OPEC's oil embargo in the '70s, that pushed toward achieving U.S. energy independence.

The following chart shows how as domestic production increased, our imports decreased.[21]

---

[20] "Kaskida Oil Field." *Wikipedia*. <https://en.wikipedia.org/wiki/Kaskida_Oil_Field>.
[21] U.S. Energy Information Administration (EIA), Monthly Energy Review, Figure 3.1 Petroleum Overview (Millions Barrels per Day) https://www.eia.gov/totalenergy/data/monthly/pdf/sec3_2.pdf .

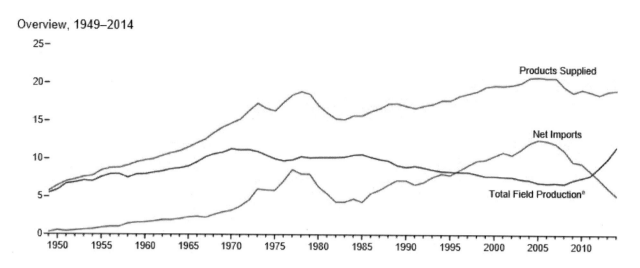

Figure 8. U.S. Petroleum Overview, 1949-2014

Looking at "energy independence" another way, the following chart relates domestic energy production to consumption.[22] (Remember, if consumption exceeds domestic production, imports make up the difference.) Using a number of analytical cases, the Energy Information Agency (on this graph) predicts energy independence somewhere around year 2030!

---

[22] U.S. EIA Outlook 2016, "Energy Production, Imports, and Exports." <http://www.eia.gov/forecasts/AEO/section_energyprod.cfm>.

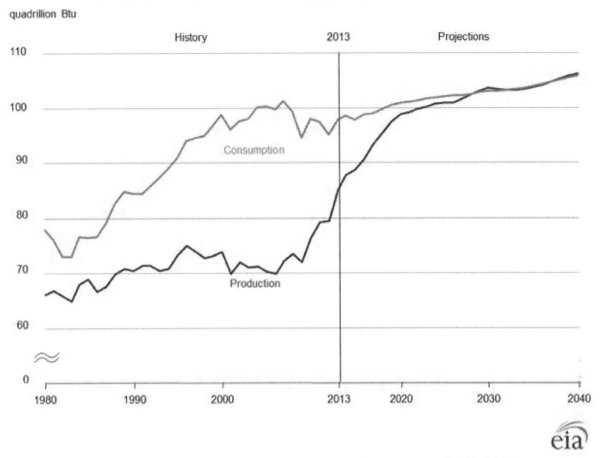

Figure 9. Total Energy Production and Consumption in the Reference Case. (1980-2040)

This chart also illustrates the effect of actual domestic production on imports.[23] Note that, for the first time in years, domestic crude oil production exceeded crude oil net imports.

---

[23] "U.S. Crude Oil Surpasses Net Imports." Energy.gov. <http://energy.gov/maps/us-crude-oil-production-surpasses-net-imports>.

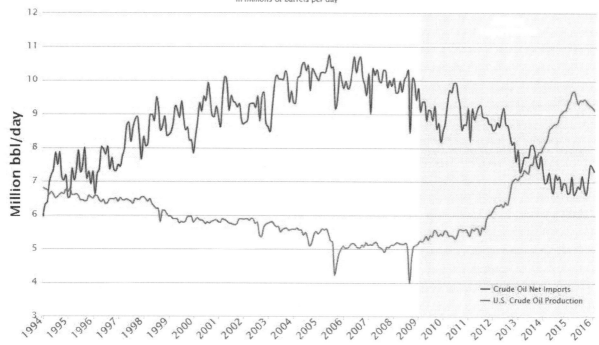

Figure 10. US Oil Production and Imports

> October 20, 2008. Freedom Field: Well depth, 29,980 feet, water depth, 6,100 feet. **Find:** 550 net feet of hydrocarbon-bearing sands

The Freedom Field find in the Middle and Lower Miocene reservoirs was estimated to contain between 90-325 MBOE. The field, renamed Gunflint, was developed and began producing in 2016 at a minimum production rate of 20,000 BOE/d.

> December 2008. Kodiak field: Another exploratory well at a depth of 31,146 feet, water depth 4,743 feet. **Find:** Another 500 net feet of hydrocarbon-bearing sands proving the significance of the Kodiak field in terms of large-scale reserves

> August 25, 2009. Tibor Field in the Keathley Canyon: Well depth 35,055 feet, water depth of 4,132 feet. **Find:** Oil found in multiple Lower Tertiary (Paleogene) reservoirs

This find was 7.42 miles from the drillship to the bottom of the well! This was the deepest offshore well in the world at that time, and 5,000 feet farther than the rig's maximum drilling specification. Arguably the "Mack-daddy" of them all, still believed to be the largest GoM discovery to date, the Tiber Field was described as a "giant" find, and estimated to contain 4–6 BBOE.[24] While the find was huge, extracting oil from the Paleogene geology is still in development. In fact, in 2015, three majors—BP, Chevron, and Conoco—joined forces to develop a network of production wells

---

[24] "Tiber Oil Field." *Wikipedia*. <https://en.wikipedia.org/wiki/Tiber_Oil_Field>.

and tiebacks to link major discoveries in the Keathley Canyon (Tibor, Guadalupe, Gila Discoveries, and the Gibson Prospect). This collaboration was considered necessary to make fields in the Paleogene rock commercially viable. They are still working on that development today.

> <u>January 2010</u>. Kodiak Field: Another exploratory well depth of 31,150 feet, water depth 4,883 feet. **Find:** Over 400 net feet of Middle and Lower Miocene oil sands

This was the last discovery by the *Deepwater Horizon* and her crew before she was ordered to the fateful Macondo well. In her nine-year career, the *Deepwater Horizon* and crew made incredible discoveries, some still producing today, some just now coming into production, and others yet to be developed. When combined, the sum of these finds contributed and continue to contribute to the increased domestic oil and gas production that is leading the United States of America to energy independence. Until the accident, the ship and her crew were described as "lucky" and "charmed" by others drilling exploratory wells in the Gulf. But the number and significance of the *Deepwater Horizon* discoveries earned the reign as King of the Gulf during a stellar career cut short.

Jed

Uncle Jed didn't just clear out the drill shack. Even with the positive ventilation of the space to make it EX-classed, he could, and did, set off the gas detectors in that shack. Multiple times! Now that's talent.

Ron Guidry

I flew in with cousin Jed once and the helicopter pilot threatened to turn around if he ripped another one. The only man I ever seen could burn out a gas detector.

Michael Cook

Gettin' to the Office

"Being safe is the only way you can go home looking like this. There is not but one of me and you can't go home looking like me."
~~Van Williams, OIM, *Deepwater Horizon*

After almost missing pre-tour, Dale, Van, and I hustled to the TV room for the briefing and filled the few seats left at the very front of the room. The on-tour Toolpusher, Jason Anderson (33), from Bay City, Texas, gave the rundown of what was going on outside (basically, the major activities planned on and around the drilling deck) for the drilling department. Once Jason finished up, Deckpusher, Steve Curtis (37), from Georgetown, Louisiana, picked up where Jason left off with the deck operations, then handed it back to Jason. Jason added anything pertinent to the deck operations, and then handed it over to the BP Company Man, Ronnie Sepulvado (59) from Zwolle, Louisiana. Ronnie went through operations and gave us the lowdown on the next twenty-four hours, and what we needed to plan for later on down the road. BP Logistics Coordinator, Nick Wilson (38), from McComb, Mississippi, went through what boats were on location and the comings and goings of helicopters and personnel arriving today and tomorrow; he also highlighted important equipment being delivered. Bo Votaw discussed Transocean topics and any changes since we had left for field break. Finally, he handed it over to Van for the final comment.

Van had a presence, and when he spoke, the whole room listened. His 30 years in the industry, having gone through the ranks of every job in the drilling department, commanded respect. Van was tough, but he was fair. If anyone decided to have a private conversation while he was speaking, Van would simply stop talking and look straight at whomever was interrupting *his* meeting. It reminded me of my childhood days in Southern Baptist Churches when the preacher stopped preaching to put a stop to whispering during his sermon. Van always had a great way of closing a meeting.

"Gentlemen and Ladies, welcome back. As you walk outside of the living quarters, I want you to remember one thing. I want you to go home exactly the same way you are right now. Look around you. Look at your crew mates. Look at what they look like. Do you want them to look the same way when they leave?"

Voices in the room agreed, "Yes." Heads nodded in approval.

Van continued. "Well, being *safe* is the only way you can go home looking like this. There is not but one of me and you can't go home looking like me." The entire room lit up with laughter as he concluded, "That's all I got."

As we filed out of the TV room, I went back downstairs to my room. During my time on the rig between 2001 and 2008, I have bunked in four different rooms, three downstairs and one upstairs. The downstairs accommodations were two-room cabins designed for shift rotation work: One person plus one relief. If we both had to be in there at the same time, it could get a little crowded, but it was manageable.

The rooms had off-white colored walls and tan doors. The back of the door listed our emergency responsibilities and mapped our transit path to the lifeboats. Each room had two bunks. At the foot of the bunks were four lockers, one for each crew member that stayed in the room rotating over a four-week period.

Whomever made the mattress purchase orders for newly constructed vessels must love to sleep on the ground or on concrete. Fortunately, our mattresses had been changed out and weren't as bad. We usually had either a blue- or a tan-colored blanket that covered the bed; some folks brought their own pillows from home, and some folks kept pillows in their lockers. Beds were always made military-style, tight enough to bounce a quarter. The top bunk had a roll-stop rail that always seemed to find its way to my elbow in the middle of the night. The floors were covered with a mint-speckled carpet that after six years was beginning to show its wear.

One of the nice things the newer rigs had were rooms with individual showers and restrooms. There is much comfort in having a personal shower instead washing in a community gathering when tired and aching to go to sleep. The combination bathroom and shower, though, was fairly tight, especially for a bigger guy like me. When I stood inside, I had room to change my mind, but definitely not enough room to change my clothes! The floors were covered with white tiles and the walls were the same color as the room. There was a raised tile lip just before the shower to keep the water, and as you stepped out of the shower, there was a full mirror and sink with a small toilet affixed to the wall.

Reaching into my locker, I grabbed my tally book, and slipped a pack of gum, pen and pencils, and a fresh can of Copenhagen into my right pockets. The changing room I'd been using since I got on the rig in 2001 was now just across from my room, next to the gym and the sauna. I walked just outside my room, took a step to the right and opened the door to the gym. The off-tour Toolpusher, Andrew Kent, from Austin, Texas, was in a full-fledged sprint on one of the stationary bicycles.

"You just got here, Andrew, and you're giving it hell already!"

"I know, right?" We both smiled and I headed into the change room. The change room was lined with lockers on every wall much like a high school gym locker room. with two wooden benches in the middle of the room. The only two showers were there for anyone who got covered in chemicals or synthetic-based mud. Easy access showers in the lockers allowed for getting that stuff off quicker, and avoided messing up that soiled hand's personal shower or even waking a sleeping relief. From the looks of it, neither shower had been used in a while. In fact, only one was usable and ready, while the other appeared to serve as a makeshift closet for stowing cleaning supplies.

Locker #36. This had been my personal locker for years. Sitting down on the bench and touching the combination lock was always a moment to give me pause. I knew I had 13 more days to open that lock. But after my conversation with Van, I wasn't sure what the rest of the hitch held in store.

The locker had three sets of shelves: The top was where I stored my completed tally books, full of notes going back to the time I started roughnecking onboard. They were priceless to me. I could always go back and review notes about certain lines, where they went and how many valves were in them, shortcuts to computer programs, equipment specifics that the ordinary person would never know unless they had worked with it. Anyone will tell you a good tally book can get you out of a hard spot. Next to the stack of full tally books was a set of Pilot G2 1mm pens. 1.0s are my favorite size pen because I write a lot and the smaller ones seemed to never get enough ink out when I write fast; the 1.0 flowed ink when I needed it.

The second shelf had a change of clothes with my hardhat hung just above them. On top of my folded clothes was my shoulder bag. Years before, I used my safety points to buy my black leather bag with "Transocean *Deepwater Horizon*" in black writing on the side. I kept my pipe calipers, measuring tapes, sheave gauges, calculators, a pair of gloves, a binder with a clipboard, a back-up tally book, and candy. I added a few extra cans of Copenhagen and some gum, and sat down to get my boots from the bottom shelf. I put on my boots, slid my sneakers in the locker, grabbed my safety glasses from inside the hardhat, donned the glasses, locked my locker, grabbed my bag, walked over to the door, and popped in earplugs. The door on this side of the locker room opened just a few feet from the hydraulic pump room, the AHU (air-handling unit) room, and the materials office.

During the summer, the air in the AHU room would heat up from the hot hydraulic oil running through the system, but during the winter months and into spring, it was mild. At that spot, I was standing 113 feet above the bottom of the pontoons. As the door closed behind me, the room purge air bumped the door back open, so I had to slam it closed. I took the walkway just to the right of the AHUs that led up to a bulkhead door of the airlock between the machinery space and the "moonpool"— so-named because on calm nights, the water under the rig reflected the moonlight like a swimming pool. I closed and dogged the watertight door down behind me, cranking the wheel until locked. The light in the airlock was faint, like it was about to go out, the lens having been clouded from years of operation.

There was another bulkhead door that lead out of the airlock to the outside area with the moonpool. I grabbed the door wheel handle and turned until it opened. The cool air from outside entered the airlock as I stepped out onto the deck and dogged the door down behind me. In the front of me was the moonpool—30 feet wide and 115 feet long. Just to my left were the trip-tank pumps and the processing pumps for the shaker house. To my right were stairs going up to a smaller deck, then another set of stairs going up to the main deck.

In our current operation, the BOP was deployed and latched-up (on the sea floor) with the slip-joint installed. There were tons of gear in this area to deploy the BOP and LMRP (lower marine riser package) to the seafloor and retrieve them to the surface: the under-hull guidance systems, BOP transporter, and the capture systems. The slip-joint was connected to what was called a termination joint. This termination joint had a huge ring we called the "super dog collar", officially the SDC ring, which was connected to the end of the marine riser tensioners. Once we set the riser string down on the SDC ring, we then scoped out our slip-joint and connected our diverter and reinstalled it all back in the diverter housing. Pretty extensive, but it was very robust and well-built.

As I started climbing the stairway leading up to the smaller deck, some of the deck crew was heading down for lunch.

"Made it back, Greg?" someone hollered.

"Yeah, can't stay gone long or I would be broke, son." They laughed and continued past me down the stairs as I continued up.

I would always stop a second or two on the smaller deck and look down into the moonpool, check out the water coming from around the inner barrel, the sea state, the color of the water, the surroundings and overall conditions. There's a lot going on down there in that space, and if something malfunctions or even looks like it's going to malfunction, it makes your day all bad. After checking everything out, I made my way up the last stairs out onto the main deck. Here I faced the starboard forward pipe rack. On my left was the hydraulic skid for the rotary table and the APV (air pressure vessel) bottles under the conveyor deck.

I turned right facing starboard, the sun glaring straight in my face, and headed down the black walkway toward the stairs up to the drill floor. Walking along the walkway, I recalled roughnecking in 2002 for our Driller, Dalton Kennedy. As we were working on the drill floor, I heard a rig-wide page come across the speakers from a voice I recognized immediately as Antonio Hall from Columbia, Mississippi. Antonio was better known as "Preacher Man" or "Rev", nicknames he earned working and singing on the *Horizon* decks and often reciting Bible verses.

The decks were well-maintained and the crane crews made sure they were clean. The crew had been on the riser deck mopping up after we'd finished running riser—always messy when we got finished. One thing about a small spot of mud on the deck of a rig: If you walk through it, you'll track it around for miles. This day was one of those days. The crew had mopped up and had drilling tools laid out on the riser deck to be programmed by the Schlumberger MWD (Measurement While Drilling) hands. The MWD guys were walking back and forth working on their tools, and had made their way through one of the mud puddles on the riser deck tracking mud back and forth across the main deck. I can still hear Antonio "Preacher Man's" page crystal clear in my mind: "If you are out on main deck today, *please* use the black walkways provided for you because we are out here busting our asses mopping this gray deck and you are tracking it up. So please, stay on the black walkways unless you have business in that area. If you track up the deck, do your friendly Roustabouts a favor and mop up behind yourself." Antonio's words always were a reminder that if I didn't have business there, to stay off those gray decks because these guys worked hard to keep them clean, and we all needed to work together to keep the house up.

As I walked down the walkway, I faced the starboard crane pedestal and the rigging rail. The rigging rail is where the deck crew kept all their slings and gear for working with boats and moving general lifts around on deck. We were drilling the last portion of the well, so the deck was not full of much casing except for the very last section we were currently drilling. I grabbed the handrail for the stairs going up to the rig floor. A light breeze was blowing, and in the distance, I could see small white caps breaking in the water. I was now 150 feet above the bottom of the pontoons. At drilling draft, this was roughly 75 feet above the sea surface. At the top of the stairs to my right was the rear entrance into the Assistant Drillers' cabin and the offline Cyberchair #3 operator's station.

Straight ahead of me was the heavy tool room and some of my Roughnecks were handing over with their reliefs. The rig floor was normally in sight of more people coming and going, so the cleaning focus tended to be outside on the rig floor. The heavy tool room was one of those areas that was easily forgotten; but, today the room smelled like Pine-Sol® mixed with WD40 and the place was *sparkling*. On my right was a set of shelves that kept our wiper rubbers, rebuilt swivel packings, some float equipment, and general items. Today, it looked like someone had rounded up every safety harness on the rig because the hook was full. Safety harnesses were used all over, and it normally took someone all day going around the entire rig with a checklist to find and bring them all back.

There was a large opening through the heavy tool room to the starboard side of the rig floor with a five-ton trolley rail running above to move large equipment in and out. This rail extended all the way out in front of the standpipe manifold just behind the draw-works, the main hoisting mechanism for lifting and lowering the equipment in the derrick during all well construction operations on the rig floor. It consisted of a drum, gearbox, AC or DC electrical motors, and steel cable that ran up to the crown, went through multiple sheave assemblies, and was anchored on what is called a deadman. This enabled the Driller to pick up and lower drill pipe and casing strings into the well. The *Deepwater Horizon's* draw-works were powered by six AHD1000 AC motors, each providing 1,000 constant horsepower.

The AHD (Active Heave Draw-works) was a game-changer in drilling equipment when the first set of these were installed on the *Deepwater Pathfinder* in 1998. Through many years of proven operations and trials, it became the draw-works of choice—tough, strong and resilient. The braking capacity of four million pounds (double the payload that the derrick could hold) provided redundancy and enabled planned maintenance without having to shut down critical path operations.

The choke and kill manifold—an assembly of lines and valves used during well construction to pump mud down to or take up from the well—was located in the starboard aft corner of the drill floor, directly behind the Drillers' cabin. It had 40 valves with pressure ratings ranging from 10-15,000 psi, and housed two automatic and two manual 3-1/16-inch chokes. Lines from the manifold ran down into the moonpool through the rig floor and connected to a termination joint just below the slip joint. The purpose of this manifold was to manage any unanticipated influx—liquid or gas that entered the wellbore. It provided a conduit necessary to manage bottom-hole pressures, and provided the ability to stabilize wellbore pressures and recover an influx to surface.

As I paused outside the door to the Driller's cabin, I could hear the blowers on the draw-works motors and the motors ramping up. We were drilling on the Kodiak prospect and getting close to finishing drilling. By this sound, I knew that Jed was making a connection.

Sisterhood

Miss Joyce (DWH Radio Operator) was talking about hurricane evacuations and how she was going to miss them because we didn't need to evacuate. She said she had polished a lot of belt buckles during hurricane parties. There was this pregnant pause; the entire room went dead silent. No one knew what to say.

Turns out she was talking about dancing.

Richard Kennedy

I recall the guys making the sign for my door, double-sided. One with an angel, and one with a devil. Whoever came in first would flip the sign when he left to warn the others.

Cyndi Johnston

Precursors:
A Brief Summary of the Contractual History of the Companies & Entities Involved in the Macondo Well

"She might be on the bottom of the gulf, but she is still the best rig in the gulf!"
~~Daniel Hobson, *Deepwater Horizon*

As the *Deepwater Horizon* crew was performing final well completion activities on the Macondo well on April 20th, 2010, the rig suffered a catastrophic loss of well control due to an undetected influx in the wellbore. After exhaustive investigations by private, industry, academic, and governmental groups, there is at least one common known: Decisions affected the outcome. From the well planning and engineering, the review and approval of those plans, changing and deviating from approved plans, and finally, executing the well completion activities that ended in explosions and fires that claimed the lives of 11 good hands, and injured many others. All along the way, *decisions*. And common to all decisions? *People*. People with different badges, different roles, different experience, people onshore and off-.

To better appreciate and understand it, we can examine some factors that set the stage, so to speak, for that event to "play" out the way it did. There were many entities involved in the Macondo well in April 2010; however, they did not all simply converge on what the *Horizon* crew dubbed "the well from Hell" in the Gulf of Mexico 50 miles off the coast of Louisiana with their company badges and cultures. There is a history of creations, mergers, acquisitions, contracts, charters, constructions, schedules, expansions, and the like that brought together numerous factors to drive decisions with profound history-making implications. Examining some of these in should provide an appreciation and perhaps context of *how* and *why* events played out as they did.

Since the 1920s, Southern Oil Natural Gas, or SONAT, with its main office in Birmingham, Alabama, was heavily involved in marketing natural resources. It wasn't until later years, however, that it became involved in offshore drilling. During the mid-80s, a new generation of semi-submersibles came onto the market and SONAT led the field with its innovation. These rigs would become some of the finest drilling vessels the world would ever know. In 1987, the SONAT GVA-4500 design rig, *Pratt Rather,* entered into service. A year later, SONAT added a sister ship, the *George Richardson*. Both these vessels were built, oddly enough, just down the road from where the *Deepwater Horizon* was built, at Daewoo Shipbuilding in Okpo, South Korea. The *Richardson* and the *Rather* would be known as the *Big R* and the *Little R* by all that worked their decks. Both rigs went on to long contracts with Shell in the GoM. As SONAT started growing, there were many crew members from these vessels who went on to fill SONAT management positions, and later Transocean.

In the late '90s I worked with some of these rigs' crew. Jason Anderson was one of them; he worked as a Derrickhand before transferring to Transocean's *Cajun Express.* He resigned from Transocean to take a position with R&B Falcon Drilling on the *Deepwater Horizon*. But he soon was back working for Transocean (still on the *Horizon*) when they merged with R&B Falcon. Many of the team members from the *Horizon* had ties to R&B Falcon, Transocean, SONAT, Falcon, and Sedco Forex. It was a blending pot of people from every predecessor company that made-up Transocean.

Recall, RBS-8D, later named *Deepwater Horizon*, was contracted in December 1998 by R&B Falcon Drilling (International & Deepwater), Inc. to be built by HHI and completed in 2000. The date of this build is important, not because of what might have been going on within the walls of R&B Falcon or HHI, but because of what was just starting to take off across the deepwater oil and gas industry.

When the *Deepwater Horizon* was being built, the industry itself was going through what might be described as growing pains. The oil and gas industry was rapidly moving toward deeper waters in the late 1990s with a continued rapid growth into the 2000s. This growth drove the need for new rigs, as well as crews to man them.

On December 14, 1998, R&B Falcon Drilling contracted RBS-8D (*Deepwater Horizon*) to Vastar Resources, Inc. for its first exploration to commence August 2001. This was known as a "bareboat" charter, with Vastar leasing the rig that R&B Falcon owned and operated. What is amazing is that this same charter—while amended many times—traded hands multiple times for the next 12 years!

Just prior to the order to build RBS-8D and the charter with Vastar, R&B Falcon merged with Cliffs Drilling Co., adding a variety of 23 marine rigs to its fleet. R&B Falcon Corp. at that point operated the largest fleet of marine-based rigs for the international oil and gas industry—118 marine-based drilling rigs.

The R&B Falcon merger with Cliffs Drilling Co. took place on August 21, 1998; however, it was overshadowed by the largest merger in the oil industry's history: BP bought Amoco for $48.2 billion a week earlier on August 12th. (Interestingly, BP and Amoco both had corporate history roots to the Rockefeller Superior Oil Co., broken up circa 1911 under U.S. antitrust actions finally decided by the U.S. Supreme Court.)

If 1998 wasn't dynamic enough with entire companies changing hands and names, 1999-2000 were years that largely set the stage for the key actors in 2010. Transocean merged with Sedco Forex to become one of the largest offshore drillers in the world. BP-Amoco followed when it bought Arco on April 18, 2000. By May of the same year, BP purchased the remaining Vastar stock to complete that merger called the "Arco union". Then on August 28, 2000, Transocean made a move buying out R&B Falcon for $8.8B, making Transocean the third largest oilfield service company in the world. In October, BP assumed the old Vastar charter with R&B

Falcon, now Transocean for the services of *Deepwater Horizon*. Rounding out mergers, in November 2001, Global Marine, Inc. merged with Santa Fe International Corp. to form GlobalSantaFe, one of the world's largest drilling contractors providing offshore drilling services to oil and gas companies.

Throughout the 2000s, there were numerous changes with the *Deepwater Horizon* charter and the companies involved, primarily changes in the dayrates for the rig (based upon market and utilization), and "ownership" (oftentimes referred to as "flags of convenience"). Regarding the latter, Transocean spun off Transocean Holdings, Inc. (based in Delaware, U.S.), Transocean Offshore International Ventures (based in Cayman Islands), Triton Hungary Asset Management, LLC (based in Hungary), and finally, Triton Asset Leasing, GmbH (based in Switzerland).

To give an idea of the value of some of these asset shuffling moves, the estimated income for all Triton Hungary Asset Management rigs in the U.S. Gulf of Mexico in *2006* was nearly $364 million! The 2009 "sale value" of the assets from Triton Hungary to Triton Asset Leasing was more than CHF 1 trillion (Swiss Francs)!

However, 2008 was a strange year for Transocean. It had been in a legal dispute with GlobalSantaFe (GSF) over the use of the "Dual Activity" patent that Transocean had invented in the late 1990s.[25] The "Dual Activity" system was a drilling system designed to conduct parallel activities on a single drilling rig. On the drill floor, it meant two drilling systems matched pound-for-pound. There were 50 feet between rotary tables, 215 feet in the air, and they carried the same crown-mounted compensators to allow them to drill in rough weather. Sitting to the port side of the drill floor was the Driller's Control Room or "Drillers' Shack" as us old-school guys called it. Unlike many systems currently used, this room housed four stations: Forward Driller and Assistant Driller, Aft Driller and Assistant Driller. Each of these stations were matched all the way down to the floorplate bolts that mounted the chairs. In the derrick hung matched travelling systems that could hoist two million pounds. The drilling system itself was rated for 750 tons (or 1.5 million pounds). The term "dual activity" refers to one rotary called "well center", which sat on the marine riser that connected the rig to the BOPs. The other rotary was called the "offline rotary" used for making up tubulars of different sizes and planning for well construction. Each drilling shift had independent teams that operated each side of the system. The Tourpusher and his right-hand man, the Forward Driller, oversaw the entire operation.

Dual Activity rig designs were built to break records. They were built to be efficient and they ushered in an entire new era of drilling sequences and processes. GSF had just recently built and delivered the *Development Driller 1* and *Development Driller 2*. These semi-submersibles were the second generation of the "dual activity" systems that had been installed on the "E Class", or "Enterprise Class", drillships

---

[25] I had the good fortune to be able to work with guys who'd been involved in those original projects and benefitted tremendously from their knowledge and experience.

Transocean had patented and delivered into the market in 1999. With these GSF systems using two different rotaries and drilling packages, GSF was infringing on Transocean's patented system. But that didn't stop people from leaving Transocean and joining GSF, sharing knowledge they had learned from Transocean's systems and taking advantage of the promotion opportunities to make career jumps. Transocean filed its lawsuit against GSF for infringing on its patent, and were in the final stages of this legal action against GlobalSantaFe when the two companies merged on January 1, 2009, as Transocean.

The 2009 Transocean–GlobalSantaFe merger, an estimated $18 billion deal, created—as described by an NBCNews.com announcement—"an energy services behemoth"[26] worth an estimated $53 billion with a fleet of 146 rigs. Per a Transocean press release announcing the deal, the merged company planned to target a range of cost-reduction opportunities of $100-150 million a year by 2010. During this merger, profits for drilling companies were hitting record highs and wells could not be drilled fast enough with the assets available. Transocean, Inc. was now the largest offshore drilling company in the world, and oil and gas companies were begging drilling companies to contract before their drilling rights on leases expired. Drilling rigs under construction already had a backlog of work for several years out.

One month before the accident, in March 2010, BP claimed to be the largest oil and gas operator in the U.S. Gulf of Mexico. However, earlier that year, BP also claimed to only *own* its Thunderhorse operation; the remainder of BP's assets were leased MODUs operated by Transocean. In fact, worldwide, BP was Transocean's largest client with Transocean managing seventy-five percent of BP's global MODU drilling operations.

To gain insight into the offshore environment in 2010, we need to relook at what was happening when industry started really expanding about 2005: New marine drilling rigs were being built as fast they could be designed, fabricated, tested, and sailed to their delivery location. Each new rig needed a crew, and crews needed to be experienced to operate successfully. That experience not only means "time in position" to develop *individual* competencies, but also time working together to build team cohesion and *crew* competencies. However, both time-in-position and team cohesion were being upended as the industry was exploding.

With mergers and takeovers, the demand for more drilling rigs to drill more and drill deeper—not to mention the financial successes by small, independent companies in deepwater explorations—companies were making plays right and left on arguably the industry's most precious resource: people. People who were still learning their positions would be hired by other companies that had critical needs

---

[26] NBCNews.com Oil & Energy, "Oil drillers Transocean, GlobalSantaFe to merge" (AP Houston, dated July 23, 2007, http://www.nbcnews.com/id/19911184/ns/business-oil_and_energy/t/oil-drillers-transocean-globalsantafe-merge/#.WS-K17pFzIU

for personnel, companies that were willing to pay whatever it took to get enough of the right people just to get a rig working. It was a worker's market, to be sure. I recollect an industry expert estimating that between 2005 to 2015, 18,000 *new* people would be needed in the offshore drilling industry, both to replace "old hand" attrition and to crew-up new rigs being built. This posed a huge paradigm shift in how crews had traditionally acquired the experience necessary (i.e. *time-in-position*) to just putting people into positions where they could either sink or swim, so to speak. Team cohesion, an attribute that can only be forged by years of working together as a crew, seemed like a casualty of war.

Add to what was taking place on the rig decks, the mergers from the late 1990s and early 2000s brought with them different processes and systems, even corporate cultures, that people were attempting to "beat-to-fit" together. In a way, the uncertainty and loss of experience and cohesion on drilling rigs was also being played out in various corporate headquarter operations far removed from the deepwater exploration and development operations. Former rivals were now on the same team; new lease operators now had new clients.

As an example, BP and Transocean each had its own safety management system (SMS), but agreed that Transocean's SMS would govern well-drilling operations on the *Deepwater Horizon*, as supplemented by BP. It was a period of tumult and change, marked by rapid transitions of personnel into new roles, in the Gulf and "on the beach", as we say.

And where was the IADC in all of this? Well, as discussed earlier, the IADC did not have the representation of technical people, at least at the "helm". The IADC board membership was (and is) made of CEOs and other corporate board members whose interests are to protect their industry's (and thereby their companies') financial interests. They are not interested in, per se, technology and processes that might even save lives or might save a well. When it comes to innovation, the *modus operandi* of the IADC seems to be "Don't rock the boat".

The U.S. Government's management and oversight of GoM operations at this time, especially the Department of Interior Minerals Management Service (MMS), should also be considered. The MMS was responsible for awarding leases for offshore drilling in the Outer Continental Shelf (OCS) of the Gulf of Mexico. It was also charged with providing regulatory oversight, as well as approving drilling permits. During this period, as the industry was growing and exploration and drilling were booming, the MMS was woefully oversubscribed in terms of sheer demands on personnel, and a lack of in-house technical competencies. In essence, the MMS was charged with an impossible mission of providing meaningful oversight to the very industry from which it collected drilling lease revenues.

Simply looking back at the history leading up to 2010—all the mergers and shuffling and changes to people and processes—and the economic engine driving a dynamic that was thrashing traditional "checks and balances", we should have a deeper, understanding and appreciation of the backdrop to the stage.

People make decisions. People don't live in a vacuum. Decisions aren't made in a vacuum. Examining the context helps us to understand. While we may not have all the answers, understanding the context of the *Deepwater Horizon* in 2010, and the crews aboard and those supporting from on-shore, helps us appreciate the *hows* and the *whys* to the tragic events that happened the way they did.

Rumors

The helibeacon antenna wire ran around the helideck and was always getting torn up by the crane. We got a single whip antenna to replace it to mount on the forward lifeboat deck. Wilfred Boudreaux, the Welder, had to make the mounting post, and he was like, "What's this antenna for?"

I didn't tell him it was to replace the broken one. I told him it was the overseas antenna, and that any rig going to Africa had to have one. That's all I said, and I only said it to him.

The next day the whole rig was in an uproar about the rig going to Africa. People were coming up to me and asking if it was true that the rig was going to Africa, and a bunch were saying they would quit if the rig went to Africa. I let it go on for about a day, then told everyone the rig wasn't going to Africa, that I was just messing with Boudreaux.

Peter Cyr

Getting in the Seat

*"I can imagine that material was not made for Roughnecks' listening
pleasure. Not enough curse words or deer in it!"*

As I pulled open the back door to the Drillers' cabin, Terry Bass (34), Assistant Driller from Zwolle, Louisiana, was sitting in the AD chair looking through the window just above his head.

"You got it?" he asked Jed.

"Yeah, man. I got it." Jed confirmed that a stand of drill pipe had just been handed from the pipe-racker to the top-drive. This was common Driller-AD communications.

The *Deepwater Horizon* had two Varco PRS (pipe-rack system) 6i models, which are each made-up of two PRS4s stacked one on top of the other. The pipe-rackers Jed was referring to had another rig's name, the *Peregrine 3,* stenciled on the sides of both.

The *Peregrine 3* was a drillship that was part of the Reading & Bates fleet prior to the Transocean-R&B merger. It was an older ship, a 1976 model built in the Netherlands. When the *Peregrine* was due to be re-fitted, these pipe-rackers were stored on the *Deepwater Horizon*. Although the original lower sections were meant to have a different home, they somehow ended up permanently on the *Horizon*. Since that time, the *Peregrine 3* drillship has been renamed *Aban Abraham* and is still working for India's Oil and Natural Gas Corporation Limited (ONGC).

The *Horizon's* Varco PRS6i was designed for tubular sizes from 3- to 13-5/8-inch. Both PRS4s were affixed to a lower traveling assembly that had a rack-and-pinion system hidden under two sections of track raised just above the height of the rig floor. The upper tower had a travel assembly much like the lower section, but it did not contain a drive motor. Rather, it was held in place by a horizontal assembly and the gear assembly ran across the teeth as the lower assembly drove it back and forth across the lower tracks.

The *Horizon's* PRS was versatile, easy to use, and easy to maintain. But, like any other machine, it had its weak points, too. The drive shaft that extended through the center of the column was more than 100 feet long and had a coupling in the center. When the rig first began operations, the crew determined there was no way to inspect that critical coupling, so windows were cut to allow for visual inspections. On other systems of the same design, these long shafts have sheared off—the lower drive assembly "driving out" from underneath the upper assembly—causing the racker to fall over in the derrick. This is no minor "hiccup" and actually has happened on several Transocean installations. Thankfully, we kept ours well-maintained and it never happened on *Horizon*.

To make up a drilling connection, the PRS operator extended the arms of the system into what is called the fingerboard, a row of horizontal metal fingers in which the drill pipe or tubulars are racked. Tubulars were placed into the fingerboard in sequential order, and each stand was accounted for in a log called the "Pipe Tally".

The PRS operator assigned the grip function on the racker, then hoisted a stand from its position. He then functioned the latch to the OPEN position. Each stand of drill pipe had a latch; some had two, depending on the size and position in the racking board. The operator then fully retracted the arms of the PRS, watching the camera screen closely as he retracted. He had to make sure that the latch behind the stand being retrieved wouldn't come up and cause the stand directly behind it to fall across the derrick. Nobody wants this to happen during a drilling connection. Bad news.

Once the operator had the stand in the fully retracted position, he rotated the PRS clockwise and faced the traveling system operated by the Driller. Years earlier, the older version of this PRS rotation used to move counter-clockwise in what Randy Ezell from Purvis, Mississippi, used to call the "stir and pour". As it rotated, the arms extended the stand around the electric traveling assembly on the lower drive. This was a design flaw that added an additional five seconds to each stand being removed from the fingerboard. Once this was changed, the operator could just simply turn clockwise, alleviating all the "stir and pour" dancing.

The operator next moved the PRS to well center. By this time, the Driller had retracted the traveling equipment and was hoisting up to connection height. The AD deployed the RBS (raised backup system); this guided the stand over the connection area. The operator then extended the arms of the PRS, retracted the guide on the RBS, lowered the stand down until it went into the box of the other joint in the rotary. The Driller then extended the traveling equipment. On the lower portion of the traveling equipment, there was a piece called the elevator, so-called because in the "golden years" of oil and gas, Derrickhands used to ride them up to the fingerboards, or "monkeyboards" as they called them. The current ones are hydraulic and have bushings inside that fit around the pipe. As the Driller was extending out, he ARMED the elevators: This was a signal sent from the top button of the right joystick to the PLC (programmable logic controller), then to the Cyberbase control system, and finally out to a bank of solenoid valves. When the valve closed, the elevators were "armed". To close the elevators, something needed to touch the lower part of the middle bushing that contained a "trigger". As the Driller extended the traveling equipment, the elevators would swing a little and bump into the stand and close the elevators. That's when the Driller would announce, "I got it."

Terry and Jed were looking at their screens intently. Not wanting to disturb them, I set my bag down next to the Driller's chair. I eyed the coffee pot, wondering how old the coffee was.

Ever since I started working in the Drillers' cabin, I've heard more rig life from the debates, stories, jokes, and gossip we had around the coffee pot than most any other place on the rig. It's kind of like our modern usage of "scuttlebutt", used now to mean "the word on the street" or around the office. On the wooden sailing ships of yore, a scuttlebutt was a cask of fresh water. When sailors were given their break to go get a drink, the stories, news, and gossip was exchanged around the ship's scuttlebutt.

Terry looked just about ready to break. "Ta-Ray," I asked in my best Forrest Gump impersonation, "no fresh coffee, buddy?"

"I'll get some made in just a few minutes," Terry answered, never taking his eyes off the screens. "Let me get this stand."

I watched Jed as he made his connection. He was chewing on a piece of gum looking over the tops of his glasses. He wore dentures most of the time, but not when he was drilling. So, he would be gumming his gum just as intensely as he was watching the Cyberbase screens.

To make a connection on this system, there were more than 30 electronic functions required during a five-minute window for the Driller to add a stand to continue to make hole. And, if he didn't make these functions in the correct order, he had to start over again. It took concentration and good memory muscle to remember where the buttons on the controls were without looking at them. Doing this allowed our hands to move faster while focusing our eyes on the screens, and at the same time watching the equipment through the window. Any distraction in the room—telephone, people-chatter in the background, or doors opening and closing—could break a Driller's concentration.

A Driller never wants to "be stuck" or to "get stuck" while making a connection. During the actual drilling, the rock and dirt (a.k.a. "cuttings") come up the well and are suspended in drilling mud while the pumps are moving the fluid. Once the Driller stops the pumps, the fluid stops moving. Sometimes, if the mud is not properly conditioned, these cuttings will slowly start to fall down around the drill bit. Time is of the essence when making a connection in what we call an "open hole", or when there is a section of the well open without any casing in it. Every Driller needs to have all his little duckies in a row when it comes connection time. I have seen that five-minute connection window turn into days and days of what is called "jarring" or "fishing", remedial operations after having gotten stuck: The Driller still needs to move forward, but just can't move the pipe. If we "twist off" or break the assembly, we generally have to put cement into the hole to cover what is left. As you can imagine, with the cost to drill a deepwater well, this is not an inexpensive failure.

After finishing his connection, Terry got up and picked up the coffee pot from the warmer, grabbed the door handle, and drew back to toss the old coffee out *just* as

Don came in the back door. Don instinctively recoiled back after almost catching a face full of old, hot coffee. "Hey man!"

"You almost got it, son," Terry snickered.

Don put his bag down beside the AD's chair as Terry scraped around the bottom of the coffee can for the last few remnants of fresh coffee.

Jed picked up and got the pumps back going. The telephone rang, and Jed answered, "You get it? Good, here we go." He had just pumped up a survey and it was the MWD (Measurement While Drilling) hand telling Jed that they got it and it was good.

Downhole tools have the capability to tell which direction a Driller is headed. These tools can be steered from the surface with pump pressure, rotation, and weight. All of the data is measured 24 hours a day in the MWD cabin, located just off of the rig floor. When work is critical and the client wants to be spot-on, a Directional Driller is brought in to steer the assembly to its final target. During the process of bringing the pumps back up, the mud flowing through the tool acts like a large conductor and the tool sends pulses back to surface from which data can be retrieved. When the MWD hand calls the Driller, he will tell him that he got the survey and it's good, or to bring the pumps back down to try again.

Jed got the rotary speed back up and began slacking off the string. Once he got a little bit of weight back on bottom, he reached over, swapped screens, and assigned the AUTO-ROP (Automatic Rate of Penetration). AUTO-ROP allows the Driller to go hands-free to monitor gauges. From the gauge data, the Driller fills out a trend sheet.

Jed turned and looked at me. "How ya doing brother-in-law? How was your days off?"

"They were good, Jed," I said. "Was glad to get back to work. If I stay home too long, it don't feel right." We both smiled. Jed went through what he had been seeing with the well: It was slick on the pick-up and the slack-off. No real drag. Hole was in good shape. Not a lot of background gas or connection gas. Basically, nice and quiet. All the pits were leveled out. Adding a little bit of chemicals to the mud. All-in-all, a good time to handover.

Jed was the guy who had taught me how to run the rig, and most of what I know about how to run 5th-generation drilling equipment. Once I understood the concept, I sucked the rest of it up like a sponge. I wanted to know more about each piece of equipment we had. I read operator's manuals on all the gear we used on the drill floor, looked for ways to make it more efficient and ways to save us time, to give the client the best product possible.

We were masters of identifying problems before they became problems and putting preventative measures in place to keep NPT (non-productive time) from occurring. During 2007-2008, the *Deepwater Horizon's* average monthly performance efficiency was 99 to 100 percent. It had been getting increasingly better the previous years and we were at the top of our game.

All the Drillers and ADs made sure they shared with each other any lessons they learned. Notes were captured and procedures updated on each task we were doing. Each new task we did, we wrote the procedure and edited it until we got it perfect. This is the way it should be on every rig in the world, with any equipment and with any operation. Drillers also cross-trained with each of our ADs, teaching everything that each of us knew. Some of us were good with the equipment and some of us were good with the numbers and calculations. We shared this information openly and it created a family atmosphere. We all wanted to see each other do well. Now don't get me wrong, it wasn't always "Kum-bai-yah Shangri-La time"; we also our squabbles like everyone else, and our "oops moments", too.

I remember, it was in 2006 when I was promoted to Driller on the *Deepwater Horizon's* A-Crew. I was about halfway through my days off when Van called me at home. "Hey, I need to you to come back to the rig."

"Is everything ok?"

"Yes, everything is fine son," he paused for a moment. "You just got promoted to Driller on A-crew. Jason got promoted up to Toolpusher, so we need you to take his place. Can you do that?"

"Does a grizzly bear shit in the woods?" I asked, rhetorically. He laughed and told me to be at the heliport the following Thursday for crew change.

"Van?" I added. "Thanks for considering me for the position."

"Son, you earned it. Keep up the good work, and see you when you get out here."

At that time, we were drilling in Keathley Canyon Block 292 on the Kaskida prospect. This prospect yielded 800 net feet of hydrocarbon-bearing sands and was one of our largest discoveries while I was onboard. At the time this well was drilled and yielded potential, it was the world's first Lower Tertiary discovery. It was estimated that the reserve held *three billion* barrels of oil!

Anyone's first day as a brand-new Driller has challenges without adding any equipment issues or problems. On my first day, I had a *big* problem. The crews had been running casing for almost two days, and that day, they were running a long string of 13-5/8-inch casing. They ran casing through our short change, and when I came on at midnight that night, I took over what was left of the running. When I sat down in the chair, I had nine stands of 13-5/8-inch left in the derrick. After that, we planned to swap over to the landing string. I handed over from Jed, and the other crew left the floor. Everyone was called inside the cabin for a safety meeting prior to starting the job. It was dark and sometimes doing large casing jobs like this at night is a bit harder because of the visibility, but the main thing this night was the weight of the casing string. One wrong move with the elevators or the slips would mean that the string could be damaged or potentially lost. So, special care was needed when setting the slips and taking weight onto the elevators—slow and steady.

I ran seven of the stands out-derrick. Don lowered stand-8 down into the string, and I lowered the casing elevators over the top of the stand. I watched in the camera until the fill-up tool and the elevators had gone down to the marked position. I had a visual mark or a distance I used to live by when running casing.

The derrick camera sat at a pitched angle above the Drillers' cabin about 100 feet up looking down onto the floor. As the camera zoomed-in, some of the clarity would be lost, and it was sometimes a struggle to see clearly at night. So, I used a reference of light to gauge when I was low enough: The view of the pipe handler back-up clamp and how much light was shining through the opening. As I slacked off, the opening would close and only a sliver of light passed through that the derrick camera would pick up.

Don moved the PRS and I looked outside to make sure that the Weatherford Crew Chief, Lance John, from Crowley, Louisiana, was ready to go. He radioed in with his distinctive, "All good, Greg." Lance possessed one of the most distinct Cajun accents I have ever heard, and I'm from Louisiana!

I slowly lifted the string as the elevators took the complete weight. I hoisted an extra amount when the operator opened the slips because I've had them hang-up on me when I was AD and almost ruined some casing. Once the slips opened, I got the green indicator, and started down with the string, slowly. I cut the mud pumps on to fill the stand as I lowered it. As I neared the drill floor with the elevators and top-drive, I could hear the draw-works roll back the last layer of drill line. It made a very distinct sound as the motors would begin to ramp down, almost like letting off the gas after revving a car engine high.

I brought the string to a complete stop at the proper make-up height for the next stand of casing. I flagged Lance to set the slips. As he set the slips, I began to slack off the casing string transferring the weight to them. As the weight indicator changed over to the weight being applied to the slips, I could see the elevators on the casing just barely moving away from the bails. (The bails are what the elevators hung on.) I could see an inch or so of room and I flagged Lance to open the elevators. He opened the elevators, and I let the rest of the mud empty out of the top-drive and fill-up tool. I would usually give it about 10-15 seconds. Sometimes these casing fill-up tools had a valve inside of them, and if they got stuck open, mud got all over the deck of the rig. This 10- to 15-second pause would keep that from happening and was a small effort to "keep the house in order".

As we were sitting for a moment waiting, the entire rig floor shook all of a sudden—like it bounced up and down in the water. Then there was another movement; but this time, the entire casing string disappeared. I looked where the casing had been sitting in the slips and I could see the end of the fill-up tool hanging just above the rotary. I retracted the block and top-drive back out of the way. Then there was a mud plume that shot above the slips about eight feet into the air for about three seconds, and then it stopped.

Ron had the radio at the time and walked over and peered in the hole. "What do you want me to do?" he asked. I told him to put the hole cover over the slips. I turned and looked at Andrew and told him he needed to call Dwight Nunley, the BP Company Man, to let him know that we had dropped the casing.

He just laughed.

"I'm dead serious," I said.

Andrew, mouth wide-open, stood up, came over to the chair, and looked over my shoulder at the weight indicator.

"You're still showing the hook-load," he said.

"Now, Andrew, that's the weight-on-bit," I explained matter-of-factly.

The phone rang and it was the Dynamic Positioning Officer (DPO) on the bridge. "What did you just do?" he asked.

"I lost the string," I reported. "A string of casing."

"What do you mean, *lost it*?" he asked. I told him it dropped out of the slips. He informed me that the rig came up eight inches on the draft. The string weight (without the traveling equipment) was 980,000 pounds!

We spent the next few days running a hydrostatic bailer, which works like a vacuum cleaner, to recover the inserts that had fallen out of the slips into the hole. We recovered 61 of the 63 dies. We'd calculate the hydrostatic pressure of the depth to "suck-up", then run a certain amount of pipe dry into the well. Once we got to the bottom of the well, we simply touched it with a small amount of weight, and the mud from the outside would rush inside, capturing any junk along with it.

We then ran a spear and a casing patch on the last stand of casing in the derrick. This had to be within three feet of tolerance. Trust me, in deepwater, blindly reaching that deep into a hole, three feet is not much. We had some extensive discussions regarding the wellhead datum before finally deciding we were ready to go. We latched into the string that was on bottom, pulled the string weight back up to the 980,000 pounds, set the casing patch, and hung it off in the wellhead. It was amazing to have seen that operate so perfectly. It was one of those jobs that no one ever wants to do, but also a job that a Driller wouldn't want to miss just for the sake of the experience.

We ran in, drilled out the shoe, and performed a cement squeeze job through the bit. We were successful on all counts. When we drilled out, we realized I had made an additional seven feet of hole when the casing hit bottom at terminal velocity. Those two inserts that we left behind haunted me. Every time I would pull out from BOP tests, or anything that required work in the wellhead, I was always worried that those two little inserts were just dancing a jig down there waiting to hang me up. We made a very successful well, albeit with some time required to recover the dropped 13-5/8-inch casings. From that day on, I was known as the Driller that ran the fastest string of 13-5/8-inch casing...*ever*!

"So, I hear HR has tried to get their meat hooks in you," Jed smiled with his toothless grin as he got up and I sat down. I opened my tally book and logged the depth for handover while we continued to talk. He handed Terry his tally book so that he could start working on his section of the IADC Report.

"Yeah, but I ain't so sure about any of that yet," I confessed. "Van was supposed to send some stuff up here to the rig floor computer so I could look at it. Some kind of 'CAPM stuff' that they are working on in Greenway." [Transocean's Corporate Office location in Houston] I could hear Terry trying to read Jed's handwriting and Don trying to decipher it. Then we all busted out laughing. The only one not laughing was Jed.

"Hell, you know hillbillies can't write," he conceded. "We can barely read!" Then we all laughed again. As we finished the handing-over, Jed told Terry, "Hey Hotdog, get off the computer. I'll finish that report downstairs." I used to call Terry lots of things when we were roughnecking years back but "hotdog" wasn't one of them.

Another Day at the Office

"That boy is a cleaning fool, son!"
~~Karl Kleppinger, Shakerhand, *Deepwater Horizon*, about Roy Kemp, Floorhand

It was one of those calm cool days—small whitecaps cresting across the water, the reflection from the sun shining on the rig floor's puddles from the guys cleaning. Don and I were in the Drillers' cabin, and I could see Shane and Roy laughing about something on the far side of the rig floor close to the safety harness box. It was a good start to the day. I told Don to call the guys in the pit room and have them bring me a copy of the pit log.

The phone rang on the desk just behind us. Don answered. "Rig floor. Yes sir. Okay, I will tell him."

Don turned to me. "That was Van. He sent you an email."

"Okay, forward it to my email, if you don't mind, Don."

"You got it, brother."

Whenever we knew we had a long drilling section, we'd try to get as much equipment maintenance done as we could. During days like these—drilling ahead, watching the logs, volumes, and monitoring the hole for changes—we also tried to do as much training with our personnel as we could. We wanted our ADs working with the Floorhands to get them ready to move up to the next slots in the shakers, pit room, and, hopefully, one day, sitting in the Drillers' chair running a crew. I would pull training records to see who needed what and whether they were behind on anything. Still, I told my guys *they* had to be responsible for *their own* development, that they couldn't rely on someone else. I would tell them they had to dig for it, be hungry, be the best they can be.

Out of the corner of my eye I saw Jason coming through the doorway on the port side next to the riser skate. He always made it a habit to stop halfway across the floor to look up at the top-drive and the pipe as we were drilling. Jason looked at the swivel packing and listened to the AC motors whirring on the top-drive. By listening closely, he could also hear the two small cam rollers running on the internal blow out preventer (IBOP) actuator shell. Sometimes when they were starting to wear, they made a faint tapping as the pipe was turning. These cams were connected to an actuator that was controlled from the Driller's chair. When making a connection, or disconnecting the top-drive from the string for any reason, the Driller would close this to keep the mud from getting all over the rig. However, the IBOP's primary function was to close-off the drill-string in the event an influx entered the wellbore and was coming up the drillpipe. This was a very important piece of the top-drive, and we had to pay close attention to the cam rollers to make sure they stayed 100-percent operational.

The IBOP design concept dates back to 1899 with the first patent by Samuel Haigh of Cincinnati, Ohio. The design continued to evolve until the version used on most every system in the world was invented in 2010 by Slawomir Kukielka of National Oilwell Varco. It is widely known as the best valve on the market today.

Our design had a ball inside. On either IBOP side was an opening we called a keyway. The actuator shell fit across the keyway where two keys were installed, one on each side, giving the Driller push-button OPEN/CLOSE control of the valve.

There was a specific way to install the actuator shell. If it was installed upside down, it would swap the Driller's OPEN and CLOSE functions. I have been on the receiving end of this more than once as an AD or Driller. The guys would just get finished making up the new assembly, and I would relieve over. They would tell me all was good, and I would trip in the hole and get to where I needed to fill up the pipe for the first time. When I went to pressure up the manifold, I'd rupture the mud pumps' relief valves. This is not a good feeling when you have the service crew standing behind you as you are shallow-testing their downhole tools. So, to make sure things were put back correctly, we started spray-painting lines down the assembly—one color on one side and another color on the opposite side—and then match those lines back up when reinstalling. A color mismatch simply required turning around the actuator shell. Easy fix.

Jason grabbed the door handle coming into the Drillers' cabin, and, as he opened the door, I could hear the top-drive running normally. "Hey fella, how's the hole?" he asked.

"As far as I can tell, at the moment, everything is going good," I said. "Looking through the trend sheets, looks pretty mundane."

"Well, the Geologist says there is a break coming up soon," Jason explained. "At this rate, you will be there by tomorrow."

"That's what I am talking about." I continued, "What are we looking for?"

"They are looking for a certain bug in the formation that will tell them exactly where that line runs," he relayed. "It is supposed to be a big show, but that's from them. It's business as usual for us though." He smiled and took his hardhat off and poured a cup of coffee.

"That's fresh, brother," Don piped in. "I just made it."

"Yeah, I could tell the difference in the smell when I came in," Jason said. "It didn't smell like burnt rubber."

Don, who was standing just next to the Driller's chair, started cracking up. Whenever Don laughed, he couldn't help bending over with his left hand and grabbing his knee so he could just laugh as hard as he could. He always had a toothpick in his mouth, and sometimes when he laughed, it looked like it was about to fall out. But he would recapture it and slowly walk away. Still laughing, Don said, "Alright, Big Daddy, Jason is here. I'm going to go down and make some rounds and check everything out."

"Sure enough, Don," I said.

Jason added, "Yeah, get on out of here and go check on the tribe."

As the back door closed, Jason got up and sat in the chair next to my Driller's chair. He turned it slightly so he could see outside, leaned over with his left arm across the fire extinguisher. For him, the fire extinguisher served as a good prop for his elbow. He placed his coffee on the window ledge just behind the large monitor, put his right hand on his knee, cocked his head back, and looked at me.

"What?" I asked.

"I hear through the mill that you may be leaving us," Jason probed.

"Brother," I said, "they haven't told me anything yet."

"Van told me that we didn't have a choice," Jason continued like it was a done deal, "that we were going to have to give you up."

"You would think *I* might have a say-so in this matter, at the very least." I was starting to feel resistance was futile.

"Well, Greg, I am happy for you whichever way you decide to go," Jason continued. "You deserve whatever comes to you. You have worked hard for it. I wish we had a spot here for a Pushing position. You were involved in the decision the last time one came open and you agreed to let Mr. Deshotel fill that one because of his time with the company. That was mighty fine of you to do that then, but what are *you* thinking about now?"

"Man, a new rig, with new people? I would love to push tools here, with my family and friends, but I also know that making that decision will be based on a few things. One, would be who I'd be working with—Pushers, Seniors, and OIMs. The other would be the rig itself and how long the contract was on it."

"It's the *Clear Leader*, right?" Jason asked.

"I guess so. That's what Van said, but I was shell-shocked when he told me. I'm planning on talking to him about it later on."

"What about this C-A-P-M thing?" Jason continued his questioning, enunciating each letter.

"I have no idea, Jason. He was going to talk about that as well. He sent me up a mail. It's in the Driller's mailbox on Outlook and you can look at it and tell me what it is, if you want."

Jason smiled. "I might just do that then."

We went on to talk about our days off. He was planning on hitching up the camper and going down to the river with Shelley and the kids when he got home. He always said there was nothing like sitting on the river with a cold beer just listening to the water run. I would have to agree with him—peaceful and tranquil. The way we worked on the rig with so much interaction each day, with multiple people, and every task under the sun going on, it made a welcomed break of serenity when you could just sit—no phones, no reports, no personnel—just you, your family and nature.

Jason and I had been friends on the rig for some time. We found it cool that his daughter was named Lacie and mine, Macy. He said one day, "Yeah, that girl of mine, Lacie..."

I interrupted with, "Lacie?"

"Yeah, Lacie."

I said, "Hell, my daughter's name is Macy!"

"Well," Jason said, "ain't that something." We talked about how we came up with the girls' names, and how proud each of us was to have a daughter. I had two boys at the time and Macy was my only girl.

Jason logged onto the computer. "You got two mails here, Greg, from Thom Keeton. Didn't he used to teach Well Control at Park 10?"

"Yeah, that's the same one," I said, putting a dip in my mouth. "He was one of my first OIMs when I went to work for Transocean on the *DF96*. We called him 'Pappy' back then."

"Pappy? He didn't look that old during the Well Control course I was in."

"Nah, just a nickname. He was from Alabama and loved Harleys, so I am sure that was a motorcycle club name from somewhere."

"'Please pass on this additional information to Greg Williams. Thanks in advance,'" Jason read the email aloud. "There are two attachments. You want me to open them?"

"Sure thing, buddy."

The first one was a PowerPoint of the organizational chart of the Performance and Technology Group at Greenway. "There's some brass in this org chart, fella," Jason said, as he was perusing the names.

"Who do they all run up to?"

"Steve Hand," Jason answered like he was reading my mind.

"I don't know him. What's the other attachment?"

"It's an Excel document. Hold on. I just clicked on it. It's a contact sheet for all of the guys on the org chart."

"Do you recognize any names in there?"

"Yeah, more brassy than before," he laughed. "Larry McMahon, Walter Cubacio, Eddy Redd. Hey, those guys have been around for a while. What you gettin' into here, Willis?" Jason did his rendition of JJ from the television sitcom, "Good Times", then chuckled, "Hell, ole boy, I'm afraid to open this other email."

"Well, I haven't talked to anyone other than Van about the whole thing, so I am not sure what's going on, to be honest."

He read the next email. "'Jimmy and/or Van, didn't you guys change out today? Please pass this info to Greg Williams: Greg, you can print the presentations and some of the drawings become easier to read. In any case, I've got 11 by 17 foldouts of the surface equipment, etc., which you can access when you arrive in Houston. As noted, please regard this info as 'Confidential'. Regards, Thom Keeton.'"

"This email will self-destruct in five seconds," Jason laughed! "Man, this sounds like some serious stuff."

"What's attached?" I asked, now really curious.

"You have three. Tell me which one you want to open: CAPM-BP Presentation, CAPM-T, and CAPM-Offshore Supervisor?"

"I don't know, Jason."

The phone rang next to Jason. He stood up and grabbed it like a shotgun out of a truck. He stood with his right hand on his hip in his best colonel stance looking outside. "RIG FLOOR!"

I turned back to the Cyberbase screens and continued to monitor the well while Jason continued speaking on the phone. "Yeah, I know. Well, yeah, just tell him to get it out of the warehouse. I will get the work order in just a few minutes." He was obviously talking to Don or John, the ADs, but I wasn't sure which one. I waited to ask until he hung up the phone.

"What's going on?"

"Oh, nothing. The guys are just getting the stuff ready to break down the fluid end of Pump Number 3 when we get finished drilling so we can start tripping out of the hole."

"That's sounds good." Steve Curtis, the Deckpusher, was coming up the stairs. Steve normally got to the top and stopped on the small platform, looked out across the riser deck to see if there was anything that needed to be done before coming onto the rig floor. He looked back toward the Drillers' cabin and smiled. I gave him the "come on in" wave and he came inside.

"What the hell are you doing up here?" Jason poked, smiling.

"Look, if you guys would get me a job up here, you wouldn't have to ask me that question."

"Steve, I talked to Randy and Bo both last hitch," I said, "and told them you were interested. I also mentioned it to Van, even though he didn't say anything back except 'Uh-huh'. We're still getting the word out."

Jason added, "Hey brother-in-law, it will come. Just hold your horses; don't rush."

Steve took off his dark safety glasses and looked at me, sweat dripping down his face, and said, "I've been holding those horses for a few years now."

"We know," I said. "But, you got to give us some time, and we will work on it for you. With those other rigs coming out, I am sure a spot will open up and you'll be first in line for it."

He smiled and stepped back on one foot and pointed his finger in my direction, saying, "That's what I'm talking about!" He cocked his hardhat back on his head, pulled a rag from his pocket to wipe his face, put his safety glasses back on, looked at Jason and said, "Unless you got something for me, I'm outta here."

Jason said, "Hit the road, Curtis."

"I will see you guys later."

"Alright, partner," I ended as Steve opened the door, walked out and pushed it closed.

I looked at Jason, "Steve is a good hand. We need to work with him a bit, but he is 'jam-up'." ["Jam-up" is a slang reference to being a good hand, a hard worker.]

"Yeah, I know. But he has got to wait a bit longer and we'll rope it in for him." Jason changed the subject and asked, "You alright? I need to pee."

"I'm fine. Go ahead."

As soon as Jason closed the Drillers' cabin back door, Bo came through the door leading outside to the rig floor. Bo was a bear-sized man, with a large barrel chest, and was close to seven feet tall. He filled the entire doorway as he stepped onto the rig floor. Walking up to the Drillers' cabin with his hands in his pockets, he also stopped for a minute. He held his hand on the back of his hardhat to keep it from falling off, scrunched up his nose under his glasses, and looked up at the top-drive with his mouth slightly open.

As he pulled open the Drillers' cabin door, he asked, "You alone in here, biggun?"

"Well, yes sir, at the moment I am. But, Jason just hit the head and he'll be right back."

"Alright." Bo took his hardhat off, set it down, his balding head shining in the cabin lights. He poured a cup of coffee, took a small cloth out of his pocket and wiped his prescription glasses, and turned to see if *his* chair was available. We had a special-ordered chair just for Bo—extra sturdy! He sat down, crossed his legs, sipped his coffee and stared out the Drillers' cabin windows at the rig floor. Finally, he said, "Well, I guess ole Van told you what was going on, huh?"

"Yes, sir," I answered. "Not much, but he did mention it."

"Yeah, I don't know anything about it," he said, "But I overheard you guys talking and wanted to see how you felt about all of it."

I told him the same thing I told Van: I didn't want to leave. I was happy where I was.

"I hear ya," Bo said empathetically.

"Ain't nothing like home sweet home, Bo." He just looked back at me and smiled.

Jason came through the back door and said, "Hey Bo, glad you came up. We were just talking about you."

"That's why my ears were burning," Bo said as he took another sip of coffee.

"Nah, not talking *about* you, but talking about Curtis and your name came up."

"Steve talk to y'all again about that AD job?" Bo asked.

"Yes, sir," I said.

"That youngin' has got to be patient," he said. "He will get there."

Jason and I both said in unison, "*That's what we said*!" Jason looked at me and said, "Damn, I like how we think the same." Roy opened up the back door of the cabin and looked in. Jason said, "Come on in, Roy."

Roy walked over between the AD and Driller chairs and said, "I'm going to go in and check the alarms in the diverter house."

"Hell, okay," I said. "That's good Roy. I appreciate you reminding me about that." He smiled, grabbed a radio so he could communicate with me and left the cabin.

Jason razzed, "That boy's made you a hand, hasn't he?"

"Yeah, he's done a fine job for me, and gonna make a helluva Derrickhand for somebody."

I recalled the summer of 2006 when Roy had joined the crew. I had been drilling on A-crew for a few hitches when my Floorhand, Patrick Morgan, got moved up to Derrickhand. I needed a replacement, so Roy replaced Patrick. All the new guys get to make their orientation tour; then they are brought into the Drillers' cabin and introduced to me. I would sit down with them for a bit and give them my "expectations" conversation. I learned Roy was from Jonesville and we knew some of the same people, so we shared some stories. He had been working on land rigs for the past couple of years and felt he could do better offshore. He also knew that the offshore rigs were safer than the land rigs. He was a good kid with a good future ahead of him. He worked a lot in the shaker house training with Karl, and was ahead of the curve picking things up quick. Sometimes, I teased him about being quiet, that he needed to speak up more when he was talking, but he, too, was a jam-up hand.

I watched him outside preparing to go into the diverter housing. He was dressed in an all-white Tyvek® suit and was dragging the mud vacuum line over to the opening. He set up his hand rails around the opening, removed the hole cover, and crawled in. In just a few minutes, the pollution pan alarm started flashing. Roy rang in over the radio, "That's the first one lifted up."

I replied, "Yeah, got a red light."

A few minutes later he radioed again, "That's the second one."

I looked over and the light was flashing. "Yeah, that's good Roy," I said. "Were they full?

"No," he responded. "Just a little in the bottom." There was a pause. Then he added, "I have a question."

I said, "Shoot."

"If they were full, wouldn't the alarm be going off?"

"Yeah, you got me, smartass," I said. "Now, come on out of there and get ready to clean the lights in the derrick."

Everybody heard him say, "Damn." Jason and Bo started laughing in the chairs just behind me. We always tried to have a good time and make the most out of being away from home for so long. Jed told me years before that if you couldn't enjoy what you were doing, then why keep doing it? It made so much sense that it always stuck with me. I have worked in other places where the bad attitude of people would just fill the air, in every word, in every meeting. The *Horizon* wasn't like that at all! Starting a hitch after days off was like leaving one home and walking into another.

It was getting late in the afternoon when Bo left the rig floor. John Carroll came up from the pump-room after helping the guys get all the stuff together to work on the fluid ends and I had him start on my IADC Report. Mr. Ronnie, the BP Company Man, walked up to the rig floor to make his normal afternoon check on things. He set his hardhat down and stood just behind me writing in his tally book. He asked how the connections have been.

"Slick as a whistle," I told him. "Flow-backs all looking good, nice and quiet."

"Good," he said. "Tomorrow may be a different day. You speak with the Geo hand?"

"No sir," I answered. "But Jason talked to me about the proposed depth and the bugs they were looking for."

"Yeah," Ronnie continued. "If they find anything here, it will be in the Middle or Lower Miocene layers."

"Well, I'll be watching for it."

"We will have a plan tomorrow. We will just ease into it and see what it does, pick up after a bit and pump up some data to MWD and make sure we know we are there. Don't want to go running off blind into it."

"Yes, sir."

Mr. Ronnie sat down next to me and put one leg across the other, still holding his tally book and pen. He looked out across the floor as if he wanted to say something else.

Finally, I asked, "How's Momma and the farm doing?"

"Everything's going good," he said. Then there was *the* pause. I was seeing a pattern. Everybody had *the* pause before they asked. "Hey, I heard some news earlier about you though."

"You did?" I acted surprised.

"Yes."

I looked back at the Cyberbase screens waiting for him to say something else. He was quiet for a bit longer. The seconds seemed like minutes.

I respected Ronnie. He had years of experience, and I was lucky to work for him as a Driller. He questioned the decisions I'd make. He pushed me to always keep things in a good working order. He had expectations where most Company Men let the Pushers' and the OIMs' expectations be the ones to live by. He was honest. If he didn't like something, he told you. If he didn't agree with something, he told you. In moments where you needed his guidance, he would give it to you, freely without prejudice, but he also expected you to remember it later. I knew when I first met him there was a certain point I had to work up to gain his respect.

Finally, Ronnie looked at me and said, "You going to accept that transfer to the *Clear Leader*?"

"Mr. Ronnie, I am not sure about that," I said matter-of-factly. "I just briefly spoke to Van about it. But at this time, I do . . . not . . . know."

"Well, it's a newer rig with newer equipment," Ronnie advised, "Do good to learn some of that. These rigs are only getting smarter and it will take smart people to run them."

"Yes, sir," I said, "I know, but I feel I still have a lot to learn here before I go anywhere else."

He smiled and looked back out the window across the floor again. Then he asked, "What about this CAPM system that BP's interested in?"

"Mr. Ronnie," I answered, "I don't have any idea about that one either. I was asked about that the same time I was asked about the *Clear Leader*, and Van told me he would talk to me later about it."

"Son, if I was your age, I would take advantage of any new technology that they offered me. It's the future."

"Yessir."

"You can always drill wells anywhere in the world, but why not drill them smarter and drill them safer?"

"That makes total sense, Mr. Ronnie," I said, "but, I don't have *any idea* what the CAPM thing is."

He explained, "It's a dual-gradient system that lets you use two fluids in the well to lighten the hydrostatic pressure so you don't have so much trouble with the narrow margins between your pore pressure and your frac gradient."

I can only imagine the look on my face as he was saying this—like a kid in school whose teacher was sharing something that was an epiphany. I was sucking it up, listening to every word intently. I hadn't made up my mind either way on what I was going to do, but I was starting to get interested now!

He looked at my face, and then he laughed and said, "Ole Van don't want to see you go anywhere, an' neither do I. But, you have choices you will need to make soon."

"Yes, sir." The wheels in my head were cranking now.

Ronnie got up, walked to the water cooler, pressed the handle, filled up a plastic cup, and stood looking at the data board just above the Driller's desk. Then he said pensively, "Imagine if you could just push a button and change any mud weight you had in the well instantly."

"That would be something, wouldn't it?" I responded, picturing it in my mind.

"It's coming, son." Ronnie picked up his hardhat and said, "Call me if you need me. And have a good night."

"Yes, sir," I said. "You the same."

Jason and John, who were sitting in the room the entire time, never said a peep during my entire conversation with Ronnie. But both looked at me when Ronnie walked out.

"What kind of science fiction jumbo was that?" Jason said laughing.

"Change the mud weight by a push-of-a-button?" John added sarcastically.

"Sounds kinda cool to me," I thought aloud.

We all went on about our business. John relieved me for lunch, and I went downstairs, grabbed a bite to eat, smoked a quick cigarette, and headed to the Pushers' office to catch up with Bo before he knocked off.

Don

I still have the watch I bought Don the hitch before the accident. He called me when I was on my way to work and asked me to pick him a watch up because his had stopped working. He said, "Don't buy an expensive one."

So, that was my invitation to play a gag on him. I bought the smallest, cheapest kid's watch with the cartoon cars logo on it knowing good and well he couldn't wear it. So, when I got on the rig, I had called him in the office because I had his watch. So, he said, "I'll be right on down!"

When he walked in the office, I just kinda reached around, handing him the watch saying, "There you go buddy."

I kept on doing some work on my computer, and Don was like, "Man, you gotta be kidding me! I can't even fit this thing."

I said, "Well Don, you insisted on me getting the cheapest one I could find!"

He just kind of kept looking at me crazy, mumbling a little, fixing to walk out and I said, "Hold on Don, I'm just kidding. I have you a good Timex in my bag, but I didn't mind spending an extra ten dollars to get a good laugh out of you."

He just started grinning, and went back to work!

Dennis Martinez

How about when we put that bird in Don Clark's locker? It came out and he went nuts!!!

Mark Whittle

Workin' Nights

"It's hotter 'n' a six-shooter in there, son!"
~~Jed Williamson, Driller, Deepwater Horizon, describing the Bucking Machine

As I came around the corner, Van was standing in the hallway looking through the Senior Toolpusher's door. I heard him say, "And that's a fact, Jack."

"What's a fact?" I interjected.

"If I told you a chicken dipped snuff," Van said, looking at me squarely in the eye, "would you look under his wing for the can?"

I stood there, not sure how to respond, so I just said, "Yes, sir!"

Van looked back into the office and said, "That boy's goin' places, Bo. Better watch him." He edged by me in the hallway and said, "I got to go call Codyman."

"Have a good one, Van."

He turned and looked at me. "Keep 'em safe. I'm a call away."

"I will boss." I turned toward Bo and gave him the hitchhiking sign.

Bo just shrugged his shoulders. "I have no idea what he's talking about."

"Yeah, me neither. You need anything, big guy?" I asked Bo.

"Just keep it in the road and I'll see you in the morning."

"Alright, have a good one." I grabbed my boots and hard hat and headed to the sack room. I was going to make a round to see all the boys while I was out.

Bright lights and the forklift backup warning greeted me as I entered. Ron was on the forklift moving pallets around with my guys in the sack room. The thick smell of rig wash used to mop the floors still lingered in the air. I paused a minute to recall when I started working down there back in 2000.

I was transferred to *Deepwater Horizon* when Transocean sold the *DF96*. Two other guys, Kevin Delcour (33) from Breaux Bridge, Louisiana, and Danny Smith (30) from Hazard, Kentucky, also started around the same time, but they came from the *Amirante*, which had been stacked. We were all displaced Derrickhands and had taken a reduction in pay to step back to Floorhands, but at least we still had jobs. Like every other "new hand" that joins this rig, I was amazed by the new gadgets and equipment, and was overwhelmed by the overall size. We had all come from smaller crews on smaller 3rd- and 4th-generation floaters—which were mostly all manual except for some of the pipe-racking equipment. These floaters still ran anchors and did not have dynamic positioning systems (DPS).

The *Horizon* had the biggest mud system I had ever worked. It was massive. I knew that I had to learn the pit systems and line-ups. The number of valves each pit had on the *Horizon* was staggering. With the suction headers in the pump-room, I needed to really think about what I was doing before I jumped in there and started opening and closing valves. If it hadn't been for a good guy by the name of Steve Ogden (42) from Wichita, Kansas, helping me out, I surely would have bit the dust. Steve and I worked well together. He showed me around and we got in sync like an old sewing machine. We flat got it done.

Ron was still running the forklift in the sack room, so I decided to take the stairway up to the pit room to visit Patrick Morgan. Next to that stairway was the Simrad™ unit that monitored the reserve pits, bulk system, and power consumption. To my left were the hoppers, and, in the middle, a door that opened up to a long walkway on the outside bulkhead that stretched the entire length of the pit room. I traversed the walkway and stopped just above mud pumps number 2 and number 3, located between the pit room and engine rooms, as they were operating. Beyond that was the ET (Electronic Technician) shop and the ECR (engine control room). I walked past the long stairs leading down into the pump room and went to the far door that opened on the pit room port side.

The door was cracked, and I could see Patrick walking from the sink over to the log book and back. He was weighting mud in each of his pits and logging it. With the purge air on and the vent fans running, I knew I could sneak into the room. While he had his back turned, I slowly opened the door and walked up behind him. Patrick was a short fella we'd nicknamed "Stumpy". He was as honest and hardworking as they come—jam up as we say—and had a very dry sense of humor. He had a joke about everything, and was just plain good to be around. So today, I was going to scare the shit out of him.

He was slowly pouring the mud into the marsh funnel. I eased closer, just an a few inches away from him now. His hardhat was just below my chin and I was looking down waiting for him to turn around. As he reached to dip the marsh funnel in the bucket of base oil, I moved with him so that he wouldn't see my shadow on the floor. As he turned back to the sink, I turned with him again. He cleaned the lid to the mud scale and placed it back on the balance, and turned around and yelled, "Jesus Christ! How in the hell can someone as big as you hide behind me?"

I busted out laughing! "Look brother, if you weren't so dedicated to your job, you would have seen me."

"Yeah, and if I was a bit taller, I would kick you in the ass!"

"Want me to get you a bucket?" I asked, patting him on the shoulder, still laughing. As I headed for the door, I looked back and he was still smiling. I thought to myself, *How perfect this room is for Stumpy. He's not tall enough to hit the lines in the ceiling.* I rubbed my neck, remembering how many times I had slammed my head off one of the valve handles in that room by being "unconsciously tall".

I walked through the bulkhead door and closed it behind me. I turned the wheel extra tight, and snickered. *He'll have to man-up to open this!* I walked back across the walkway, waved at Keith as I passed, and stepped through the sack room door. Ron was finished moving pallets and was standing at the Simrad™ as I walked by. The guys were getting ready to bring up mud from the reserve pits.

The *Deepwater Horizon* reserve mud tanks were in a league of their own. Originally designed to be chain lockers like its sister ship, *Deepwater Nautilus*, it had four tanks with a total capacity of 10,316 barrels. In "normal people" terms, these tanks had the capacity to hold 433,272 gallons of milk! That's more than enough volume to take the entire displacement of riser in 10,000 feet of water depth—something that most rigs could not even get close to achieving at that time! The bottoms of these tanks were some 70 feet below the Derrickhands' feet, inboard of the two aft columns—*Deepwater Horizon's* signature "legs"—on the port and starboard sides of the rig.

When Kevin Delcour and I first started on the *Horizon*, we were put under Pumphand, Jesse Harbin (35) from Hallettsville, Texas, and we were assigned pit-cleaning duty for our first two weeks. After orientation, we went down to check these pits out. I remember thinking, *Pit-cleaning won't be that bad for a bit. Let's learn the rig and the guys*. I had no idea the pits would be *this* big!

We descended in the column elevator and stepped out onto the deck, 53 feet above the thrusters and 20 feet below sea level. The space had been vented for days in preparation for our entry. We donned our gear and setup the tripod for retrieval in case one of us became incapacitated and had to be winched out. I had never used one of these winches before coming to the *Horizon* and thought to myself *that better be a hell of a winch if I go down*. Both of us had a radio to speak to our Hole-Watch. We put on our safety harnesses and entered the tank. We got down to what we thought was the bottom of the tank. But, we weren't even close.

They lowered down explosion-proof lighting, and we rigged it up on the ladders so we could see better. We also carried flashlights. As I looked around, I could see what looked like a big fan blade about 30 feet from me. It was a new generation agitator called a "Flygt". There were two of these Flygts in each mud tank. The one I was looking at was less than two feet from the top of the settled mud. There was another one in the far-right corner of the tank that was about six feet from the top of the mud. What we were standing on was solid, settled-out barite build-up from the original mud that had been in the tank on the transit from Korea months earlier. And, when I say it was solid, it was solid. This stuff made the long ride over from Korea, splashing about with a really long time to settle. "Man, shit, this is a lot of barite," Kevin said as he looked in my direction. Neither of us had seen this much barite in a tank in our lives. We walked around a bit and came up with a game plan.

We climbed back up to the top of the tank, told Jesse what we were going to need, and took off after the equipment.

We needed to assemble enough lines and pumps to be able to pump the barite and wash-water up to the main deck, some 82 feet above us. We used the spiral stairways going up and down the column to stage three-inch air-driven pumps in three different locations. We then connected the plastic-covered, wire coil line between these pumps. The final pump placed inside of the reserve tank with 100 feet of hose gave us the ability to position the suction anywhere we needed while we were cleaning.

On the surface, the wash fluid would be retention-tested and pumped overboard. The client was allowed a certain amount of discharge per the drilling permit. Once we reached that limit, we would have to pump it into cutting boxes to be transported to shore for disposal.

We rigged up a waterline from the fire main and went to work. We cut a ditch as deep as we could through the center of the mountain of barite, put the suction line in the middle of the ditch, and began working the outermost edges, pushing all the wash water toward the ditch. We worked on this for what seemed like weeks: every day, same routine, in and out of the tank.

It wasn't until a couple weeks elapsed—when we'd gotten it down to a manageable level—that we had our first hiccup: One of the lines blew off of a pump in the stairway. Mud was cascading down the stairs filling up the elevator shaft before we got the pump shut down. That created a heck of a mess to clean up.

Some days later, we finally saw the bottom of this tank. We then repeated the entire process on the other starboard side pit. The two port side pits were both fine and didn't need to be worked.

To eliminate the settling issues, the Pushers decided not to put fluid into those reserve pits heavier than ten pounds per gallon (10ppg). Instead, we used one side for synthetic-based muds and the other side for water-based muds to keep the two fluids separated. If synthetic- and water-based muds get combined, the water is immediately soaked up and the whole mess turns into a mud that looks like "chocolate pudding" and does not mix.

To prevent this from happening, the *Horizon* Team modified the reserve pits by installing jetting lines into the pit bottoms. We also added a line to the transfer pumps so we could circulate the tank while the mud wasn't being used. It's a long way to the surface to transfer that mud, so we had to learn to be patient with it before the system was primed to transport it back up. When running these pumps, we always made inspection rounds down to the transfer pumps to make sure the packings were not leaking and filling the room with mud. This happened once or twice, and that was a bitch to clean up. Suffice it to say, no one wants that kind of day, so we checked them when these recirc pumps were running.

Back in the sack room, I walked over to the Simrad™ and watched Ron line up the valves on the screen. I patted him on the shoulder and walked up the stairs to the main deck. It was dark outside now, nearing 1900 hours. I knew Karl would be back from lunch, so I could swing by and visit him.

The purge was tight on the doors to the shaker house. I had to hold the door to keep it from sucking back in on me as I tried to enter the space. With the shakers running, no one could really hear the doors opening and closing. But even with all the shaker noise, the sound of the small metal gate that stayed closed at the top of the stairs was somehow audible. I grabbed the metal gate, pushed it open, then let it close back making a banging noise. Karl was at the sink, and although he didn't see me, he knew it was me, and shot back his "Vanilla Gorilla" grin. This was our thing. I was the only one that banged that gate, but never came down. Simple little things like banging a metal gate and not coming down would be things we would do working together as a crew. It may be difficult to relate to if you've not experienced close working relationships with a tight crew, but these were things that people got used to. After he saw me, I did go down.

"All good Big Daddy?"

"I'm straight brother," Karl smiled. "No problems down here."

It was always cool in the shaker house. From the first time I stepped foot on the *Horizon*, I enjoyed it in there. On older rigs, the mud coming back out of the hole was 100 degrees Fahrenheit, or more. It was so hot that steam would come out of the shaker house on cold days. During a cold snap it was nice and warm, but during the summer, it could suffocate the strongest! On these big rigs, the mud travelled through the riser, all the way down and back up again. In deep water, the riser becomes a really long cooling path bringing mud back to the surface at 68 degrees F or so—the same temperature as the sea water surrounding the riser at those lower depths. Condensation dripped from the mud lines in the shaker house. So, whenever we were drilling, the shaker house was cool in the summer and mild in the winter.

I smiled, looked around, and said, "Damn, it's clean in here! You keepin' Roy hooked up when he's in here?"

Karl shot back, "That boy is a cleaning fool, son!"

"Good deal, big guy. If you need anything, I'm a call away." I headed back to the stairs and out onto the main deck.

There was a cool breeze blowing outside, and I could smell the exhaust of the engines. The sky was so clear I could make out the navigation lights on the planes overhead. On this steel island, so many miles out on the water, one can see many things in the night sky. It is very serene. I turned to the port side of the rig and passed in front of the air intake. To my left was the riser deck and the bucking machine.

I recalled back when I was a Floorhand, we received what they called a "bucking machine"—a machine that makes and breaks tubular connections. BP had purchased the unit from Offshore Energy Services (OES, formally Garber) so we could make up drilling equipment on deck and pick up long pieces of bottom hole assembly (BHA) with minimum time disruption on the critical path.

One hot August day in 2002, Jed was on the deck running the bucking unit and I was working as a gopher—"go fer this, go fer that"—helping him with whatever he needed on deck. The AC unit was not working in the bucking unit control cabin and it was hot. *Very* hot! The deck had a topcoat of light gray that reflected the sun like a mirror. With the sun beating down from above and the deck reflecting heat up from below, it turned this cab into a rotisserie. The summer heat is relentless offshore. Some days, there is not even a mouse-fart of a breeze, not the tiniest hint of air movement. The Gulf would be dead calm, and we'd say that the water looked like a mill pond. A mill pond is a retention pond that collects lumber-yard or wood processing run-off. There is no movement at all on a mill pond, and this is what it looks like sometimes when you are looking out across the Gulf of Mexico.

I was bringing Jed water, but it looked like he was about to pass out. He hollered at me to get inside of the cab so he could teach me how to run it. I hopped in while Jed stood just outside of the door drenched in sweat, and yelled, "It's hotter than a six-shooter in there, son!" I could already feel my skin tingling from the heat, and I just nodded in agreement. I didn't care how hot it was. I was going to learn how to run this machine. The noise from the hydraulic pump inside of the cabin was deafening, so we had to communicate over that wearing ear plugs and muffs. As he showed me the push-pull, break-out, and make-up controls, the sweat was just pouring down my arm and dripping onto the console. Later, when I would look at sheets for making up tubulars filled out on-deck by guys in the bucking machine, I knew why the ink was always smeared and runny—because the guys would sweat all over the paper. That was years ago, but every time I see that bucking machine, I remember that first day learning how to run that beast.

Over the walkway was the riser skate that extended from the riser deck into the rig floor that enabled us to run riser attached to the BOPs. The riser is the large-bore pipe between the rig and the BOP down on the seafloor wellhead through which we all subsea work is done.

The gantry crane was parked all the way to port side and it was as quiet as a mouse back there—only the sounds of the electrical power generation engines and my heartbeat in my ears because of the ear plugs.

I went up the stairs and entered the rig floor door. I could hear the blower motor running on the top-drive as it was getting closer to the floor. This sound told me that it was almost time to make a "hook", or a drilling connection. Jason and both ADs were in the Drillers' cabin: Don Clark was sitting in the Driller's chair, while John Carroll was sitting in the AD's chair filling in the last log in the Driller's trend.

"Boys, y'all gonna make this connection?" I asked.

Don was looking intently at the Cyberbase screen. "As long as you're sitting right here where Jason is, then we will," he laughed.

"Well, hell, I might as well get up then," Jason said as he stood up. "Andrew will be back in a minute anyway. He ran out back to the Geo cabin. You are good either way. So slide on in here." He walked over to the desk and sat down.

I took my hardhat and glasses off, set them on my bag next to the Driller's chair, slid the chair back and sat down.

"Big daddy, you okay with me making a connection?" Don asked.

"Absolutely." I took a quick look outside and told him, "Kick your elevators back before they smack the floor.

"I was just about to do that shit when you said it."

"Good. Make it happen."

Don kicked the elevators back on the TDS8, cut the AUTO-WOB off, and began to drill the last few feet by hand. The elevators eased closer, barely touching the floor. "Have you been backreaming before making the connection?" he asked.

"Yeah, I have been working it up a single, unless I see something, and bringing it back down to connection-height without rotary to see if there was any drag behind me."

"Okay here we go."

I could hear the PRS kick-on outside. John was going after another stand of drill pipe to get ready to hand-off to Don. Don slowed the rotary down and began to pick the pipe up. It was slick. He worked it up about 50 feet and turned the rotary off. He slacked off slowly watching the weight indicator—not a bobble. It got down to about twelve feet and Don cut the mud pumps off. As the pumps were coming down, the Mudlogger put the flow-back screen up on the left-hand side of the Driller's display. Karl was also watching the flowline in the shaker house. Once the trend broke over and started following the other connections, I said, "Alright Don, go for it."

Andrew came in the back door of the Drillers' cabin. "Good to see Don making a connection," he said.

Don signaled for Shane, Roy, and Alvin to throw the slips in, then Karl pushed the talk-back button UP next to the flowline, and announced, "No flow."

Don slacked the drill string weight off on the slips and broke the top-drive out, working his way through the buttons of the Cyberbase. Every few seconds or so, he would look back at me.

"I won't let you mess anything up, brother," I reassured him. "You go for it."

Making a connection in open hole, this deep, on one of these rigs is a *big deal*. There are multiple things that can go wrong, and you need to be ready for anything. Everything went as planned. Jason left the Drillers' cabin and went downstairs. Don got the bit back on bottom, and we were set for the rest of the night to drill ahead.

Hearing Loss

I remember the older fella, Donald Breaux, who used to come out from Houma and service the bucking machine. I had to go wake him up one night because something he did to the unit before he knocked off wouldn't let her get kicked-on and running.

So, I find which cabin he was in, and bang on the door. Man, many, oh Lord, many times! I finally just opened it up. And if anyone remembers, this cat was hard of hearing. So, I see the drapes on the bunks pulled across, so I just started knocking on the bunks, the one that didn't pull open the curtain, I knew it was him. I finally opened his curtain, turned on his bunk light, got him awake and one of those Life Alert tags was around his neck, one of the push-button kinds. I told him, "Hey, got some problems with the unit. Need you on deck." As I was headed out, I was thinking to myself, I hope he knows that Life Alert won't work out here. It must've just been a habit to wear it, but I found it strange.

But, he got me back a few hitches later. He was also the one that ran the flowback tool that BP rented from OES. I was on the rig floor with Mike Sepulvado and Walter Wojciechowski. The routine was I was supposed to let him know when to scope-up the tool when the pipe was empty so we could go get another stand. Well, when he got on the slips, I reached up to check to make sure the pipe was empty and he scoped the tool out. I was brown from the waist to the top of my hardhat with oil-based mud. I took my safety glasses off and turned around, and I could hear Walter Wojciechowski laughing, "Hell, yeah!"

Greg Williams

Cramming: It's Not Just for School

"With what education I had, I had to get mine the hard way. And you know I try to instill that with my kids: Education is great, college is great, and my kids will finish school! My Momma and Daddy begged me to finish school, but no, I wanted to go to work. We was just raised in that atmosphere that it was okay as long as you was working."
~~Jerry Isaac, Mechanical Supervisor, *Deepwater Horizon*

Just after the pre-tour, guys from B-Crew started wandering up to the floor. We were still drilling ahead. Jed grabbed the handle to the Drillers' cabin, stepped in and went straight for the coffee pot. Don had just made a fresh pot. It smelled like relief time.

"Hey, ole man, watcha know good?" I asked Jed.

"Oh, not much," he replied. "Better get down there and grab some of that meatloaf they got made down there. Its good!"

"I hear ya."

"How's the ole hole doin'?" Jed asked.

"Oh, not bad," I said. "No drag. Nice and slick. Basically, the same way you left it."

"Good." We continued chatting for a few minutes.

I leaned over, still talking to Jed, and handed my tally book back to Don who had started working on the IADC report. "Well, ole pal, I'm going to leave it with you and get over there with Don and get that report knocked out."

"Go ahead, buddy," he said. "I gotcha."

I grabbed my bag, got a cup of coffee, and sat behind Don as he worked on the report. Terry was sitting in the AD's chair going through the checklist, making sure everything was good to go. Hunting season had been over for a couple of months by this time and Terry, a big hunter, *always* had plenty of stories to tell about running down big hogs with the barkers in their bullet-proof jackets—dogs with Kevlar vests to protect their chests from wild hogs. But for now, we just all listened to Don single-key-pecking away on the keyboard.

We were using a software system called GRS. It had an imbedded software licensed by the IADC that allowed us to report electronically instead of handwriting each single activity into a log with three duplicate copies attached. The digital version remedied a lot of issues that Drillers had previously had with written copy: Corrections, readability and portability, getting reports ashore for analyses, and not least on the list, storage!

Many years before, when I worked onshore for Nabors, I was roughnecking for a Driller who had trouble writing his IADC report. I offered to help, and ended up becoming the official scribe of the IADC report for his tour every day. This allowed me to learn drilling shorthand way early in my career. But, I also learned that I was working with some people in the oil and gas industry who struggled to read and write. This latter lesson allowed me to offer some help a couple of years later when applying for a job offshore with Hercules.

I was sitting in the lobby filling out my application when three fellas came in and spoke with the secretary who gave them applications and directed them to the lobby to fill them out. They all wore typical rig clothes—overalls, tee shirts (some with stains and some without), and steel-toed boots. As they sat down, I realized they were struggling, so I went over and asked if they could use some help. They expressed their appreciation, and I sat down next to them. We went through each application, line-by-line. None of them had graduated from school; all of them had trouble reading; only one could spell his name. They had been employed up until the week before for a small land rig company. When their company cut back, these guys were going to give it their best shot going offshore. Situations like this made me thankful for the privilege of being able to attend school and learn. Many guys are forced much too early in life to give up their education to help provide for their families, and spend most of their lives farming, fishing, and working in oil and gas.

Don pecked the last key, finishing up the report, and I said, "All right boys, I will be in the life boat if you need me." Everybody laughed.

"Don't plan on any kind of stuff like that while I am up here," Jed added.

I laughed and said, "Hell, I know. It's always a good reminder though. Be good."

I opened the door, and a cool breeze hit my face as I stepped outside onto the rig floor. I was eager to get down to my quarters and read the emails Jason had forwarded to me earlier. On slow drilling days, we never saw much of the Maintenance Crew, so I decided to drop in and visit a few of the boys for a few minutes. I used the port side main deck entrance just next to the port crane, and went down the stairs. At the bottom was Jerry Isaac, (39) from Monroe, Louisiana. "Where ya headed, brother?" he asked.

"Hell babe," I said, "I'm knocking off."

"Yeah, I know. Just messing with ya."

"How y'all doing down here?" I asked.

"Man, it's been a good, quiet day. Got lots of PMs [preventive maintenance tasks] done and closed-out."

"That's good," I said. "Keep some of this shit running."

The *Deepwater Horizon* was the only rig I had ever been on that didn't have an us-versus-them mentality. At most installations or places where I've worked or visited, there was a feeling of separation between departments, where folks felt that certain jobs were owned by the Mechanics or the Electricians, Big Wire, Small Wire—and *everyone* had their opinions about the Drill Crew! Folks on other rigs seemed to share a perception that most Drillers just tore stuff up all day, and then *they* were the ones who had to fix it. There was probably some truth that Drillers tear stuff up when they're drilling—that's life. But the folks on *Horizon* were family. When we left home to come to work for these long periods of time, we came back to another family, and that made coming back to work not so bad. For some of the guys, the rig was actually a better environment. Some of them were rough characters when they were at home, and the rig kept them sober, out of handcuffs, healthier, and wealthier.

A page came across the intercom. "Jerry, Rig Mechanic, call the shop."

Jerry gave me a 'sayonara salute'. "Alright brother, let me step in here and see what they want."

"Ok, buddy. Will see ya tomorrow." I turned and walked toward the lower set of stairs which led down to the second deck change room. This was most of my guys' change room. The coffee shop was just above with two flights of stairs between the change room, coffee shop and the main deck. It was just easier to grab a locker here, grab a smoke above, and then be on deck in just a few minutes.

I went inside. The room was completely empty, and the smell of Go-Jo hand cleaner and mopping solution was in the air. They kept the quarters around 65 degrees F, so it was like a freezer when I walked in. I took off my hardhat and safety glasses, put the glasses inside the hardhat, slipped my boots off, picked up all my gear and headed down the hallway to my change room. My feet were always super-warm inside my boots, so after I walked down the hall, my sweat-prints followed me all the way down the off-white floor. I passed my bedroom. The door was open, bunk made, fresh towel on the bed—always an inviting thing to see. I passed through the gym and into the change room, opened my locker, unloaded my boots, hardhat, and bag.

As I went into my cabin, started the shower, got all the stuff out of my pockets and threw it onto the desk, I thought, *What a hell of a day. Not only was there one new job offer, but two. Why would they want me? Why not someone else?* I struggled with this as I was never a person that was out for myself. I was more interested in the performance our team. One person represents a single point of view and cannot humanly account for everything. The power and strength of a good team is immeasurable. *This was my family—these were my friends, my co-workers, my guys, my crews with whom I had invested so much. How could I ever leave my team?*

I had been thrust into the position of having to make decisions over the next few days I didn't want to make. I threw on my pajama pants and blue Transocean T-shirt and sneakers, went out on the back deck, and grabbed a quick smoke. I gazed out across the water. There were small reflections of light in the distance, but as far out as we were, I would never expect to see anything other than another drill ship or semi [semisubmersible drill rig]. The air was cool and crisp against my freshly showered skin, and chill bumps ran up my neck and the hair stood up on my arms. I felt excited and worried at the same time. I don't really know how that works. The last time I felt this way was when I received a call from the OIM, Ken Reed, from Lafayette, Louisiana, about my AD job.

That was back in August 2003. We had planned a vacation to Florida while my two oldest were still little guys: Tristan was six and Macy had just turned three. It would be our first trip to Disney World and we were all looking forward to it. I had been working 14 days on and 14 off, so a trip like this had to be planned around my off-schedule. When I arrived home from my hitch, we loaded up the four-door 2000 Dodge Ram with extended cab and headed east on a 13-hour drive to Florida. There was plenty of room in the cab for four people and the bed of the truck had a waterproof cover that locked—the perfect place for luggage. We left late at night so the kids would sleep through most of the trip.

Just as we were hitting the Orlando city limits around 9:00 a.m., my cell phone rang. I looked down and saw the number. It was the rig. It started raining as I pulled over to answer the phone.

"Greg, this is Ken on the rig. How are you?"

"I'm good Ken. We just got into Florida taking the kids on vacation. What's going on?"

"Well, when are you going to be back home?"

I looked at my watch. "Ken, I can be back at home in about 13 hours if you need me." I got a nasty stare from my wife. The kids started waking up.

"No, I don't need you right now, but will in about a week."

"Ken, I can be back home in a week. Watcha got?" The hair started raising on the back of my neck—that excited-worried feeling taking hold. *Was this the job I had been waiting on for so long?*

"We need an Assistant Driller on D-Crew and you're next up, Greg."

"Ken, I can come back as soon as you need me to, and I appreciate the promotion."

"You're welcome. The Pushers picked you, Greg. You worked hard for it. Let me know when you get back home and we'll work the schedule out."

I finished up my cigarette, thinking about that call five years ago. I wondered how this was all gonna play out? With a headful of thoughts, I went upstairs to the galley to grab a bite to eat before heading over to the Pusher's office. Just as Jed had advised, the meatloaf was good—strong with onions, just the way it had been for the last six years. It seemed most of the meals never changed very much. I learned later in my career that the OIMs picked the meals and agreed on the menus with the Camp Boss. A lot of their personal tastes went into it; that was just another perk of being an OIM. If the crew didn't like what was on the menu, to whom would they complain? Certainly, not the OIM because they might be complaining about one of his favorite meals!

Honestly, the rig's menu was one topic I avoided. We had the best jobs in the world: We got paid to work, got our clothes washed, a bed to sleep in, good friends (on most days) to talk to, and food to eat—not a whole lot to complain about, especially considering the conditions much of our military work under. Yes, our jobs were dangerous, but it was danger that we knew, anticipated, and could control with proper techniques and experience. Our counterparts in the Armed Forces sometimes do not have the luxury of being able to control the danger that lurks just around the corner. So, most of us never complained. That always seemed like biting the hand that fed you. Literally.

I finished up the meatloaf and deliberately made my way to the ice cream cooler. There it was, the signature pralines and cream that always seemed to make it onto the supply list. I'm not sure whose favorite this was, but I was sure glad it was someone's. I filled my cup to the brim, closed the cooler, and left the galley.

Everything was quiet on the floor. The Company Man's TV all the way down on the other end of the hallway was playing. I wondered if Teddy Reed, the night Company Man, was watching the TV on full-blast because he was hard of hearing. Most of us had some type of hearing loss from the work we did because in days past, we didn't have the proper protection. Years back, we only had two things to protect our hearing: our left and right fingers! And those tended to be mostly engaged in some sort of work anytime you really needed hearing protection. The opportunities to utilize fingers to close off your ears were slim-to-none. Today, the requirement to use hearing protection—single- and double- barriers of protection from high noise—is enforced 100 percent, a good change in the industry.

I turned the corner next to the OIM's bedroom and looked into the Maintenance office. It was vacant as all those guys—Maintenance Supervisor, Electrical Supervisor, and Mechanical Supervisor—all worked 6-to-6 shifts. It sure was a tiny office for three senior supervisors to work in.

Stepping into the Senior Tourpusher's office, Don was tapping on the computer keyboard looking at the IADC report on RMS. "Hey, Big Daddy," he greeted me.

"Hey brother," I said, "Checking the report out?"

"Yeah. I was having some problems getting this BHA [bottom hole assembly] put into the report."

"Let me look," I said as I slid in. Sometimes the system locked-up if the operator stayed on one page too long. It was necessary to refresh and save it again so the data would replicate correctly. An entire page could be filled out, the report finished, but didn't get refreshed and saved again. Then at 5:00 a.m., the Senior Pusher would be calling the on-tour AD or Driller wondering why the report wasn't completed. This happened to me more than once as an AD, and it was a hard lesson! So, whenever I was doing the reports, I would save multiple times throughout so that my work wouldn't get erased. Tricks of the trade—the more you use it, the more you got used to it.

I slid my chair over to the Senior Pusher's computer. The password had been changed, so I dug around, and pulled the keyboard tray further out. People usually had a Post-it with the password written on it just to the left of the keyboard. Sure enough, there it was. I logged in and went to my Yahoo Mail.

As I searched my emails, my excitement grew. I opened the first one and read the attachments. I read each name of CAPM Project Team on the PowerPoint presentation. There were a few placeholders for some of the positions, one being the Offshore Supervisor, which was presumably me. I closed the PowerPoint and opened the Offshore Supervisor Job Description and started reading.

Each task on a Transocean job description had a 1, 2, or 3 Level of Authority. Level 1 was 'act at will'; Level 2 was 'act, but inform the person that you report to'; Level 3 was 'consult before acting'. Most of the tasks for the Offshore Supervisor were Level 1, meaning I needed to learn *a lot* about the position, and there were no references—this was a newly created position for someone to monitor and supervise the offshore operations' portion of the project. Most of it used terms and nomenclature common to any other offshore job description...*except* for a few points that related to equipment testing and installation, and monitoring the process. There was also a section on teaching drilling crews how to operate the system. It definitely needed more than a cursory look.

I opened the second email and looked at the surface equipment setup and the last PowerPoint that had been prepared for the management update. This equipment was completely foreign to me, other than the centrifuges and the large-bore manifold. I would have to learn about everything else from scratch. All of this was a bit overwhelming. Of course, I also knew I still had the option of heading over to Korea to pick up the *Clear Leader*.

Getting the *Clear Leader* added as a functioning offshore drilling unit was equally important to the company. But as challenging as assuming a new rig and crew was to me professionally, the CAPM Project was what had really captured my attention. I had a chance to do something cutting-edge, and I was looking forward to hearing more about it. I forwarded the emails to my home email so that my wife could read about both projects, and, hopefully, we could talk about them over the next few days. I signed off and looked around. Don was long gone. I was so engrossed studying about CAPM that I hadn't even heard him leave. I locked the computer, got up and walked down to my room. I slipped into the freshly washed sheets, turned out the lights, and lay there for a minute. Listening to the hull vibrating put me to sleep almost instantly.

Oops! (Part II)

When the rig flooded, me, Big A, and Jerry Pitts were mopping water three levels up from the pontoon. I asked them what should we do with the mop water? We decided to dump it down the elevator shaft because Karl Rhodes was vacuuming it up at the bottom. I looked down there and saw Karl's head stick out into the elevator shaft and I dumped a full bucket of saltwater and spit on his head. From three levels up, it was enough to knock his hat off.

All I heard was "Gawdda$& it, Matt!" Then heard steps like a cartoon when Yosemite Sam is chasin' Bugs Bunny. It was Karl running up the steps. He ran all the way up there just to ask why.

I said, "You needed to cool off!"

Matt Hughes

I remember when we picked the rig up in Cape Town to take it to Curacao. Most of us had shown up the night before, but one flight was delayed and didn't show up until that morning and the guys on it had to go directly from the airport to the harbor. When the bus of late arriving crew showed up, me, Mack Silas, Richard Kennedy and a bunch of others who'd been together in Korea were standing around shooting the breeze while waiting to be taken out to the rig. A new hand came up and joined us and listened to the conversations for a while.

When there was a break in the conversation he said, "So what do you guys all do?"

I was like, "Oh, we work on an oil rig."

He said, "No shit. I mean what do you do on the rig besides being a smart ass?"

I stuck out my hand to shake his and said, "Hey, I'm just messing with you man. I'm Pete, the Chief Mate. And who are you?"

He said, "I'm Jeremy the AB [Able-Bodied Seaman]."

I said, "Really? So, in addition to being a smart ass, I'm also your boss." You should have seen the look on his face. His chin just about hit the ground. Mack almost fell over clutching his gut he was laughing so hard. Everyone had a good laugh at this, including myself.

We joined the rig and carried on with our business. Of course, everyone on the DWH knows we all got on just fine, but it was months later when Jeremy confided in me that on that day, he had felt like just turning around and getting back on the bus.

Peter Cyr

Going with My Gut: No, Thank You

"Yeah. Geo was down here giving us the run-down on how old the formation was and what was in it as far as microscopic bugs. Man, I almost fell asleep! It was like watchin' grass grow!"
~~Jed Williamson, Driller, *Deepwater Horizon*

I awoke around 8:00 a.m. Once I got back to life on the rig, it always took a few days for me to reset my internal clock. I lay in bed for a moment, and knew we weren't tripping because I the motion wasn't there. Whenever they were tripping on the rig floor, I could feel the rig bob up and down from the momentum of picking up and lowering the traveling equipment. I grabbed the remote and turned the TV to the rig floor. *Still drilling*. Seeing it on TV just confirmed what I already knew. I changed the channel to the Mud Logger screen to see what their depth was and how much longer we had to drill. *Still plenty of hole left*. I was excited. I should be crossing a sand today based on the information provided by "Paleo", a discipline of oil geologists who specialize in correlating micropaleontology findings in cuttings to the presence of hydrocarbons [27].

I crawled down from my top bunk. This was always kind of a balancing act for me. I hated the ladder because the rungs were made for people with small feet and mine weren't. So, I usually bypassed the ladder and just put my foot on the side of the bottom bunk. "One giant step for man", and I'm on the floor. I grabbed a towel and showered, put on my Carhartt jeans and a button-down shirt, slipped on my tennis shoes, grabbed my tally book, and headed upstairs to the Pushers' office. I left the door ajar so the Bedroom Staff hands could easily get in to clean before pre-tour.

At the top of the stairs I passed Van in the hallway.

"Hey, need you to come talk in a few minutes."

"Hell, Van, we can talk now." I said. "I'm good."

"Well, come on then."

I followed him down the hallway to his office. Van closed the door behind me and sat down at his desk. He pulled the phone over between us, pushed buttons, and the phone started ringing.

"This is John," my Rig Manager, John Keeton, answered.

"Hey John, I got Greg in here," Van started, "and we are calling you about this CAPM stuff."

"Alright. Well, let's talk."

---

[27] PetroWiki, "Paleontology in Petroleum Geology", http://petrowiki.org/Paleontology_in_petroleum_geology

"Greg, you seen the mails, son," Van said directing the conversation to me. "What's on your mind?"

For me, this was big, and I was a little bit awestruck. Here I was talking to both the OIM and the Rig Manager, and they were asking me what *I* thought about something!

I finally answered, "I'm interested in learning more about it before I accept the position."

"Well," John advised, "if you don't take this one, you are going to the *Clear Leader*. So, you best make your mind up soon, or HR will put you where *they* want to. Look, how about we get that fella, JP, and Thom Keeton on a call later on and talk about it? How would that be?"

"That will work," I responded, feeling a little bit better. "At least I can ask a few questions then."

"Good enough, John," Van said. "Let me know what time and we will give you a call back."

"I will give them a call *now*. Stand by."

The phone went silent and Van picked up the receiver and set it back down. He looked at me and said "Greg, I hate to lose you, son. But I haven't been able to argue this one out. It's either the *Clear Leader* or this CAPM Project."

"I know, Van," I said. "I just want to make sure I am doing the right thing for me, that's all."

"Like I said," Van continued, "I just wanted you to know how I felt."

The phone rang. "Hey guys, got a pen? Here's the number to call," John said. Van wrote the number down. "Give us about 15 minutes and call that number."

"Alright," Van concluded. The phone went silent again.

"Van," I said, "I'm going to burn one real quick."

"Hell, I will come with ya." We left his office and headed down to the coffee shop.

This time of day on the *Horizon's* schedule could be described as the calm before the storm. It was just before the 9:00 a.m. break and preparation for lunchtime. At 10:00 a.m., helicopters would start coming and going, then the busyness of new people checking into quarters. Crew change days meant that guys who only see each other two times a month piled into hallways to catch up about what they did on their days off.

I followed Van into the coffee shop, and we stopped and poured a coffee. I could tell by the way the creamer mixed in that it was far from fresh. I opened the door to a strong order of nicotine floating in a cloud of smoke. In the porthole of this small space was an ivy plant, which was cared for by the Catering Crew. Its leaves were a mixture of dark green and chocolate brown showing the accumulation of the nicotine and tar from the smoky air. How it managed to survive all those years in the coffee shop was beyond me.

Newspapers were always laying on the table—some from the day before, some from the day. After the helicopter arrived, that day's papers would find their way to the coffee shop table, compliments of the BP Dispatcher, which was always a nice touch. Gene Frevele (50) from Pittsburg, Kansas, our Chief ET—formerly an Electronics Warfare Technician in the Navy—was sitting with his "48"-quart coffee cup reading a newspaper spread out on the table, scrutinizing each section line-by-line. On the wall, just behind Gene were picture print-outs of some of the rig crew on their motorcycles in different parts of the world. The comradery remained strong regardless of where guys were.

When you have been working with the same people for so long, it becomes instinctive to ask about family, friends, pets, or whatever else comes to mind. General conversations about topics of the day were always a quick way to strike up a Marlboro. I should say Gene and I. Van never brought up anything. He would flip through the newspaper and laugh when we said something that warranted a smile. Today's conversation was about Pamela Anderson's latest divorce. We laughed about Tommy Lee being the DJ for her next wedding, and how the Baywatch cast could come back as the servers. And then afterwards, they could all do a reunion tour together. Yeah, conversations like that were normal on the *Horizon*.

Van looked at his watch. "Alright boy. Let's head back to the office."

"Alright." I put out my smoke out and followed. Van was a fast walker. He once told me, "You must walk with purpose in this business." I never asked him why. I just assumed it was something that he had used as part of his appearance when he was pushing tools. We sat back down at his desk and Van dialed on-speaker.

"Hey Van, I have myself, Thom, and JP here," John answered.

"Well, it's myself and Mr. Williams on this side."

"Hey guys," I jumped in. "Thom, it's been a long time, a few years at least."

Thom "Pappy" Keeton, from Mobile, Alabama, was acting as an advisor for the CAPM Project in this current role. He knew a lot of people in the industry and spoke the language necessary to blend in with the rig supervisors. I first met Thom ten years earlier on the *DF96*. He was my first OIM I had in deepwater, although it was considered mid-water, or "other". We had built a relationship over the years. Thom was the first Well Control Instructor with Transocean to become IADC-certified so he could teach Fundamental and Supervisor courses in Houston. I first took his course when I was a Derrickhand on the *Horizon*, and stopped by his house once or twice during the week to visit with him and his family. Thom had 30 years in the industry and was well-respected by many going all the way back to the Wilrig and Penrod days in the 1980s.

"Hey Greg," Thom answered. "John said you have some questions about the project?"

"Yeah, just a few, Thom."

JP interjected, "Gents, just a reminder that anything we discuss over this call about the Project is confidential and needs to be kept in-house."

"Okay JP, that's not a problem," John said,

JP continued, "Let me introduce myself. You guys know Thom, so I will get started. My name is JP Buisine. I am the manager of the CAPM Project. CAPM is Transocean's answer to the pore pressure and fracture gradient problem that we currently face in the deepwater market. It's a combination of equipment and theory that will allow us to drill wells safer, more efficiently, and well under budget. Greg, I trust that you have reviewed the mails that Thom has sent you?"

"Yes sir, I have. Looks very interesting and I'd like to learn more about it."

"Well, once you get here and get sorted out in Houston," JP advised, "we can get up to speed on everything."

"Okay."

"What other questions do you have, Greg?" John asked.

"How is the pay going to work being in Houston?"

"You will be paid the same as you are on the rig," JP clarified. "The only difference will be that this will be a full-time position until you have a relief in place. We had two candidates, but the other candidate had an accident prior to us being able to interview him. So, we will do this at a later time. But we need to get the first Supervisor onboard now so that we can get started with the training and interface."

Thom added, "We have your laptop and phone here. Just needs to be activated when you take your seat. Your apartment is also ready for your arrival."

Van muted the phone. "Boy, they pullin' the whole wagon out here." He took the phone off mute

John picked up, "So everything will be taken care of, mileage, travel, all of that."

"Yes," Thom added. "Normal company exemptions will be applied and paid like they are now."

I looked around the room. My heart was beating much harder now. There was a hunting show playing on the Outdoors Channel on the TV. Van had the TV muted during the call, but two guys in camo stood there holding one of the biggest turkeys I had ever seen. Without muting the phone, Van whispered, "Look at the beard on that bad boy!"

There was a quiet pause on the other end. Then John jumped in, "Hey boys, y'all still with us?" We could hear Thom and JP laughing on the other end.

"We were wondering what you guys were watching on the TV," Thom said. "I then remembered how much Van liked to hunt and realized he was talking about a turkey!"

We could hear all of them carrying on a conversation in Houston. It was obvious that the team had had prior discussions about this position. Van and I were only privy to this part of it.

John brought the focus back, "Greg, you have any more questions?"

"No sir," I answered. "Not right now."

"Greg, you'll need to call James Penny and tell him you are accepting this position so that HR will know."

"Me?"

"Yes, you."

"Yes sir. Will do," I responded. "Does anyone have his number?"

"I will send it to Van after this phone call."

"Alright guys," Van took over, "we are going to let you go."

The guys thanked us for calling in and hung up. Van picked up the handset and set it back down. He looked at me across the desk and said, "Well, I guess that's it, huh?"

"I guess so."

"You just have to call HR," he reminded me.

Me call HR? I haven't talked to HR since I hired on 10 years ago! While we were sitting there, John emailed the number to Van who wrote it down and handed it to me. I figured I might as well get this over with and excused myself.

"Van, I'm going to step over here to the Senior Pushers' office and call Mr. Penny."

"Alright, son" he said.

I walked around the corner, sort of dragging my feet, holding the piece of paper in my hand with the name "Penny" and a Houston number scribbled on it. I kind of felt like a child who'd been sent to visit the principal. In the office, the sun was shining brightly through the porthole and reflecting off the plastic binders on the shelf just behind the Senior Pushers' office chair. I sat down, took a deep breath, picked up the hand set, and pushed each push button deliberately. It only rang a half-ring before someone answered.

"This is James."

"James, this is Greg Williams from the *Horizon*. How are you?"

"I'm good. Thanks for calling me back." James said politely. "I'm busy trying to crew-up this newbuild and you are *hot* on my list. Have you talked to Van or John?"

"I have, James, but *you are* aware that the CAPM Project is asking for me as well, right?"

"Yes I am." There was a moment of silence. Then he asked, "What do you think about that?"

"James, to be honest, it sounds interesting, but I wanted to talk with you first before making my final decision. I have some questions."

"Okay," he said. "Shoot."

I went on, "Who all do you have slotted for *Clear Leader* so far?"

"Well..." James sounded like he was rocking back in his chair. "That's the funny thing. We only have you and two other people at the moment, and they are wanting you guys to fly over to Korea next week."

"Who are the other two guys?" I asked. My curiosity had perked up.

"Terry Johnson and Bobby Blansett," James responded without hesitation. Those had been familiar names for years. I had worked as a Derrickhand for Terry's brother, Scott, on the *DF96*. I respected the family and knew about from Terry from small talk. It was much the same for Bobby, as well. When you work with a company in the oil and gas business for any length of time, names of people you may have never met will get mentioned in general discussions, some folks asking if you know this person or another. I also knew that Terry had been a Toolpusher on the *Deep Seas* when it came out of Spain, and that he had been on that rig for a long time. Bobby, on the other hand, I wasn't that sure about, even though I had heard his name mentioned a few times.

"Well, James," I said, "I am going to have to decline the *Clear Leader* offer."

James was quick to advise, "Greg, this spot won't be open for long. How long is this CAPM project going to last?"

I, of course, never thought to ask this question on the phone call. I jotted it down to ask Thom later. I told James, "I am not sure, but I can find out and let you know later, if you like?"

We both hung up the phone, and I leaned back in the chair, put my hands behind my head, and looked over the top of the computer screen. The headphones hanging around the announcement extension just behind the screen were rocking slowly back and forth with the rig motion.

Van stepped into the doorway. "Did you call him?"

"Yes, sir."

"Good. I can let Keeton know." Van stepped back out and walked down the hallway. I sat there for another few minutes in thought before heading out to start my day.

DPOs

*When we washed and scrubbed the decks, whenever we needed to get rid of the water, I'd call the bridge ask for help. Eight out of ten calls, they could "tilt" rig. I remember the DPO, Hugh, calling me saying, "Are **we** done cleaning the rig?"*

He just pushed a single button! But yes, technically speaking, he did help clean the rig.

Jaime Rene Serna

A ballasting story:

One time I was chatting with the DPO at the stability computer. The phone rang and it was the Driller, and he wanted me to ballast the rig to starboard. I said, "Okay." I hung up and continued my stability conversation with the DPO. I totally forgot about the ballasting.

Five minutes later the phone rang and it was the Driller again, saying I'd gone too far. I said, "No problem. I'll fix it." I turned to the DPO and told him I was about to teach him something very important about ballasting the rig. I sat down in the chair next to the phone and put my hands in my lap.

After about three minutes, the phone rang and it was the Driller, again, telling me that was perfect. I said, "Okay. I'm all-stop on ballasting operations." I'd never touched a button.

Peter Cyr

Drillers Drill—That's What We Do

"As a Driller, the most conscious act that happens when you are drilling is 'to drill', to drill the well, whatever it takes."
~~Greg Williams, Driller, *Deepwater Horizon*

I stepped into the pre-tour and grabbed a seat as the room started filling up. The guys laughed and joked as they were getting seated, some poking fun at others. Some good joking around amongst the team was always a sign that the mood was good for the day. Today's meeting put more emphasis on the drilling side as we were encroaching into the zone flagged by Paleo. This meant that we would drill for a while, circulate, drill for a while, and circulate throughout the day until Paleo was happy with the findings, or with the "show"—a term used when there is an indication of oil in the formation. They felt good about this one. We would find out soon enough.

I went down to the third deck smoking area, finished up my smoke, and headed up to the rig floor. I took the stairs onto the deck and walked toward the remotely operated vehicle (ROV) unit. The ROV Team was just finishing its weekly inspection, and I noted in my tally book to put that in the "Comments" on my report. Even though it was on the A-tour's "watch", I would still make a point to mention it so that one of us would log it. I stood and watched for a moment as the thimble broke the surface of the water. The sun reflected from its wet surface as the small thrusters spun.

Back in 2004, I got to drive the ROV when I was filling in for Jed as AD during the Atlantis Project. It was late evening and I had a few minutes to spare, so I called up Jason Garic, Lead ROV Tech from Katy, Texas. He was doing seabed surveys for the Development Team. He had served as an Aviation Electronics Technician in the Navy before joining Oceaneering to come offshore.

"Hey buddy, you guys just doing a milk run?"

"Yeah," Jason answered. "You comin' for a visit?"

"I want to drive that thing!"

"Come on, let's do it!"

The ROV unit comprised two stacked steel container boxes: the ROV control van on top, loaded with instrumentation and controls, and the ROV shop on the bottom. As I climbed the small set of stairs and entered the ROV control van, Jason flipped on the lights. It reminded me of the interior of the PLC (programmable logic controller) cabinets in the AD cabin on the rig floor: four equipment racks, a small desk, two pull-out laptops, and controls with a mouse that had looked like it had another mouse on top of it.

Jason taught me which control moves which ROV component, but it was not easy to pick-up and run. He moved the sub forward and backwards and turned the camera back to look at the tether. "Make sure to always, *always* know where your tether is. If you get that wrapped up, you'll have to immediately call the rig floor and give them the 'ALL-STOP'," he warned. "Here, come get it."

I slowly put my hand on the controls and started to move the sub. The smallest hand movement made the sub react. There was almost no delay in controls-to-movement, so much different than what I was used to. One quick ROV dip to the side and I handed the controls back. "Here, I will leave this to the professional." Throughout my years, I'd say Jason was probably one of the best ROV Techs *ever*! I stood behind him watching as he effortlessly and smoothly ran the ROV around the seabed. We were in a development field so there were a lot of obstacles: multiple wells, pilings and 30 or more 36-inch structures sticking 10 to 12 feet above the seabed. If he made a wrong move with the ROV, he could catch the tether on the rotating drill string from well center. The effect would be like reeling in the line on a fishing reel—and it would happen quick.

I walked across the starboard side, went up the stairs, entered the heavy tool room, and made my way around the draw-works to the back door of the Drillers' cabin. Jed had just made a connection, so he now had me setup for an hour or so of drilling. I took off my hardhat and glasses, set my bag down, and strolled to the coffee pot. Freshly brewed! I looked over at Terry in the AD chair and he looked back at me smiling, indicating that *he* was the one that had made the fresh pot.

I grinned back, "Thanks, Ta-Ray for the fresh pot."

"See, we trainin' him up, brother," Jed piped in. I smiled and sat down in the chair next to Jed. He handed me the daily work instructions and said, "Mr. Ronnie said to call him when you get to that depth at the top."

I took the work instructions, sat back in the chair, and started to read them over. There was a depth penciled in at the top above all the computer printouts. "They expecting something pretty good-size here I believe," I surmised.

Jed agreed. "Yeah. Geo was down here giving us the rundown on how old the formation was and what was in it as far as microscopic bugs. Man, I almost fell asleep! It was like watchin' grass grow!"

"Almost?" Terry corrected! "I had to wake Jed up three times What are you talking about, 'almost fell asleep'? Greg, he had that cup of coffee sitting back there in that chair in front of the computer and his big ole head kept dropping!"

Jed looked over at me and ran his tongue across his lips as he smiled and started laughing. With his dentures out, he sure did make a funny face. He called himself a hillbilly. But, being born and raised in north central Louisiana, to me he was more of a redneck with no teeth.

"I can imagine that material was not made for Roughnecks' listening pleasure," I concluded in agreement. "Not enough curse words or deer in it!" We all laughed.

Since starting my drilling role on the *Horizon*, I was part of finding three large sands. There had been a total of twelve since the rig started in the Gulf of Mexico. And every time we got close to one, it was like Christmas morning with anticipation, surprise, and just a little bit of fear. Not fear as in fearing for your life—fear as in not wanting to make any mistakes, wanting to do a good job for the client.

As a Driller, the most conscious act that happens when you are drilling is to "drill", to drill the well doing whatever it takes. I have gotten some in-depth instructions from clients. I have also had Company Men look at me and tell me do whatever I needed to make it drill. Sometimes this meant bending a few Laws of Physics. But, when you're working with the kind of downhole pressures we were, it was good to give the well a reminder that you were there and on your game.

The tools used to let us know whether we're getting close to sands are called "logging" tools: Gamma and Resistivity. Both have been around for many years. Gamma goes back to the '70s and Resistivity, all the way back to the '20s. The Electrical Resistivity logging technology is credited to Marcel and Conrad Schlumberger. The success of this innovation propelled Schlumberger to the Fortune 500 company it is today, providing oil and gas servicing all over the world.

Electrical Resistivity is ascertained by sending out a pulse into the formation. Each geological layer has a resistance to electrical current, depending on porosity and permeability. Data received by the downhole drilling tool is returned to the surface by electrical pulses through the mud column inside of the drilling string. Gamma relies on the radiation signature unique to each geological layer millions of years old. When either of these tools passes through a formation during drilling, it will send data to the surface to be recorded on a log for the Driller to see. The only problem with these techniques? Neither is real-time.

The ability to provide at-the-bit real-time data logging is something industry researchers have been working to develop for years. There are tools on the market that get close; but currently, there is nothing that can pinpoint exactly what the drill is "seeing" *as* the Driller is drilling. That means, a Driller must rely on experience, client data, and a host of drilling indicators while drilling to know the "where's" and "what's", <u>always</u>! Most of the Gamma and Resistivity tools on the market sit about 15 to 20 feet behind the actual drill bit. This means a Driller must drill at least 15 to 20 feet of new formation before either of these tools can get into the formation to analyze what has been drilled. This brings its own inherent risks that the Driller cannot see.

There are tools to help combat the unexpected and the *Horizon* was well armed to combat the unexpected. Absolutely critical in the Driller's arsenal when drilling is the circulating system. A simple analogy is your car's circulating system that circulates oil while it's running. Oil is pumped up from the oil pan through a tube, run through an oil filter to filter particulate before passing into the engine. The oil is gravity-flowed back, through oil ports into the crankshaft and bearing cylinders, into the oil pan where heat is rejected before circulating again through the oil filter into the engine.

With well-drilling circulating systems, we use drilling mud. This is a weighted fluid; the weight is specifically mixed based on the pressures in the drilling formation. This weighted mud in the well holds back thousands of pounds of pressure being applied by the tremendous downhole geological forces. The drilling mud is pumped from the mud tank by a mud pump and goes down the drill string, out through the drill bit, and exits into the well bore. The pressure that is being applied by the mud pump pushes the mud back to surface up through the return line. The mud then goes through filters to clean out the dirt and trash (such as drill cuttings) before returning to the mud tank. Anything that enters the system that is not accounted for will give the Driller's team an indicator that something is not right.

As he got up from his chair, Jed handed me the drilling trend then headed back to the desk to work on his report. It was time to review the setup on the Cyberbase. I had learned from Jed and many of the guys how to set-up the systems' monitors and alarms so that even the smallest of changes would be noticeable. Arguably the most important alarm is called "gain and loss". This setting has high and low threshold alarms for the tanks from which the mud is pumped.

The system runs similar to how swimming pool levels are monitored. If a pool has an overflow tank equipped with a level, this information can be used to refill or even drain some of the pool water to maintain a fine range—not too full and not too low. The amount of water used, added, or unexpectedly gained from an unknown source requiring investigation, can be measured with high fidelity.

On a much larger scale, a Driller uses a similar tank and monitor design concept. If a Driller is drilling along and the level rises in the tank, this is an indicator that something has changed. What could it be? Any number of reasons might cause this, but we will concentrate on what happens while drilling. Unlike a swimming pool system, the drilling mud tanks are fixed to a ship floating on the ocean surface and subject to environmental forces, such as wind, waves, and sea currents. This makes the tanks rock back and forth, called pitch and roll. The rig lifting and lowering due to wave action is called heave. Pitch, roll, and/or heave can cause the tank to experience false indications. A Driller must know the entire system as well as the sea conditions to set the alarms correctly.

Whenever I set the alarms up for drilling, I used what's called a "totalizer". I would take all the tanks or pits onboard the rig and assign all of them as ACTIVE. This means that every drop of drilling fluid onboard the rig was accounted for. During normal operations, this worked fine. Occasionally, a sensor might malfunction, but for the most part, with this set-up, any other fluid that entered the system would raise the amount of fluid in the "totalizer". The totalizer is a single number calculated from all the volumes in all the pits put into one easy-to-read digital display. It keeps the Driller from having to look up fifteen other volume numbers.

An unwanted intrusion from the formation being drilled—be it gas, oil, water, or a mix—is called an *influx*. This set-up will pick-up any influx into the open circulating system. Hence, that gain and loss alarm is the most important to set up and watch.

Jed had his gain and loss set at five barrels on the high and low. I moved it to ten as I watched the rig movement. I could tell that the seas were picking up and the pitch and roll would start to make a difference in the active pits. The design of the semi-submersible or drillship plays a big role in how pits will be affected by sea conditions, as do the placement of the return line and the distance fluid must travel to get to the active pits. The heave can give a difference of plus or minus ten barrels depending on sea conditions. A Driller must watch the trend closely and set the system up to accommodate conditions.

For example, if drilling in a salt formation for the last 1,500 feet, and there is a small amount of seepage into the formation and the hole is gun barrel straight—no cutting beds or anything of this nature—the gain and loss close can be set five high and five low with calm seas. On the same hole section the following day, it may have to be set at a different mark based on the heading of the ship and the sea conditions.

In addition, the crane loading and unloading the rig to and from a supply vessel will also affect stability. If the load is heavy enough, it will shift the vessel to increase tank loss or gain indications. With all these ongoing activities affecting an open circulating system, crew communications are critical. Anytime the DPO (dynamic positioning officer) moves the vessel, it affects the loss and gain indicators. The Driller and the DPO must have constant communications with any rig movement. The DPO will also be in contact with the Crane Operators to know where large lifts will be made, and the large lifts must be communicated to the Driller so he knows how it will affect his readings.

On the other side of the gain is the loss: For each new foot of hole that's drilled, a foot of mud must be added to replace it. I would pre-calculate each foot of hole that I would be drilling, and then log this on the trend sheet throughout the day. I would know how much mud I lost (i.e. filled the hole with) as I drilled. There would be no surprises at the end of the day when I logged how much mud the well had taken during my tour.

Without tracking this, the well could take more mud than needed and I could be unknowingly moving into an over-balance condition. A well over-balance is when too much pressure is being exerted from the mud column onto the formation; this greatly increases the chances of breaking down the formation (i.e. exceeding the fracture gradient) and losing mud. Lose too much mud and the pressure (i.e. pore pressure) drops in the mud column, which opens the door for an influx to enter the wellbore. On wells that are finely balanced between pore pressure and fracture ("frac") gradient, it is very important to visually maintain this.

Using the automobile analogy, when failing to monitor the gain and loss on a car's oil circulating system, should it go too high or too low, there could be damage to the engine and most likely a high-dollar mechanic's bill. Unlike a car, however, an undetected influx during drilling operations can really ruin the day. As the Driller, I am the single person that stands between the well and the people sleeping in the living quarters behind me. Should I fail to detect an influx, it could mean disaster for everyone.

As I moved through the screens on the Cyberbase, it was no surprise that they were set up almost perfectly. Each Driller sets them up a bit differently, but the main indicators for seeing a change in formation are drilling rate, pump pressure, and drilling torque.

Without going into what some might call "the romantic parts" of drilling machinery, the drilling rate is, in large part, determined by the force required to drill through different formations. There's a lot of science that goes into this. But, to simplify, imagine pushing a heavy box around a ceramic tile dining room floor. The box slides easily without too much force. And, given the same amount of force, a constant rate of slide or progress can be achieved. However, when transitioning from the tile floor to carpet, the amount of force required to move the box will increase significantly, and the rate of progress will likely change. This is similar to drilling, except you know what it takes to push that box across the floor. This oftentimes is not the case, however, when downhole drilling. The force required, measured in WOB, or "weight-on-bit", as well as RPMs (revolutions per minute) to drill a formation changes when formations change; these affect the drilling rate. It comes down to experience and knowing what works best with the formation being drilled. It's kind of funny, maybe in a sad way, but by the time Driller's become *good* Drillers, gaining the experience and mastering that knowledge of what works best in different formations, they get promoted and then it's time to teach someone else.

Jed had set the system on "AUTO-WOB," which allows the Driller to take his hand off the system that applies weight and speed to the drill string. The computer automatically keeps the same weight applied to the drill string and the Driller sets his monitor and alarm up to watch the ROP (rate of penetration). If it speeds up or slows down, he knows he has a change in formation. As the bit leaves one layer and goes into the next, a momentary increase in speed will be seen. Then, this will drop back off and the speed will begin to change until the bit finds a speed it's happy with. A sandy formation will harden up when transitioning out of another formation. There may be a reduction or an increase in weight needed, depending on its purity.

The pump pressure trend shows us how well we're cleaning the well. As I said before, for each foot drilled, a foot of mud is added; but also, one foot of formation is now being added to the mud column. I know this may seem to be confusing to a "non-Driller". Perhaps an easier way to imagine the concept is to take a clean glass of water, weigh it, and then add dirt to it. The glass of water will become heavier if you do not remove the dirt. That is the function of the filters or shakers, to filter out cuttings when the mud comes back to surface. If pump-rates are not being monitored and we are drilling faster than we can pump the dirt out, it will lead to some other issues like stuck pipe, large cutting beds in deviated holes, and over-balances.

There is also a fancy tool downhole called an ECD (equivalent circulating density). This tool works real-time as we are drilling: The pressure in the column of fluid is read by a sensor on-bottom, which, in turn, correlates to a given weight. As we drill and add formation pieces or "dirt" to the mud, this number will change. Once we've stopped drilling and circulate the hole clean (also called "backreaming"), this number will be relative to what we are pumping back into the well (i.e. clean mud) from the surface. Some companies drill with a certain directive on ECDs and use these for finely "walking the line" between gains and losses, or for navigating the line between pore pressure and frac gradient.

All these indicators are significantly changed when a well is placed on a "closed system"—*much different* than an open system which is not pressured up. An open system relies on gravity and the atmospheric pressures to derive information. This can be misleading if not properly understood by the Driller.

Now that I was in the Driller's chair and everything had been set up, I hid my kid-like, Christmas morning excitement. I got settled in for the day, plenty of gum and tobacco in my bag to last the tour. It felt like Showtime.

We Live for This!

"Oh, you're not going to explode, or anything, but you will become a fat-ass!"
~~Jim Spizale, BP Company Man, *Deepwater Horizon*

When I was an AD for Jed, I was once told by the Company Man, Jim Spizale, from New Orleans, that I better enjoy my days as an AD, because when I moved into that Driller's chair, I would gain weight. I looked at him with a blank stare on my face that conveyed, *What are you talking about? I am not going to gain weight.*

"Oh, you're not going to explode, or anything," he said with a chuckle, "but you *will* become a fat-ass!"

"Nah, not me," I laughed. I soon found out the hard way that the worst thing about being a 5th- or 6th-generation Driller is the time one must remain locked to that console during a tour. During my first year, I gained 40 pounds! I couldn't believe it happened to *me*, just like Jim had predicted. Of course, there's a lot to say about being inactive for such a long time, and then there's an entire discussion about the mental and stress-related aspects of the job. I certainly had put more of my time and energy into my job than I did my health and didn't go to the gym like I should have. This ultimately earned me that extra 40 pounds. Nonetheless, I learned from it, and I've been passing the lesson on, repeating the message from the conversation Jim had with me years before.

Today, John decided he was going to work outside and Don would help me inside the cabin. It was a rule that when the BOPs were latched up, a minimum of two people needed to be inside the Drillers' cabin at all times to monitor the well. Only under special circumstances approved by the Toolpushers were we allowed to have only one person inside, and this was usually during wireline logging, and never when there was a drill string below the seabed or BOPs.

I called Patrick and chatted with him for a few minutes to ask him what the Mud Engineer had him adding. I was just double-checking all the bases. It was logged on the trend sheet, but even the smallest addition would add up in the mud weight and needed to be accounted for.

I rang up Karl in the shaker house to see if he was okay with everything going on down there, and to make sure he didn't have any screens that needed to be repaired or changed. Sometimes when drilling a long section, the bottom shaker screens would get loaded up in the far back, meaning that the cuttings or sediment coming from the well would stick to the screens in the very back bed of the shaker. This could cause the screen to tear allowing cuttings to get back to the mud pits. No one wants this to happen as the cuttings would be recirculated into the hole and could possibly plug the discharge screens on the mud pump and affect pumping pressure or plug downhole tools. Again, I was double-checking with everybody to try to head off any surprises.

We flushed through the choke and kill lines on the BOPs, got slow pump rates, fresh mud, and the lines were ready to use if we needed them. We flushed through the manifold on the degasser and checked all our pressure gauges. We were getting ourselves ready for anything that could happen, getting ready to cut into a new sand.

I called the DPO and requested no positioning moves be made unless it was necessary, and asked that all cranes remain cradled until further notice. Steve's hands didn't mind this at all. But Steve preferred to be outside running the crews getting stuff done. My request put him in the position of working on paperwork instead, and he hated paperwork. But, even on a drilling rig, paperwork is part of the job.

I was thirty feet away from making a connection when the phone rang. It was Mr. Ronnie. "Greg, when you drill this stand down, circulate the cuttings above the BOPs so we can see what the ECDs will do before we drill ahead."

"Yes sir. Will do." Circulating is needed, of course, but I would much rather be drilling. Circulating and hole-cleaning are very important because no one wants fill on-bottom once TD (i.e. total depth) of the drilling section is reached. Circulating can also show how well the pieces of the formation are being suspended in the fluid once the circulation is stopped. Some clients liked to use "wiper trips" to check this and to clean out cutting beds if they were thought to be building up.

At any rate, circulating it was. I roughly calculated the time: I had just come on tour, so I would spend about the next six hours getting the cuttings above the BOPs. That would still leave me with another five or so hours of drilling, so that was good. I finished drilling down the last bit of the stand. Then I began backreaming up. No drag while rotating. I reached the upper limit on the traveling equipment and then started back down. Once I got about thirty feet from the rig floor, I cut off the rotary and slowed the pumps down so I could get a good pick-up and slack-off in case I needed to "fire the jars" later. Depending on the deviation (i.e. angle) of the well, the technique I used may not always have been the best, but for this, it worked fine.

When we transition from one formation to another, there tends to be what I would describe as a "rubble zone", or a zone of unconsolidated formation. This can cause the drill bit to stick and the rotary to torque-up and stall-out. Drillers have gotten their string stuck, or twisted it off, when crossing formation zones.

When a Driller gets hung up or stuck, there is a tool called a drilling jar installed in the drill string. The drilling jar works like the end of a ballpoint pen. When the pen is clicked, it stores energy in the compressed spring. When clicked again, the spring energy is released upwards retracting the ballpoint tip.

The drilling jar, when a given amount of weight is applied to it, stores energy. When the string is pulled upwards or pushed downwards, once the jars are "cocked" or "loaded", they will fire or release this energy, causing the string to move in the opposite direction in which it was cocked or loaded. If the Driller gets stuck and needs to get free, he will need to know what weight to apply to cock the jars. The only way to know this is to make sure to record the BHA (bottom hole assembly) weight on the surface prior to installing the jars. When the string gets stuck, the Driller slows the pumps down, slacks off the required weight to cock the jars, then pulls the drill string back up to neutral weight (plus or minus) and waits for the jars to fire. It doesn't always work the first time, so this may need to be done more than once. Before the Driller fires the jars, he must clear the rig floor to protect crew from falling objects from the derrick. No one is allowed to be outside or near the rotary table when firing the jars.

I got my pick-up and slack-off, started my pumps and rotary back up, and set the system to AUTO-ROP. This allowed me to assign a maximum rate of penetration for the drill string to travel with a certain weight applied. This mode was perfect for backreaming and circulating, freeing up my hands to keep up with the trends, answer phone calls, and take notes. All we had to do now was sit and wait until the cuttings were circulated past the BOPs.

Not many people in the world sit in this position. Nerves begin to take a beating waiting for the circulation to finish. In the back of my mind, I'd go through a mental checklist of everything I had done that day and the days just before. I'd start to think about the things that could go wrong, the action I'd want to take if they did, and as much preventive action I could put into place before something happened. *Were there any indicators I missed*?

As the pump strokes clicked away, some momentary gas circulated up in very small volumes—just enough to register on the gas detector in the shaker house. These smaller volumes are little areas that may have been just small pockets of gas that were trapped when we cut though them that day. Some of the gas registering on a gas detector may never record on the instrumentation because it is vented to atmosphere. Because of the force of the drilling mud being applied by the mud pump within a given area, nothing is pushing back. When something does push back, depending upon the situation, the Driller must react to what he sees. He relies on monitors, gauges, logging equipment, downhole equipment—that arsenal of tools at his disposal. There is only one issue with all of this in an open system: lag time! The deeper we are working, the greater the time delay between the moment we make a change on the surface to the effect on the bottom.

A home internet connection can provide a rough analogy to drilling a well. One can have the fastest equipment money can buy to receive the signal and process it. However, if the internet provider decides to do maintenance on their side slowing down the bandwidth while a large file is being downloaded, there will be a period of time from the second the command is sent until the file is actually downloaded. This is lag time—what's happening is not real-time.

Lag-time is an issue Drillers face every day. The data they are seeing on surface is delayed, or has a certain amount of lag time from when and where it was recorded. This lag time can affect the Driller's ability to detect an influx in time. Considering the motion of the vessel, the calibration of the gauges, and the total amount of fluid moving through the system, the Driller's ability to make a small mistake and miss something is very real. He has to be ready.

We can preplan as much as possible. Our strokes are calculated and we know how much time it takes to move a volume of fluid from point A to point B. We also know, at any moment, how fast that fluid will be travelling until the gas that has entered our wellbore gets entrained in our drilling fluid. At certain pumping rates, how it can become masked until the pressure being applied within the wellbore is no longer enough, or the pressure inside some "bubble" can overcome the pressure that is pressing down on top of it. Then the gas will become free, expand rapidly, and move in one volume and unload, or move all the fluid above it out of the way. Why? Because we are circulating through an open system, vented to the atmosphere. We rely on gravity, precision weighting in every single drop of the fluid in the well, and pressure from a mud pump applied in one direction. And this mud has to travel all the way down the wellbore then back up.

We were 20 minutes from having the cuttings up to the BOPs. I picked up the phone and called Mr. Ronnie. The phone rang a few times and then I looked up from the console, and saw him coming through the door on the port side of the rig floor. He knew exactly what time the strokes were going to be past the BOPs as well and was always prepared. I hung up the phone.

He opened the door and asked, "Just about there?"

"Yes sir!"

He picked up the phone near the Driller's computer and called up to the Logging cabin and asked, "How many strokes you showing?" He paused, then asked, "Okay, so what depth was that?" I assumed he was talking about the small amount of gas that had surfaced during the circulation. He hung up the phone and pulled the chair up to just behind the Driller's chair where he could see the stroke counters and the pressure gauges. As I worked the drill string back down to the last 20 feet, I turned the rotary off and slacked off until I tagged bottom while slowing down my pumps. The hole was nice and clean—no fill on bottom—and we were in a good place. I had enough room to make a connection.

This time, we were going to pick up a single joint of drill pipe instead of making a full three-joint connection. That gave me plenty of room to work the drill string up and down in case we needed to work the pipe multiple times or cock the jars if the well got a little sticky as we transitioned from one formation to another. The twenty minutes had elapsed and I asked, "Mr. Ronnie? You ready?"

"Sure thing," he shot back.

I slacked off the pipe. Roy, Shane, and Alvin set the slips. As I broke the connection on the top-drive, out of the corner of my eye I could see the riser feed machine, or riser skate, on the aft side of the drill floor begin to come in.

I knew I had a connection or tool joint fifteen feet from my middle pipe rams in the BOP on the seabed, nearly a mile below my Driller's chair. It was imperative to use extreme caution to avoid the chance of damaging the pipe rams since they are not designed to seal around tool joints. Damaging the rams or sticking the tool joint and keeping the rams from fully opening back up would mean a halt to all well operations. The drilling assembly would then have to be pulled, temporary plug and abandonment operations performed to secure the well, and all the drilling mud displaced to retrieve and repair the damaged BOP. In deepwater drilling, that scenario would cost millions of dollars, not to mention the hit to the project schedule.

I lifted the top-drive, latched the elevators onto the drill pipe single on the riser skate, and began to hoist it up. John deployed the RBS (raised backup system) so we could use the stab feature. I hoisted the top-drive and pulled the single from the riser skate. Roy grabbed the lower part of the pipe as it came over to well-center, removed the thread protector, and painted the threads with pipe dope (i.e. thread compound). Then he swung the pipe back and shoved it forward to get it into the RBS stabbing arm. I hoisted up the single and turned the elevators around while John activated the stabbing arm. Pulling the single back, I slacked off the top-drive into the box of the joint in the rotary. I spun in the joint as I was assigning torque to the top-drive, and I kicked my mud pumps on to slowly start filling the pipe while making the connection.

Once the joint was torqued, John removed the RBS. I slowly picked up to make sure there was no torque on the drill string. With this weight, I wasn't expecting any, but I always made sure there was nothing that could make the slips hit the guys' hands outside. As the pipe moved up, the guys grabbed the slips and pulled them from the rotary. I slowly started up the rotary. The torque on the string began to climb, and it got up to 14,000 foot-pounds before breaking-over. When we stop the drilling motion of the pipe spinning in the well, there is always a certain amount of energy needed to restart this movement again. If the well is starting to give us any issues, we will be able to see an increase in break-over torque or off-bottom torque.

As the torque began to fall off, I stepped-up the mud pumps' speed—incrementally increasing speed in steps. Similar to the increased torque required to get the pipe spinning from stationary to drill speed, the fluid system requires increased force to get the drilling muds from static to full-circulating. This was also something that I needed to monitor: If I brought the pressure up too fast, I could break the formation down and begin to lose drilling fluids. This is called "blowing the bottom out of the well". As I stepped-up the pumps, I stopped at each increment for five or ten minutes to allow the pressure to stabilize. I worked the drill string up slowly trying to break down some of the additional friction being applied by the well, to give it kind of a boost. Finally, the pressure stabilized, the mud was circulating, and we were ready to start drilling.

I got the bit back on bottom and slowly started to apply weight. I wanted to find that original cut where I'd left bottom. Sometimes finding this bit pattern is a little tricky; but, starting slow and light, gradually increasing the speed and weight, the bit will usually fall right back into place.

Each drill bit has a certain cutting pattern, regardless of the weight that is being applied; the bit will only cut one way if it continues spinning to the right. Any time you are spinning to the left, you'll be having bigger problems than bit pattern! That was a little Driller's humor. About the only time a Driller might slightly turn his drill-string to the left (counter-clockwise) is to release trapped torque. There should be no reason to make a turn to the left unless you are doing something with a specific tool down-hole, but *never* with a drilling assembly! This is because all drill-pipe is tightened together in a right-hand, clockwise direction, or right-hand threads. If the drill-string is turned counter-clockwise, it would "unscrew" or break a connection downhole. Right-hand motion—good; left-hand motion—bad.

We were finally drilling ahead now. Each inch we cut could be a new formation. No cranes were moving outside, no changes from the Bridge. All pit markers were level, no transfers of fluid, nothing that might distract me from seeing what was happening downhole.

In the room, anticipation was heavy. Minutes turned into hours. And then, finally, there it was. The rate of penetration (ROP) began to decrease and the bit weight began to increase. I knew we had a change. I deselected AUTO-ROP and went manual. The sticks were cold to the touch, but I knew each curve in them by feel. I knew exactly where that small hole was on the back of the joystick that faced the monitors. It had a screw inside of it that retained the button-control on top of the stick. I would always position my middle finger across this hole and press lightly—kind of a nervous tick I had while running the rig.

I asked Don to zero out my pump strokes so I could see what was coming back on the cuttings from this spot. I figured I was most likely on a cap. Beneath, it could be over-pressured (meaning influx) or under-pressured (meaning loss of returns). To slowly start peeling away layers, I slowed the rotary down to 50 RPMs and stacked another 10,000 pounds on a bit that already had 15,000 pounds. In the back of my mind, I was thinking, *if this bit falls through, how much stretch am I working with? If there is a hole there, or nothing, how far will I drop? How much mud will I lose?* As Driller, I have to concentrate on making sure I make the best approach.

Drilling is like landing a plane in bad weather: The pilots already know the weather's not good, so they position themselves to take the best shot at a successful approach. That's how I felt when drilling into a new zone, except for a fear that always nagged me: Looming down there was an influx that got masked by lag time or rig movement. When the plane is on the ground, the pilot gets out and walks away, hopefully. For the Driller, once this cap is broken through, you're in no man's land—new ground, never touched before, never seen the light of day, and damn sure never had a drill bit punched through it!

The ROP was down to almost nothing. I picked up on the string slowly until there was no weight on bottom, and went back down and tagged bottom. I started to slowly apply more weight and got to 35,000 pounds and held it. I worked the weight back and forth from 35,000 to 10,000 pounds. Then, I added an additional 5,000, now sitting with 40,000 pounds of weight on the bit. Finally, the ROP started to move again, reading one to two feet per hour, a good indicator. I would let the bit drill and when 5-10,000 pounds would drop off the indicator, I added it back. This went on for about 15 feet and then my 40,000 pounds WOB fell off immediately. *I had broken through!*

Remember from earlier how far the Gamma and Resistivity tools were behind the bit? Now, I had to drill an additional twenty feet to get the Gamma into newly cut formation to see what we had. I picked up off-bottom, slowed down the pumps, spaced out the connections in the BOPs, and flow-checked the well. Anytime there is a change in formation, the Driller should flow-check. A Driller can flow-check whenever he feels the need. However, the only "rule" to perform flow-checks is whenever there is "a drilling break", or a transition from one formation to another. A good rule of thumb is to drill the minimum amount necessary after a break before taking a flow-check. This minimizes the time Drillers might be blind to an influx, and increases time to react and, if required, to shut-in the well.

The Mud Logger put the trend chart on my screen. I kept the rotary turning slowly to keep cuttings from building up around the bit with the pumps off, or at least to keep some movement to preclude getting stuck. A surprise influx would then just be adding bad to worse. Silently, I sat and watched as the flow began to die down. It followed the same trend as the earlier connections. This meant nothing had changed downhole between when all the previous connections had been made and now. This is called "fingerprinting".

Fingerprinting is a powerful tool and I cannot say enough that Drillers should utilize fingerprinting. Knowing the history gives Drillers real-time insight on what he's holding in his hand, and verification that there are no new sources dumping fluid, gas, sea water, or a mix into the well. If everything is the same, then go back to work. If it's different, it needs to be investigated.

The flow began to taper off, and Karl confirmed flowline status from the shaker house over the loudspeaker. "No flow."

I turned and looked at Mr. Ronnie. "Let's go see what we got," he said.

"Yes sir," I said, and got the bit back on bottom.

It didn't take much to get it drilling again. She was cutting at 30 feet an hour with only 10,000 pounds of weight-on-bit. I was confident we were transitioning through a sand. We had folks tracking the cuttings coming from the bottom of the well so that we could see what type of formation it was. At this current drilling rate, I would have the Gamma and Resistivity into the formation before the cuttings made it to the surface to be analyzed. I got another twenty feet of the formation drilled, but was at a point where we needed to make another connection. I figured roughly I had just gotten the Gamma tool into the formation, but knew we would certainly see what we were into on this next stand.

I worked the pipe all the way up one time and prepared to make a connection. We flow-checked the well and the fingerprint ran just as the others before. We were in good shape. We got the connection made, and I was back on bottom.

When we're loading data from the downhole tools onto the chart or rig floor display, it seems like forever before the small lines begin to change. Of course, when we're peering at them in anticipation, it's like watching grass grow. This one seemed to be drilling well and the updates were coming in pretty regularly.

To understand how the chart lines appear, imagine driving down a two-lane road with two straight, parallel lines, one on each side showing the shoulders. Now imagine driving up to a stretch where the road changes from a two-lane to an eight-lane highway; those shoulder lines move way outside as you drive down the middle lane.

Similarly, we were watching two roughly parallel lines on our graphs for Gamma and Resistivity logs. I would drill along and watch the lines changing on the MWD monitor. If the lines started moving outward on both the Gamma and the Resistivity logs, it meant we were in an oil sand. Jed used to compare it to an hourglass, or to a girl with a large backside. Once you got past the waist, it plumed out *beautifully*.

When I was drilling, I *knew* whenever I was getting into a sand—I could feel it, smell it, sense it—I just knew. That beautiful, hourglass shape of a good, hydrocarbon-bearing sand is pure Heaven to a Driller.

Sometimes, there might be a change or two to one or both lines indicating fine layers of formation to which the tools were reacting. If it wasn't consistent, or was messy on the chart, we described it as "ratty", indicating an unconsolidated formation. But a good clean sand is consistent. And this one wasn't ratty at all! It was sweet to watch as I drilled through it.

During the rest of my tour that day, I drilled a total of 500 feet of hydrocarbon-bearing sands in the Middle and Lower Miocene reservoir! Any time we found paydirt for the client, it gave everybody on the *Deepwater Horizon* a well-deserved and well-earned sense of pride. This was the Kodiak prospect—a huge find.

Years later, this well would be tied back to a floating production platform known as Devil's Tower spar. It would yield first oil in 2016. This well was initially drilled some eight years before by the team on the *Deepwater Horizon*.

Oops! (Part III)

Alan, the Bosun, was a cool cucumber. I remember the Welder doing some work on the front deck and a spark had lit some rags. Alan happened to be walking by and saw a Roustabout, I don't remember his name, but I think his nickname was "Bucket". He was sitting on a bucket with a fire extinguisher in front of him sound asleep. Alan woke him up and asked him what he was doing. He said he was the fire watch for the welder. Alan was like, "Well, what about that fire right next to you?"

Peter Cyr

Little Roughneck

"One of the things I learned as a 'little roughneck' was speak less and work more."
~~Greg Williams, CAPM™ Project Offshore Supervisor

After only a couple days of my hitch, I was back home in Louisiana for a week with my family before heading to Houston to assume my new role as the CAPM Project Offshore Supervisor. In addition to that time with my wife and kids, I made sure to spend some extra time visiting Mom. My mother had been battling colon cancer for about three years, but seemed healthy and undergoing routine check-ups. She hated seeing me trade those 14-days off with my family to take a regular Monday through Friday job far away in Houston. However, she also knew I was excited to learn and to be part of something new and cutting-edge. I had left the *Deepwater Horizon* Team on March 18, 2008, just after the huge find on the Kodiak Prospect, and after nearly eight years, setting sail toward something I knew very little about. Mom gave that conceding support by going out and buying my first ever dress-casual business attire, from the dress shirt down to the belt and shoes!

I treated my 200-mile drive to Houston like every other crew change, leaving my house, giving that "I love you" beep for each kid at 1:00 a.m. to be in Houston by 5:30 Monday morning. I was excited about meeting the other guys on the CAPM Team, and learning about the equipment, procedures, and the overall scope of the project. But first, I had to get there. Lesson 1: Houston is a big city! Lesson 2: Pay attention to signs. I drove around for ten minutes *after* getting to the Greenway Plaza parking garage trying to find the Greenway 4 Visitors' Center. Once I parked, I stripped off my "driving clothes" as I like to drive comfortable and hurriedly put on my new dress clothes. Buttoning up my shirt, I realized I was going to have to get used this this new "arrangement", or at least until someone figured out I wasn't as smart as they thought I was.

Thom met me at the Visitors' Center lobby to take me upstairs. As we shook hands, I realized I hadn't seen Thom since I took his Well Control class in 2004.

"Have any trouble finding this place?"

"Not at all." I figured I didn't need to start off my stint in the Transocean Corporate Headquarters "whining" about driving around the stupid parking garage for ten minutes because I didn't pay close enough attention to the signs.

"Glad you made it safely, Greg," Thom said. "Good to finally have ya on board. If you're ready, let's get up to what will be 'home' for a while."

With that, we headed down a long hall that opened into what looked like a big, pedestrian four-way intersection. Straight ahead was the first escalator I'd ever stepped foot on in my life. I had never been in a building tall enough to need one. I always wondered what would happen if something like a handle or strap got caught in an escalator. It's the little things that sometimes make me go, "Hmmm." Fortunately, I wasn't carrying anything to find out, so I just rode with Thom. As we drew closer, the huge "Transocean" sign over the front desk appeared. Our escalator ride topped out in the Transocean lobby. Impressive.

I must have looked like a big country kid staring at his first mall as I gazed at the vast, dark marble lobby floors that looked too fancy to walk on. Most impressive was the giant, polished marble globe that sat in a big granite bowl that flowed water from the bottom keeping this massive sphere suspended on a thin water layer. Anyone could go up and gently spin it if they didn't mind getting their fingers wet. The laser-etched globe must have weighed a ton or more. Still, I could easily turn it with my fingers. Amazing.

Place sure has changed in nine years, I thought. Nine years ago, when I interviewed with Transocean, I parked right outside the front doors on the street and strolled right in to HR.

Now, the Transocean offices at Greenway Plaza 4 had a "big kid on the block" feel. Transocean had the largest offices of any drilling contractor in Houston at the time—multiple floors in Greenway Plaza and then spread over several facilities in Houston alone. Just having meetings with our rig management teams meant driving through eight lanes of traffic for thirty minutes (most times). Houston is a big, big place with lots and lots of people—and more cars than most cities have people. Houston had an oilfield town feel to it, to be sure.

As we let folks off the elevator to head up, Eddy Redd got off and he and Thom spoke just a bit. Eddy Redd was a Sr. Manager at Transocean, having worked his way up from the rig floors in SONAT Offshore before it became part of the Transocean family. I didn't know Eddy at the time, but I had heard plenty of stories about his father, Odile. He was well respected, and everyone in the company had good things to say about him. As we continued up the elevator, Thom mentioned that IT had my laptop ready and that I could pick up my cell phone tomorrow. To a small-town kid who'd spent the last 15 years on rigs, it sounded to me like I had hit the lottery.

When we got out on the floor for Deepwater Operations, Non-Standard Operations, Well Control and New Technology, we walked to the Project cubicles. Thom and I walked over to his cubicle that faced Highway 59, known to locals as "the Rambo freeway". I looked out. It was still semi-dark outside, but the hustle and bustle on the freeway was just getting started. Over the next eight months, as I worked on the CAPM Project, this was the morning ritual, every day from about 6:00 to 10:00 a.m. Repeat in the afternoon—in both directions. I would learn too well why it was nicknamed the Rambo Freeway by those who had to fight through two or more times a day. I also learned that as a commuter, I had to pick the right times to start and end my days, and when to drive. Otherwise, I would have to get close and personal with my truck radio . . . for hours.

"Which one of these squares is mine?" I asked looking around to see what real estate was available.

"They're all open," Thom responded, handing me some papers to sign and the promised 11- by 17-inch drawings, "except for those over against the wall."

"Mind if I grab this one," I said pointing.

"Knock yourself out," Thom smiled. "Also, here is a manual that you will need to start reviewing. It has all the processes and procedures for installation and operation of the equipment."

I went to my new desk and started reviewing documents. One of the things I learned as a "little roughneck" was to 'speak less and work more'. The drawings were for equipment I'd never seen before. The manual had lots of blank pages, most likely awaiting input from the operations side. Presumably, that would be me. As I was looking over the documents, I saw the lights come on in Jean-Paul "JP" Buisine's office, the CAPM Project Manager. He walked in, tossed his bag on the chair, plugged his laptop into the docking station, and came straight out to Thom and me.

"You must be Greg," JP said looking straight at me as we shook hands. "I've heard a lot about you."

"I hope it wasn't *all* lies," I joked, kinda like being back on the rig. Both Thom and JP responded with laughter, which was a relief to me.

"No. When you've been with the company as long as you have, people remember. And you come highly recommended." JP smiled. "This will be a transition for you. When you get settled in over the next couple of days, I am sure that Thom will work with you on the schedule and the activities we have coming up. I've got a meeting with Steve and the team today and will let them know that our first Offshore Supervisor has joined the team!" As he finished, JP raised his hand and made a fist as if he was clinching a win after a long race. "Yes." He then stuck both hands into his front pockets and rocked back on his heels. "Well, I will leave you and Thom to it," he said nodding to each of us, and he turned and walked away.

I knew I was a fish out of water here, a Driller in an office building. And while I was thinking that any Vegas bookie would probably set high odds against my making good in this gig, I was *highly* motivated to master this new stuff. Out of fear of failing? Perhaps. That's always been an internal driver for me to perform. But I was also very conscious of JP's statement about me being "highly recommended". I *knew* what that meant. I might have to die trying, but I would not let those people down—those who mentored me, who challenged me, promoted me, and recommended me all these years. Yes, I was highly motivated to best contribute my areas of expertise to make this CAPM Project a success.

"So, what's JP's background?" I asked Thom, watching him walk away.

"He was with Schlumberger for a long time. He's an engineer by trade, but was also a Rig Manager as well. I guess you could say he's worked the best of both worlds. He's sharp and keeps up with his business."

"Seems like a good enough fella," I surmised. "Thom, how long is the project going to last?"

"What do you mean?"

"Well, I need to call James Penny," I said, "and let him know I won't be accepting the *Clear Leader* transfer."

"I thought you had done that already," Thom sounded surprised, with a hint of concern.

"No, not yet. I was waiting to ask you that question when I got here since the rig still had a few months before it comes out."

Thom looked at me with both hands on his hip. "It will be a while. You may want to give him a call."

"Okay. Will do."

Thom and I walked around the floor where he introduced me to some of the rest of the folks. I recalled a lot of the names from reading various Transocean newsletters and other documents. Some of these guys had been around since SONAT.

In each corner was the executive office for each of four department directors. The CAPM Project fell under Larry McMahon, Director of Performance and Operations, but he was out of the office when we stopped by. We did see Jimmy Moore, Director of HSE-North America.

I recalled when I first met Jimmy way back in 1999. It was a rough and windy morning aboard the *DF96*. Anadarko was our client at the time when Jimmy brought Tim Juran—a long-time Reading & Bates guy, but at that time, the Transocean HR VP—to visit the rig and discuss the merger with Sedco Forex Offshore. Everybody was packed into the *DF96*'s small TV room for the meeting.

Our OIM, Keith Freeny, from Carthage, Mississippi, stepped into the room just behind Jimmy and Tim. "Gents, sorry to disturb your meeting, but I need some guys to go down on the anchor boat and secure two joints of riser that have come loose and are moving around a lot on deck!"

"No, absolutely. Operations come first, Keith," Jimmy said, moving aside to let the OIM move in front.

"Alright boys, I need two volunteers," Keith said, looking around the room. "Raise your hand."

I also looked around the room, and no one was jumping up to volunteer. The seconds felt like minutes, so I raised my hand. *Two joints of riser shouldn't be that big a deal,* I said to myself.

"Okay, Greg," Keith directed. "Now pick a Roustabout to help you."

I looked around the room. I wanted the fastest guy we had, and looked straight at Pick, also from Carthage, Mississippi. "Hell, Pick. Come-on! Let's go." Pick was about five feet tall, weighed in at about a hundred pounds—that's soaking wet *and* with rocks in his pockets. But he *was* quick on deck, grabbing slings and going from one spot to the other like a speed-monkey.

We followed Keith out who yelled back at us as we walked, "It's pretty rough out there, boys. Take your time, and *don't get hurt*!"

"Alright Keith," I said, fully intending on keeping my end of the bargain, but having no idea how.

Pick and I headed down to the change room, got our gear on, and headed outside. The crane operator had the crane up with the personnel basket already waiting on us when we came out of the bulkhead door and stepped onto the main deck. I looked out at the water. She was brewing wicked and mean, white caps crashing back and forth. I had not seen the seas so rough in a long time.

Still onboard the *DF96,* we walked over to the handrail and looked at the anchor boat as it rocked up and down in the crests and troughs of the waves. I thought to myself, *Holy shit, what did I just volunteer for?*

The riser joints were rolling uncontrolled back and forth on the deck of the boat. When I say "uncontrolled", I mean there was nothing in their way! They were free-rolling all the way to one side and slamming against the bulwarks or the vessel side-guards that protected the service outlets and the machinery spaces.

Pick, watching the same things I was, made one of those classical long, southern drawl comments, "Man . . . shit. Look at those waves." I was thinking the same thing, but I never said a word. At the time, I was 24, in the best shape of my life—six feet-two, 250 pounds, and had been working manual drilling rigs for six years. I was ready for the challenge. Concerned? *Yes*. Scared? *No*.

Pick went off and came back a few minutes later with four helideck chocks used to chock the wheels when the choppers landed to keep them from rolling.

I looked at Pick and down at those chocks. "What you going to do with *them*, Pick?

"I'm going to put them next to the riser when they roll up next to the side of the boat and chock 'em," he answered, like a kid with a stroke of genius.

"Pick," I said, "that riser weighs a lot, brother! I don't think those chocks are going to help any."

"Hell, it's worth a try anyway," he grinned. I just shook my head and put on my work vest.

We climbed into the personnel basket and the crane operator started picking us up. Once we cleared the pilot house, the wind was howling, blowing around our basket. We narrowly missed the antennas heading over the side. The anchor boat pilot was trying to position his boat close enough so that we could land the personnel basket onto the back deck just in front of the boat's anchor catch.

This first, simple step was anything but simple. The supply boat was rising and falling with the rough water. Our crane operator was on the radio with Pick who yelled to me, "Here we go!"

I looked down as the personnel basket began to lower. The boat heaved down, so the crane operator let the basket down full-force and chased the boat down. The basket made contact and we jumped off immediately. The boat heaved back up and about fifteen feet of cable slack and the "headache ball" came down into the basket! *Whew! We haven't even made it to the hard part and barely made it!*

We froze for just a second, and as soon as there was a break in the boat heaving up, we grabbed the chocks out of the basket and threw them onto the deck. The crane operator immediately hoisted the basket back up and out of the way.

We both turned around to look at the two riser joints rolling port-to-starboard and back, stopping each time with a slam. Each one of these riser joints weighed approximately 11,000 pounds, and here they were playing bumper cars on the deck of this anchor boat. I imagined what the Captain was working with on the bridge. When you have unstable loads like this up top, depending on how much stability you have in the draft, the free movement of this kind of weight could very easily sink a boat. The boat was struggling and I could hear it. The props were coming out of the water and the smoke was boiling out of the exhaust. I thought for a second and looked up toward the front of the boat. About mid-ship, there were two large winches for securing the anchor and anchor chain while they were working on deck during anchor operations. I knew that those would be crucial to helping us sort this mess out.

Pick made a mad dash up the deck and deployed the chocks, and got out of the way just before the ship (and risers) rolled back. As I told him earlier, that was most likely not going to work. Well, it didn't. One joint rolled quickly back to the starboard side and smashed the chocks like grilled cheese sandwiches.

I motioned Pick to stay where he was, that I was going to come through the bulwarks and meet him mid-ship. I ran over to the starboard side of the ship and navigated through all the lines and catch pans that were in the way. As the riser joints rolled back toward me, the only thing that stood between me and utter destruction was the six-inch steel pipe that made up the bulwarks. They slammed up against the bulwark pipe and stayed for ten seconds or so. I was scooting quick, getting close to the first winch on the starboard side just as they rolled back to the port.

I got to the winch and told Pick that we would use them to secure the joints. I just needed him to stay there and operate the winch for me. These anchor boat winches were rated for 100 tons, so I knew they would do the trick. I grabbed the chain and hook that was made up to the end of the cable. My "plan" was to go back through the bulwarks, get down to the other end, get enough cable pulled out, and lay it down on deck. Then we'd let the riser joints roll back to the starboard side and I'd toss the cable over the joints and hook the hook back into the cable. Finally, Pick would run the winch pulling the line tight, cinching them up next to the bulwarks. *Sounds like a plan!*

I pulled the heavy chain and cable down through the bulwarks. When I say heavy, I mean *heavy*! Add to that the pitching and rolling ship in rough seas and those huge risers slamming back and forth, I had my hands full. I was nitro-fueled on adrenaline. I reached the end and pulled out another fifteen feet of slack.

I took a minute to get the timing right and rehearse my movements in my head. Then I told myself, *Well, I have to physically <u>make</u> myself go out there in the path of these wrecking balls and lay this cable down.* I saw my chance when the boat rocked and the joints rolled hard to the port side. I rushed out pulling out the cable and chain and laid it down leaving enough slack to throw the hook over the bulwarks. I hopped to the end out of the impending return path. As if on cue, they came back and the joints rolled over the hook, chain, and cable, and slammed against the starboard side. The split-second they passed by, I was scurrying out behind them as they crashed into the side and parked for a second. I grabbed the hook and threw it over the bulwarks piping, raced around the end to other side, grabbed the hook and hooked it off back into the cable, and like a calf-roper, threw up my hands flagging Pick to winch it up! I kept, what we call, "giving it the high-sign", which means "Speed up! Speed up! Pull the cables as fast as the winch will go!"

All of this was taking place in a matter of seconds, and we were working as fast and furious as we possibly could. Try to imagine the amount of time that all of this winching seemed to be taking as we waited for the inevitable rollback! Pick was pulling it in as quickly as the massive winch could spool when the joints started to roll again. They rolled *just* as Pick was pulling in the last bit of slack out of the cable. The end of the joint nearest him kicked to the left just a bit, but the winch did its job and secured the joints against the bulwarks.

We briefly thought about trying to even out the load to get one riser joint lashed up on the starboard and one on the port. But, we realized that we had already endangered our lives enough trying to secure them both to starboard. There was no way we were going to be involved with taking that rigging loose to let them roll again. We took the winch from the port side over to the starboard and snugged-in and secured the riser flanges of the ends that had kicked out. We grabbed what was left of the helo chokes, called the Crane Operator, and waved to the Captain of the boat, whom we could see giving us an applause from his cabin as we were boarding the personnel basket.

Who would have ever guessed that more than a decade later, I would be in the Transocean Worldwide Headquarters Building, high up in the Greenway Plaza, talking to the same Jimmy Moore—my new Director of Health, Safety, (and, I would like to emphasize the word "safety"), Environmental for North America (HSE-NAM)—telling the real tale of what Pick and I had volunteered for during our first brief meeting aboard the *DF96*.

Jimmy

During a casing run, I was laying in the bunk about twenty minutes before pre-tour, and I felt the rig bob. I turned to the rig camera on TV and saw all kinds of people crowded around the rotary. I got dressed and went up to the rig floor thinking, "Shit. We must've been on down time."

When I got there, Mr. Jimmy was standing by the empty rotary. I walked up. He looks at me and points his flashlight down the rotary and said, "Cookie, you see anything down there?"

I said, "Not a thing, Mr. Jimmy."

And he rocked back laughed like crazy. The slips had failed and we had lost the casing, and yet he still laughed. That's the type guy Jimmy Harrell was—never let the stress get to him.

Michael Cook

Sitting in the Drillers' shack one day, Jimmy Harrell looks at me and says, "Mitch, you ever cook any toilet paper?"

I didn't know if I understood him correctly, so I said "WHAT?!!"

Jimmy says, "Have you ever cooked any toilet paper?"

"No Jimmy I haven't."

Jimmy says, "Well, I haven't really cooked any myself, but I've browned a lot of it."

Mitch Gill

The Project:
CAPM™—Continuous Annular Pressure Management

"Imagine if you could just push a button and change any mud weight you had in the well instantly…. It's comin', son."
~~Ronnie Sepulvado, BP Company Man, *Deepwater Horizon*

My first day on-boarding was a bit of an overwhelming "learn places, people, and things" sort of experience. Later in the day, I met Ernest Windborne from Mississippi, who would be my roommate for the next year. Ernest was a Power Engineer who had retired after many, many years designing and developing 5th-Generation drilling vessels for Transocean. He had designed the entire drilling package installed on three vessels destined to become the pride of Transocean: *Discoverer Enterprise, Discoverer Spirit,* and *Discoverer Deep Seas*. These ships led the way in the new technology of dual activity drilling.

"Yeah," Earnest told me with a genuine grin and a distinct Mississippi drawl, "Transocean dug me up off the river bank like an old worm to come back." This became a signature line that he would tell every new person he met. When I realized all the accomplishments listed on this guy's resume, and that Transocean had brought him out of *retirement* just for CAPM, I started to realize how much value the company saw in this technology.

Still, even though I thought the concept sounded great and it sure looked good on paper, I had doubts about how it could be implemented successfully—how it would be rigged onto an actual system to really work. However, during the first full week of meetings, Iain Sneddon (CAPM Project Team Leader) and John MacKay (Sr. Operations Advisor), guys from Transocean's Office in Aberdeen, Scotland, made a believer out of me. They had been involved with the project for nearly two years before I was brought on and, as expected, were extremely knowledgeable and well versed in the system, and how it would be implemented and used. It didn't surprise me that both of their names are listed on the CAPM design patent.

There were many meetings, but meetings had an intensity to them—a certain energy or earnestness—that I hadn't experienced other meetings. I recall John focusing on a concept valve that was being created to help with some of the back pressures in the drill string. William "Tater" Wilkerson from Spring, Texas, another smart cookie, was our design engineer working on the filtration method that would ultimately be the heart of the CAPM design. Each meeting was chockfull of "smart cookies" who were paid to use their talents, and talented they were! I felt a little out of my league, but as I said, I was highly motivated to get up to speed quickly.

My initial mission on the project was to help flesh out the draft manual that Thom had given me, and flag any issues. Eventually, it was to become the CAPM Field Operations Manual. Soon, I would be designing the HMI (human-machine interface) displays. For 5th-gen Drillers, the HMI is, in essence, the Driller's/Assistant Drillers' collection of screens and view selections. It is largely through these screens with customizable views that Drillers/ADs see their world, and how they "communicate" with all of the systems. My mission was to make the transition from the existing drilling systems to CAPM as seamless as possible, or intuitively logical to 5th-gen Drillers. There were other tasks I would be lead on, but these were the first-ups and the big hitters.

I intently went through drawings, procedures, ran calculations, and met with vendors in Houston to speak about testing and delivery. I was the hands-on guy, who wore a polo shirt, but with a hard-hat, work gloves, and Red Wing steel-toed boots in my truck. Anytime something needed to have hands laid on it, I was the man. The guys in the shops liked when I came around because they would always tease me about how big I was.

Everything on this project was moving along at a significant pace. Transocean's design approach for dual gradient drilling (CAPM™) allowed for any Transocean drilling ship with the SDC ring to be configured with the CAPM system. The SDC ring, if you recall, is what we nicknamed the "super dog collar" in the moonpool that held the riser, which extends down below the ship and connects to the BOPs. There were other design approaches that were being explored by other companies, consortiums, and universities, but the biggest advantage of the CAPM design approach was that everything for the system was available onboard the vessel, topside. It would be easier to maintain and, if required, to troubleshoot and repair.

After the manifold had completed fabrication and testing, it was shipped from Anson Flowline in Newcastle, England, to Houston by sea freight and trucked into the Anson facility west of Houston. Thom, Ernest, and I were there to take delivery of the hardware and perform detailed inspections. We watched the large flatbed back down the long drive to the rear of the facility where we had a crane to offload the cargo onto the large concrete slab, all staring at the big, three-legged manifold with its huge chokes and bright red paint.

As I looked over the system, I inspected the choke assemblies. The first thing that struck me was just how big they were. These manifold chokes were big—the biggest I've ever seen. The second thing was how high they were from the ground. I needed to figure out how the crew could get to them to tear one apart when needed. The fabricators had provided a tool to tear down the chokes—a puller that had a balance point in it. I took notes on operational maintenance, and wrote down my questions and possible issues. But, overall, I had a good impression of the manifold and choke assemblies.

Thom checked out the tubing runs and valve labeling. Ernest was opening electrical panels. I watched as he took his pen and poked around inside the panels. Then, he took his pad out and started writing notes. I looked over his shoulder, and asked, "What's got you so intent there, Ernest?" I was curious to see what he thought about the electrical side. They don't make guys like him anymore, and I wanted to learn as much as I could.

"You see the way those wires are ran?" Ernest pointed with his pen tip. "How they are touching the inside of the panel?"

"Yessir."

"Take your hand and feel the inside of that panel." Ernest was a master teacher, knowing that literal hands-on experience sticks. I put my hand in and rubbed around. It was rough to the touch, unfinished.

"Those wires," he continued, "if left like that will vibrate and eventually wear down the sheathing on the outside of the cable. Then you will have a short go straight to ground."

We completed our acceptance inspection and met in the Anson conference room to discuss what we'd each found and to develop a "punch list", or a list of actions and issues to be resolved. We also discussed the manifold testing and filtration set-up including equipment required. Because the concrete slab was the only solid ground behind the facility and it didn't provide enough real estate for the manifold, filtration kit, pumps, and additional flow-loop required to test the system, we would have to haul in enough loads of rock to create our own terra firma for the entire set-up. As a result, we elected to move the manifold and other equipment all the way across town to Go West Fabricators to perform the manifold and filtration set-up testing.

As we left the Anson facility that day, I was excited. I'd finally gotten to touch my first piece of CAPM hardware. The project was now tangible. Something about all the drawings and meetings and design discussions turning into something I could touch and feel and smell made it more real.

It was now June. Thom, Ernest and I would be making installation survey visits to the rigs earmarked for modification. We were to physically measure out everything for the engineering and fabrication needed to implement the CAPM system on the rig. I mean everything: Electrical, structural, mechanical, human factors, even clearances for men and machines. The first up was *Deepwater Horizon*. It would be good to finally be going "home" again to see my old team.

The week of our final preparations before flying out to the *Deepwater Horizon*, Iain sent me his final document for the installation survey. Four of us—Ernest, Thom, Tater, and I—headed to PHI's heliport in Houma, Louisiana. The chopper ride was a time of introspection for me, but when we landed and boarded the *Horizon*—our *Horizon!*—it felt like coming home. A lot of smiling faces on old friends. A lot of catching up in just a handshake, a hug, or a "How's Mama and the kids?" But I knew that the four of us had a big job and a limited window of time to do it—and it had to be right. We set up in the *Horizon* conference room with drawings, manuals, and our laptops. Our CAPM HQs for a few days!

Ernest, obviously, was looking at everything required to supply enough electrical power as this beast sucked a lot of power. The mods for this alone would be significant. For example, to modify the rig for CAPM, power had to be run from the starboard aft MCC (motor control center) all the way to the moonpool and aft riser deck where "the heart" of the CAPM equipment would be laid out. This required new racks and cable trays all along the path to the connections. Then we needed to penetrate the aft riser deck to run power to the processing system.

Thom, Tater, and I worked the equipment layout to optimize where everything would be placed. We knew going in that the rig layout was going to be tight. That's an understatement! But challenging as it was, we were determined to "make the impossible possible". This modification wasn't as simple as adding a fire extinguisher to a wall. We were taking an already fixed amount of "busy" space and adding a number of large components, all connected together, in an area where people and equipment had to work. We *absolutely had* to make this system doable, where it wouldn't impact the mission, namely drilling and completing wells. The CAPM was designed to make what we do safer and even faster—not the opposite.

During all this measuring, photographing, redlining drawings and manuals, walking things out, etc., we also had to explain the process to the crew and show them, conceptually, how the system would work, how it would be operated, as well as what it would bring to the operation. There's no doubt, we needed the guys onboard *Horizon* to be "on-board" with the CAPM system.

During our close-out meeting with the rig team, we discussed a future opportunity to test one of our downhole tools being developed as part of the CAPM Project. During that discussion, I became aware of the *Horizon* crew's concern with the set-up and how CAPM would interact with the rest of the system. That's where my role came into play. I made it personal, to make sure that what the Drillers and Assistant Drillers would see on their operating screens would work. It *had* to fit. It *had* to be right!

I got up early the morning we were scheduled to catch our chopper back so I could visit some of the guys. When I walked into the OIM's office to visit with Jimmy Harrell, from Coopersville, Mississippi, he shoved his hands in his bib overalls and rocked back in his executive high-backed leather chair.

"Set down, boy, and talk with me." I sat down just across from him and his desk with piles of paper. Sunshine was glaring through the porthole behind him.

Jimmy had been with the rig few years. He'd been on every kind of rig that they made and was a hell of a hand. He came over from the *Discoverer Enterprise* and took the OIM position when Ken Reed left. Jimmy had sense of humor that would catch me off-guard from time to time. I had worked around him a lot during my time on the *Horizon* and have great memories.

Some years back, just after the morning meeting when I was Jed's AD, all the senior supervisors were headed back out onto the deck to check on their guys. Jimmy would make a round outside around 9:00 a.m. or so. We had just finished drilling out a section on the well and I was standing at the BOP panel with the doors open getting ready to flush the choke and kill lines.

Jed had been running the mud pumps while I was functioning failsafe valves on the BOPs with my back to the portside when the Drillers' cabin door opened. I looked over my shoulder and there was Jimmy.

There were a few other people in the Drillers' cabin, too. Our Subsea Engineer, Mark Hay from Saline, Louisiana, was leaning on the table just in front of the coffee pot with his hard hat kicked back and arms crossed. "Uh-oh, there's trouble," he said, poking at Jimmy, and started to laugh. "Hey there, Jimmy Wayne, what's going on?"

Jimmy walked over and put his arm up on the Driller's chair just behind Jed, and said to Mark, "What are you doing up here? Something wrong?" as he took his safety glasses off and let them hang down around his neck.

"Why, no Jimmy," Mark answered. "Just making some rounds."

Jimmy got tickled, and he had a very distinct laugh when he got tickled. It was something like a mix between a grunt and a cough, but many of them several times over. He walked over to the coffee pot, grabbed a cup, and poured some coffee,

"Well, boys," Mark said, "Jimmy's here to relieve me, so I'm going to take-off. Y'all be safe."

"Alright, Hayday", I said as Mark left.

Now, ever since I was young, I had never been able to grow any hair in the center of my chin. If I trimmed it, it would be very apparent that the hair in the center just didn't exist. So, to mess with Jimmy, I just shaved a strip right through the center and called it good. I had been waiting to do this for a while because I knew there was no way he could not say something.

Jimmy walked over to my right side and stared at me through the glass of the panel door I was holding open. "Son, who taught you how to shave?"

"Jimmy," I smiled, "I did that just for you!"

"It looks terrible and you should just shave it all off." He started that staccato laugh again. "You look like a wrestler, son. Is that what you want to be is a wrestler?"

I shot back in earnest, "No sir, I don't want to be a wrestler. I want to be an OIM! Think I can be an OIM with a goatee like this?"

I closed the panel and walked over to the water cooler. Just as soon as I put the glass to my lips, Jimmy said, "Son with a goatee like that, you may find more than an OIM's job. Looks like a cat been licking on it!"

With a mouth, full of water, I doubled-up laughing and almost choked to death. You could hear Jed in the background laughing, "Ha ha ha! Jimmy, you a cat, son." Jimmy put his dark safety glasses back on and pushed open the door and walked out giggling.

Today, though, was a new day. We both had a lot on our minds. We each had a lot at stake. But, what was best for *Our Horizon* was unspoken "common ground".

"So, what do you think about Houston?" Jimmy started the conversation as he took his hands from inside his bib overalls and began to peck on the keyboard.

"Jimmy, it's alright," I said. "I'm learning a lot and hope it can be put to good use here on the rig."

"That thing's big, ain't it?" he said, still pecking on his keys, but slowly.

"Yes sir," I said, leaning forward in my chair, "but with some good planning, we will be able to get it in there. It'll be tight, but we can do it."

"I was talking about Houston," Jimmy stopped, glancing over at me like I'd missed the first pitch badly.

"Yes, sir," I laughed.

"Well, on that CAPM stuff," he was all business now, "I'm just worried about those Derrickhands down there, and how we going to do all the mud coming and going."

"Jimmy, it would be the same on any other rig out there."

He looked over at me, and peered over the rims of his glasses. "Yeah, boy, but I ain't on any other rig." And he smiled a big smile.

"Yes sir, I know that," I answered. Knowing I had a chopper to catch, I added, "Besides that, everything else is going good? Y'all doing alright out here?"

"Yeah," he said, getting back to the keyboard. "BP is keeping us busy! Got a bunch of wells they want to drill, but the old rig needs a little work on it. But, we doin' good."

"Good," I said, standing up. "If there was anything else wrong, you *would* tell me, wouldn't you?"

"Sure would."

"I know you would," I said reaching to shake 'goodbye'. We both smiled as the Radio Operator came over the speakers announcing the chopper was five minutes out.

"Well, there's my ride, Boss. It was good to see you again."

"Same here, Greg. You take care and come back and see us."

I walked out of the OIM's office and stepped into the Senior Toolpusher's office and called the rig floor. "Rig Floor!" It was Jason.

"Hey, ole boy, I'm headed out," I answered back. "Y'all be good!"

"Sure enough. I will give you a call next week. Something I want to talk to you about." I knew Jason only had a few days left in his hitch.

"Alright, brother. Anytime. Give me a ring. You got my number."

"Take care man. We will holler at you later."

"Be safe, hear?" I said.

I headed straight to the cinema room where the departing helicopter video was being shown. Everyone was there and ready to go. I sat down next to Thom who asked right away, "Say your goodbyes to Jimmy and the boys?"

"Yes sir," I said, my head afire with thoughts. "Hope we can get the system out here. It'll be tough, but I think we can do it." Thom cocked his head back a tad to look over at me and smiled.

Back in Houston, we all worked hard to develop the implementation plan. We gave a long presentation to Steve Newman and the rest of the Transocean Management Team, going over the hardware, piece-by-piece, recommending deployment and installation options. It was starting to gel into an excellent plan.

One tall pole in the tent of "to-dos" was defining the HMI, the human-machine interface: Developing all the screens for how the rig's people would be able to receive information from and communicate to all the CAPM systems, as well as how it all worked together with the existing drilling systems. And, this all needed to be defined within the legacy software platforms of the Cyberbase® drilling control system.

I began working with our subcontractor, Cordyne, Inc., and was assigned Joel Garrett, a super-sharp guy. The CAPM Team gave me the print-outs of *every* screenshot from the Driller's Cyberbase monitors. I would take each screenshot and develop a PowerPoint slide of how I wanted the screen and adjacent screens to appear. Joel would build a computer-generated graphical user interface (GUI) and send it back to me. I would go through it and test it for functionality, making sure it was visually understandable. Of course, whenever new hardware and functions are being added to a legacy system, there are some things that will be new, and some things that users are used to, but just don't exist anymore. For example, the Cyberbase did not have any functionality for tagging—a critical CAPM parameter—so we had to create new functionality. I was always striving to get CAPM monitoring displays to match what the Drillers were used to seeing, and for new functions, I tried to make the transition easy. Every evening, I sat in my apartment and ran the screens over and over and over again, trying to make them perfect. I eventually recorded a voice-over and a video that walked the users completely through the system. Nothing felt better than being part of something that looked to be headed toward a successful start-up.

Several days after getting back to Houston, Jason finally called me as he said he would. "Hey man, what the hell's going on?" I answered.

"Hey fella," he said, "what you know good?"

"Oh, not much, just trying to get me a quick bite before heading back to work."

"Do you got a few minutes we can talk?"

"Man," I answered, rocking back a bit, "for you, yes, absolutely!"

"Look, I have been asked by Corporate to take a Well Control Instructor's position. What do you think about it?"

"Jason," I said, "that's great! They must think a lot of you to offer *that* job."

"Only problem is," he went on, "I wanted to know, since you've been in the corporate world for a little bit coming from the rig, I know you will tell me straight..."

"Yeah, well," I interrupted, "I'm still a Roughneck at heart, Jason. That will never change. But what does change is the coveralls. My coveralls now are a button-up shirt and khakis with an access badge to get to the office instead of the rig floor. But it's not bad at all, actually. If we can ever find me a relief, it would be lots better, but I'm making it for now. That weekend drive back and forth after long weeks here gets tiring, but this project is interesting and definitely keeps me busy."

"Yeah, I live about an hour and a half from Park 10," he continued weighing things out. "So that morning and afternoon drive may be rough."

Jason, Well Control Instructor. Now that will be a hell of a change for him. That time spent driving would be hard for most anyone. Maybe for short-term stuff, but for long-term jobs like that two-year minimum Well Control Instructor position, that's 48 weeks a year of an hour-and-a-half morning and hour-and-a-half afternoon *without* any traffic, and there's *always* traffic! That's over 720 hours spent behind the steering wheel of a vehicle. And, he'd have to give up his days off, which are a big plus for offshore guys. I believe in making changes to better your career, but quality-of-life needs to fit into the equation, too.

"Jason," I said, "the main thing is how is it going to affect your family life? Some people can do it and some people can't. What's Shelley said about it?"

"We haven't talked about it yet," Jason confessed. "I was doing some reconnaissance before talking to her, and trying to see if it was actually worth doing or not."

"Look," I said, "if it was me, I would do what was best for my family and stick to that. After that, if you can stomach that drive every day, then that would sew it up."

"Thanks buddy. That's good stuff. Hey, one more thing," Jason remembered.

"What's that?"

"You remember that consulting thing we talked about a few years back?"

"Of course, I do, man. I still have the logos I sent you in a folder on my desktop," I laughed.

"Well, would you be interested in kicking something like that off in the future, if things keep going good?"

"Jason, it's hard telling *where* I will be at, or *what* I will be doing by then. But, like I told you before, I will always be willing to come and work with good people!"

"Sounds good man. Well, let me let you go. You cleared up some of it for me, but next, I got to talk to Shelley."

"Let me know what she says, brother," I said. "Be good to see you around here more!"

"Oh, there *is* one more thing." Jason was on an afterthought roll, it seemed. "They wanted to know who I wanted to take my position here when I left. I recommended you. That I wanted *you* to come back if that project was going to be finished."

"Well, honestly, I would come back *whenever* they told me it was over. But, that will be a decision between Keeton and Buisine. Let me know how it goes and we will go from there."

"Sounds like a plan. Holler at me later."

"Take care Jason. Talk soon"

"You bet."

I hung up the phone, finished lunch, and headed back to the office. I myself had traded in my quality of life to work on this project, being away from my family Monday through Friday every week, and some weekends, too. As life unfolded, I look back now and wonder if I shouldn't have made other decisions. Of course, I wasn't thinking about this at the time Jason and I talked. It's just 20-20 hindsight years later.

By August 2008, we were making final preparations to function-test the flow-loop using the return manifold. We'd be test-verifying the choke algorithm using some new software, and I was excited to be testing and using some cutting-edge technology.

The manifold was now positioned in Go West Fabricators' yard in Galena Park close to the Houston Ship Channel on a white, caliche rock testbed. I know that there are hotter places in the world than Houston, Texas, during the month of August, but when that "Africa-hot" heat and humidity are piled on top of a bed of white caliche rock at high noon, it will bake your biscuits quick! It kinda reminded me of that National Grey used as topcoat on rigs, only brighter. This stuff was blinding!

We reviewed the layout. Tater had positions of the pumps, fluid processing system, flow-loop, relief valves, and the return manifold for the test set-up all drawn up. LEWCO (LeTourneau Ellis Williams Company) delivered the mud pumps and Expro came in and started setting up the flow-loop and chokes. We had the pumps hooked up to fresh water tanks, pumping out of these tanks through the suction and out the pumps' high-pressure discharge. The fluid would then be routed to the return manifold. Once the flow passed the manifold, it would enter the last part of the flow-loop back to the fresh water tanks and then the process would start over. There was a manual relief valve placed in the flow-loop just ahead of the manifold. We could open this valve to simulate a downhole loss of fluid pressure. Then we could observe the software's reaction and choke closing to manage the bottom hole pressure it was told to hold.

This sounds high-tech, but it was a bare-bones setup to prove three things:

1) That the system would be stable enough to operate with steady pressures.
2) That the system would automatically react when there was a pressure change and adjust itself.
3) That the system would operate for an extended duration before experiencing any issues.

I stood at the HMI as we turned the pumps on and started to move the fresh water through the lines. After we got the lines full of water and fluid returning to the tank, and all the lines checked for leaks, everything was ready. We input the bottom hole pressure for what we wanted to hold. A few seconds later, we could hear the chokes moving on the return manifold; they started to close. Once the choke started to restrict the fluid causing the manifold pressure to rise, it stopped at the programmed setpoint. We verified the manual gauge and the reading was the same as the HMI. We manipulated the system in every way we could imagine to see if we could make it fail, or make it fail to detect a change in the pressure profile. One hundred percent user control! The average temperature of the fluid was reaching 125 degrees F and the system was still operating perfectly. If it could work with hot temperatures, it most certainly would work at the cooler temperatures of deepwater.

Even though there were other variables (such as temperature, line sizing, flow rates, choke opening), these were conditions which could change with any vessel or drilling rig. But the constants on every operation are the user set-up point to maintain the same bottom hole pressures, and the need to make the Driller aware of any influxes, even micro-influxes that may enter the well otherwise undetected. As I discussed before, the instruments currently providing "insight" to the Driller are so far behind the drill bit, that Drillers are in new territory before they can receive any data. This CAPM equipment setup and the theory behind it provide the Driller the control to instantly manage the pressure profile. So, what's the big deal? No uncontrolled events, constant real-time monitoring, the ability to make immediate adjustments, and a better well drilled for the client. This is not a sales pitch. CAPM would do just that.

Our system testing lasted for a week. We captured all the data and planned our first post-test results review.

John MacKay, Thom, and I left out of PHI Houma, Louisiana, on Monday, October 20th, 2008, for the *Horizon* to do the downhole valve testing. Again, it was good to see my guys. The rig was stationed on the Freedom well, Mississippi Canyon Block 948. The well had reached TD (total depth), and BP had given us some time just after the plug and abandon operations. They got the riser displaced of all the mud and handed the rig over to us for a few hours. We didn't have long to perform the tests, so we were in and out pretty quickly. I had enough time to catch up with Jason, Randy, and Van before departing the *Deepwater Horizon* in the morning. I didn't know it then, but that visit was my final time aboard. I would never return, and never again be involved with any other operation with my rig and my crew on the *Deepwater Horizon*.

We traveled to Bathgate, Scotland, to participate in the FAT (factory acceptance testing) at the Oil States Klaper Limited facility. It was my first trip out of the United States, so I was all eyes and ears going everywhere, taking everything in. The FAT entailed connecting all the pieces—integrating the surface package with the control system—and functioning everything using the HMI. Naturally, I was still the "hands-on" guy, and took some ribbing from the technicians about my size, especially at Aberdeen. When they first saw me working with the equipment, they exclaimed, "Would you look at the mitts on you!" They had a funny way of talking about the size of my hands.

We spent two weeks going through the surface equipment integration, previewing the fluid weighting devices, and driving from Aberdeen to Bathgate, finally arriving in Newcastle at the facility where the return manifold had been built and tested. After a successful FAT, the system was broken down and loaded onto skids made of tough lumber treated for open water transport.

The skids for the CAPM surface package were delivered from Scotland to Transocean's yard in Amelia, Louisiana. We were there when they unloaded this precious sea freight from the boats. Much of this equipment was the only of its kind on the entire planet, and Transocean had invested a lot of time and money into it. It was paramount to all that nothing be damaged during handling. I spent the next twenty-one days working with our two new junior supervisors and first four operators. We completely assembled the entire system, installed spacer spools, labeled, checked and rechecked, and performed final testing. Then, after the final testing, the entire system would be broken apart, packaged up, and deployed for its first field test.

As we knew early on, to implement CAPM on a rig, to get everything installed, that rig would have to come off contract for an unscheduled OOS (out-of-service) period of several weeks. And that is where the CAPM Project hit a snag. While some parts of the CAPM package were "plug-and-play", a substantial amount of time was required to install new lines to process the amount of fluid—the mud pit system, bulkhead and deck penetrations—not to mention the power that was needed to supply the motors that operated it. *Deepwater Horizon's* schedule was filled with exploratory work that had expiration dates. These leases had to be explored within a certain time frame or they would expire—the client would lose the lease and Transocean would obviously lose the business.

In addition, the costs of the OOS modifications and installing the CAPM system and training the crews were super-expensive to bear alone; Transocean needed commercial agreements with BP. Those agreements between BP and Transocean for the *Horizon* OOS time to commercialize CAPM never came to the table. It appeared too costly, and ultimately, there did not appear to be enough window of opportunity to get the CAPM system installed on the *Deepwater Horizon*. We'd hit a roadblock.

The project team turned its focus onto the *Discoverer Enterprise*. That rig had its scheduled ten-year OOS coming up in mid-2009. The plan was to be ready with all of the equipment for installation and field trials completed onboard during the rig's other work to avoid impacts to the client, also BP. This would allow Transocean the option of implementing on either vessel should the commercial opportunity arise.

I cannot reveal any proprietary information about CAPM™, but there is enough pubic information on dual gradient drilling to blow one's mind for days. From my perspective, it would provide a revolutionary approach to offshore drilling, giving teams the ability to move past conventional thinking and on to new ways that would make offshore drilling lives better.

With the oil peaking at around $136 a barrel, prospects that seemed unobtainable before, due to the high costs to discover and extract, were now made possible with CAPM. What was brilliant about the system, in layman's terms, is that the entire pressure profile of the well could be changed with the touch of a button. This also meant a Driller could see tiny amounts of gas or fluid entering the wellbore. CAPM would give Drillers what they always needed: ultimate control over the well along with the ability to drill the well faster, safer, and more efficiently. While drilling the well may be the easiest part, it is also the greatest risk a Driller will ever experience. We had designed and proved a viable system that would allow for safely navigating that overbalanced (loss of drilling mud) and underbalanced (potential kicks or influx) profile. It gave that well control "trigger" to the Drillers they always needed, but were missing—real-time insight into the well. We had finally proven we could provide a solution to address this unknown, dark area that makes the hair stand up on the back of every Driller's neck.

Our approach to dual gradient drilling (i.e. CAPM™) would also reduce the overall costs of well construction by handling influxes and greatly reducing mud losses. Some of these events (i.e. mud losses or influxes) could last for days or even weeks. The average deepwater vessel dayrate in 2008 was $500,000 a day. Add to that the client costs with its service companies, combined with the drilling contractor, those dayrates could reach well over $1 million a day! Days spent on remedial work on wells that had small pressure profiles between under-balanced and over-balanced could lead to millions and millions of dollars lost.

The CAPM system was smart and made sense, but it also needed investment by both the owner and the client. BP made its decision not to take the *Deepwater Horizon* out of service for a few weeks to modify the vessel, perhaps because it couldn't see the ROI. CAPM needed somebody to bite the fiscal bullet to commercialize the work that the CAPM Project Team had accomplished. We had a viable solution. We had hardware on-dock ready to go. We'd test-verified it as a viable solution.

In light of the events that followed, and the tremendous costs in human lives, costs to the companies involved, costs to the industry, and costs to the United States, the decision not to install the CAPM system on *Deepwater Horizon* was such an incredibly short-sighted one.

Gordon, Karl, & Greg Meche

Gordon, Mud Engineer, would come out my second week. He had been there a while and he would come out with BP Company Man, Teddy Reed. Gordon and Mr. Teddy worked nights together. Mr. Teddy would always get up around 1530-1600 and get his day started. On the weekend, he would come in and watch the golf tournament and drink coffee while he was waking up. Gordon was a big golfer and he was good, so he would come in and check on the golf scores. I always made an effort on the weekends to come in. Mr. Teddy would always ask me, "Well, Mitch, how we they lookin' out there?"

"Mr. Teddy, we are looking good." And then we'd all just sit around and talk about golf. We would ask Gordon, "How do you make that kind of shot, Gordon?"

He would say, "Oh man, you got to tweak this and tweak that." That was the only real time I spent with Gordon. He was a nice guy, a good cat, and he was excited about his baby coming.

Mitch Gill

So, Gordon Jones and I had a small moment in the mud shack about not loving a Foo Fighters' song, "Wheels". It was pretty hilarious, and weirdly deep. We couldn't collectively agree, so we agreed to disagree. Then somehow, we arrived at the conclusion that the song was something that we, in fact, could agree upon. As I play this song, I cry. When I repeat the song, "Wheels", I think of my brother.

I'm an Iraq war veteran, as some of you already know. As the [DWH] anniversary approaches, I feel things that can't be explained. I've seen brothers die. I watched a brother of mine get shot in the neck. Close quarters. I signed up for that. Our DWH disaster is not for one second what we could ever fathom. I never compare the two.

I also never post. I also try my best to not get drunk. I also . . . bear with me . . . I love you all.

Greg Meche

Thank you, Greg, for your story and service to this country. My time in life with Karl was spent split between the oilfield and the Army. He served during Desert Storm/Desert Shield. There were many stories he could never voice with words to explain how he felt. He never went hunting, and many could never understand why he never taught Aaron to hunt. He simply said, when I asked him one of the first times he had the opportunity to go with a friend, that he had held enough guns and done enough killing for a lifetime and had no use to hunt unless he had to.

The military meant a lot to Karl. God bless and keep you, Greg.

Tracy Kleppinger Melton

Loss

"My brothers, rest in peace. This world has been so much less bright since we lost you all too soon."
~~Ron Guidry, Electronics Technician, Deepwater Horizon

Back in October of 2008, the week before the CAPM Team made our final visit to the *Deepwater Horizon*, I headed back home in Louisiana for the weekend. I was getting ready to take my son to ball practice when John Carroll called.

"Hey, Greg."

"Hey partner. How are ya?" I answered, glad to hear from him.

"I hate to call ya like this, Greg." There was no mistaking the seriousness to his voice. "But Jed passed away today."

Tears came like a wellspring. "Was he home?" I asked, holding my voice together.

"Yes. He was home."

I stood there on the porch, shell-shocked. I'd just talked to him last month when he told me he might be off a hitch to go get some tests run and maybe a stint.

John went on to let me know that Jed had walked down a few miles to help his youngest son fix a chimney leak, walked back, sat down with Jackie, his wife, for a coffee and took his last breath. It had been a massive heart attack.

I sat down on the edge of my porch to think a bit. Jed had been a mentor to me—not only as a Driller, but in real life, too. I didn't know when I left the rig back in March, it would be the last time I would see Jed, with that toothless grin and him giving me that big pat on the back. Then again, we never really do.

I called Jackie, and we talked for a long time. I took some bereavement time from the Project to go to Jed's funeral in Arkansas. The *Horizon* Rig Manager, John Keeton even drove up. I know Jed wouldn't have believed it himself that the Rig Manager would come to his funeral. I imagined, plain as day, Jed sounding off in that down-home, "hillbilly" way, "What are you doin' up in my neck of the woods, Keeton?"

It was a somber drive down a long, dark highway back to Louisiana. There was not much to lift my thoughts, not even recalling what seemed to be a million and one stories. But for the three beautiful kids snoring in the back seat, the drive from Jed's funeral would have been even worse. Yes, with my children, we certainly shared in the best of times; but also, in those moments in life when life gets tough, we shared those, too, and held on to each other, trying to always remember to cherish each moment we have together. I still miss ole Jed, even to this day.

In November 2009, I received more bad news. My sister called to say that she had found Mom passed out in the hallway of her house and that they were in the ER.

Mom had been going through chemo for a while, but she still continued working! During the summer, we all gathered with her on the porch of her house in Many, Louisiana. As we all sat together as a family, she told us that she just wanted to go through the holidays not feeling sick. She wanted to enjoy one Christmas out of the last seven feeling well. She told us all she'd decided to quit doing the treatments so that she could enjoy life. We all left knowing that she was making the best decision for herself.

She was released from the ER with instructions to follow-up with the oncologist the following week. When I made it back home that hitch, I went straight to see her. My step-dad was out visiting his mother, so she and I just spent some mother-son time visiting. She was up and moving around. Not a hundred percent, but she seemed like she was doing okay. She confessed she was nervous about her upcoming doctor's visit. She went back to her room, crawled into her bed, and stacked her pillows up where she could watch TV. She grabbed the remote and flipped through the channels until she got to an old episode of "Star Trek". I climbed onto the bed next to her and we just sat and talked about anything and everything. I just enjoyed spending that time with her. I laid my head in her lap and she put her hand on my head as if I was ten years old again. "Everything's going to be okay, son," Mom reassured. "Don't worry about me."

The following week, we met with the oncologist. He gave us the worst news possible. The cancer had come back and was progressing rapidly. The doctor gave her three months. I remember Mom's face when he told her. She seemed stunned. "Are you *sure*?"

"Miss Karen," the Doctor looked at Mom, "I so am sorry. But any additional options we have available for you will only make the pain worse."

"I'm not in pain," she plead, still not believing what we'd just heard.

"Cancer doesn't hurt Miss Karen," the Doctor advised. "It hurts everything else. But we promise to make you as comfortable as we can."

She looked down at the floor. It was quiet. There was a heaviness in the air. Finally, she took in a big breath and let it out. "Well then, if that's all we can do, then that's all we can do." She got up, looked at me, and said, "Y'all take me home."

My step-dad had left the room right after the news, and then came back in and asked, with desperation, "Is there *anything* else we can do?"

"I'm sorry," the doctor repeated. "But as I explained to Miss Karen, all that is left will only cause her more pain."

I just sat stunned in a daze listening to all this. I just heard a death sentence and felt helpless—totally helpless. We walked out of the hospital and got in the car. No one spoke, each one of us alone in our thoughts. My step-dad drove. I leaned my head on the window staring out, seeing nothing, not knowing what to say or do.

The tears began to fall. I was not believing that the person I'd looked up to and most respected my entire life . . . would soon be gone. The more I thought about it, the more the tears poured. I was startled for a second to hear someone else in our car crying, only to realize it was *me*. I'd gotten louder and actually startled myself with my own crying.

Mom reached back and put her hand on my knee and squeezed it tight. "I want both of you to know how much I love you, and it doesn't matter what the doctor says. If the Good Lord wants me, then He will take me."

She was the strongest person I have ever known in my life. She had gone through a groundbreaking technique the year before when they drilled into her head to eliminate some tiny spots of cancer. This first-time procedure wasn't a hundred-percent success for Mom, but it was enough to clear her brain for a while, and it opened the path to new techniques, giving doctors a new tool in their treatment protocols.

I returned to the CAPM Project, but our activities had nearly grounded to a halt. I spent most of my time reviewing procedures. The day-to-day monotony of it was driving me crazy. I emailed a friend whom I'd met working with the *Discoverer Enterprise*. He had since been moved to Brazil as the Asset Manager over the rigs in that division—sharp, intelligent, and a good contact to keep. He let me know his team was looking for a Performance Toolpusher to fill a position after the first of the year. I decided it was time for me to move on, so I made a request to JP. He advised that the CAPM Project was not in a position to release me yet, so I returned to looking through procedures and making monthly trips to Amelia to check on the CAPM hardware we had stored. In my mind, time was ticking away.

In mid-January 2010, I had come into the office super-early to beat the Friday afternoon traffic heading home. As I was just leaving Houston, nearing the freeway interchange next to the Downtown Aquarium, my sister called, sobbing softly.

"It's time," she said. "They are calling all of us together."

I began to tear up. "Is she awake?"

"No."

"Hold the phone to her ear," I requested.

"Okay, go ahead," my sister gave me the cue. I took a deep breath.

"Mom, I want you to know that you have fought the hardest and most valiant battle. Do not be afraid. You're not leaving us behind with nothing. You have taught us everything we need to know to be good people and to live our lives accordingly. You have been my friend when I didn't have any friends, and you have been my leader when I needed leadership. I love you, and I will be home soon."

My brave, hardworking, humble mother passed away on a cold, calm night, January 22, 2010. She was surrounded by family and friends, me on one side holding her hand, and my cousin, Melissa, holding the other. I am thankful now that JP didn't release me from the CAPM Project to transfer to South America. I likely would have missed sitting with my mother when she left this world.

Back on my birthday, 2009, I'd lost my grandmother; she died on her mother's (my great-grandmother's) and my birthday, and also passed away with family and friends, especially her best friend of over forty years. I was very close to my grandmother. The enormity of losing my mother felt like the mule-kick of three punches in a row—my grandmother, Jed, and now Mom. When Mom left this world, I just closed my eyes. I basically didn't open them back up for a year. I was numb. In shock. So much so that I went into depression. I didn't realize what was happening then, but looking back, I can see it clearly now. The days following her funeral were miserable for me, and all I could do was consume myself with work to fill the time. The monotonous work that I complained about before became an absolute need to make it through each day.

In late February, I was in Amelia when I met up with an old *Deepwater Horizon* friend, Harrell Pfleger (60) from Sumrall, Mississippi. Harold had been my Mechanical Supervisor years before on the *Horizon*, and was now a Project Engineer in Transocean's Upgrade and Repair Division. He told me a bit about what he was doing and said that he was going to need a relief. I thought this may be the perfect time to get away from everything for a while. I spoke to JP about my situation and told him about the opportunity.

Thanks to the CAPM Project timing, he said there may be an opportunity for me to return to the CAPM Project later when things started to move commercially, so he agreed to the transfer. Before the ink on the transfer had time to dry, I was reassigned to the *Henry Goodrich* 25-year OOS Project in Canada. I traveled to Newfoundland for this four-month project, and on to Nova Scotia for cold-water survival training in April 2010. It was during this training when I got that call from John Carroll who told me about the *Deepwater Horizon* accident. I lost eight members of my second family that night, April 20, 2010, four of whom worked directly for me. Gone.

If I had been in a tailspin before, I was now going down in flames with no parachute. I kept on working the project, but I was struggling, operating in shell-shocked, zombie mode. I finished up the *Henry Goodrich* OOS Project and headed home to Louisiana. But the home I came back to was not the same home I'd left. I walked into a house full of strangers, having been completely estranged from my wife and kids whom I'd only seen a few days in the past four months. We had become disconnected—*I* had become disconnected from everyone and everything. When I was reassigned to another project in GoM, I had hopes that things would get better. I thought things were looking a little brighter.

Instead, I was served with divorce papers. Like Ron Guidry said, "This world has been so much less bright since we lost you all too soon." To me, it was everyone so important to me, all lost in such a short span. I remember lyrics of some song along the lines of "having nothin' left to lose". In a way, at that point in my life, I had nothin'.

Karl

We were working on the pipe deck offloading pipe and it was me, Karl Kleppinger, Richard "Tiny" Booth, and I think Jeremy Clements. Anyways, we were busting ass all day and just clowning each other. Well, me and Karl got into it just like we all did bitching, and raising hell with each other. I was up on the stack of pipe and Karl was on deck flagging, and I knew just the right buttons to push to make him blow his top. He was the flagger and was trying to tell me what to do, and I was like, "You need to shut-up and worry about what you're doing!"

And it pissed him off so bad that he blew up! He was like, "I'll come up there and kick your ass!"

And I was like, "There's no way in hell you will get your big ass up here!" (Keep in mind, I'm pissing him off on purpose.)

He got so pissed at me that he started to tear-up mad, and he threw his hard hat at me. Of course, me and Tiny just laughed our asses off. But, after the work was done, it was right back to normal messing with each other.

Russ Cummings

When I very first arrived on the Horizon I think in late 2006, early 2007, I set down to eat breakfast with a couple of the guys. Karl was one of them. Karl had built quite a handsome plate of food and even had bread as sideboards. I didn't know him very well, and I just wanted to poke at him a little bit. So, I told him, "You know they let you go back for seconds, right? You don't have to eat it all in one shot."

He slid his plate toward me, pointed at it, and said, "You know, my grandfather lived to be 94 years old," and he stared right through me.

I answered back, "Did he eat big, too?"

Karl's response was, "No. He minded his own business."

I busted out laughing, and he just gave me that grin.

Mitch Gill

My initials are "PC". I try to be polite to people. Some people I know, I won't mention any names, but they would never be offended by anything I called them. They wore it like a badge of honor. Russ [Cummings] would turn to Karl and Tiny and say, "I knew I could get the Chief Mate to call me that!" And the three biggest guys on the rig all giggled like school girls. Hilarious.

Peter Cyr

O Fateful Night—The Incident
Views from the Rig

"Personally, I don't consider myself the most knowledgeable of the industry, but I do know about a few things. I knew those men. They were good at their job and they were hard workers. They were family men with people waiting on them at home…. My outlook was from inside the office, behind paperwork and emails, and still, I am proud to have been a part of the 'Green Team' and to be able to work with such well respected men and the Deepwater Horizon itself as an entire entity."
~~Andrea Roberts, Transocean "Green Team" [Onshore]

Mike Glendenning *Deepwater Horizon* Mechanic

My first rig assignment was the *Deepwater Horizon*. I was onboard the *Horizon* in October of 2008 until the fateful night of April 20th, 2010. I was onboard during the blowout, and this is my story:

The story of the Macondo well is nothing short of tragic. Those on the *Horizon* were walking tall: We were receiving our Seven-Year No-Lost-Time-Injuries Award from Transocean and BP upper management. The Macondo well changed all of that, of course, and more than likely, changed the offshore oilfield everywhere, at least for the foreseeable future. It's not that other rigs haven't had bad well blowouts, or that there hasn't been a tragedy of that scale in any waters where there was drilling. What made this one different was the fact that it was the worst offshore well blowout/accident in U.S. territorial waters. And then it was turned political by the irresponsible, agenda-driven U.S. media, and the administration in office at the time.

If I remember correctly, the Macondo well had been drilled to a depth of approximately 10,000 feet by the *Marianas* previously; but, she had to get off it because of a bad Gulf storm. We were the next to hop over to it and resume where they left off. I am no expert when it comes to well drilling, so I will not attempt to explain the technical challenges on the Macondo well. I know we had hot-work shut down for more than two weeks due to the high gas levels, and that we had stuck somewhere around 1,000 foot of drill pipe and BHA (bottom-hole assembly) because the formation collapsed. We perforated it, cemented it in, and kicked off to keep drilling. It seemed to me that we always had a large amount of gas coming back throughout the project. Once finished, we thought we were good-to-go, doing every normal thing that you would do when abandoning a well. I was completely clueless at the time that anything was amiss.

There were, however, a few things I had noticed that day. And now, when I look back on them, they make a lot more sense. But at the time, all they did was make me raise my eyebrows a little. For example, around 4:30 in the afternoon, we (the Mechanics) got a call to the rig floor to replace a leaking hydraulic hose on the iron roughneck. When I went into the drill shack to ask permission to enter the floor to perform the work, I noticed a great deal of tension among those in positions of authority. For this rig crew, that seemed odd.

We finished up our work, and I knocked off at 6:00 p.m., went to eat dinner, and went to my stateroom. Strangely, I did not get undressed, but stayed dressed in my blue living quarters coveralls. I stayed up listening to music and chatting with some old high school friends on Facebook.

I remember it was sometime after 9:00 p.m. when I first heard the well flow; however, at the time, I wasn't aware of the fact that it was flowing, because my room was Room 304, underneath the port crane and the port diverter line. As such, I was used to hearing them bleed-off well pressure after pressure-testing wells. So, when I heard it, I thought nothing of it. (Keep in mind, I also had headphones on listening to music.) When the first blast happened, I also didn't think anything of it because in my room, it honestly just felt and sounded like the crane crew had dropped something big, or landed something hard up on the main deck.

Shortly after that, though, Yancy Kepplinger came over the PA system instructing everyone that there was a fire, and for all hands to muster at their inside muster stations. Even then, I remember saying out loud, "You have got to be kidding me! I hope this is over quick!" When I stepped out of my room, that's when I realized that something had gone terribly wrong. There were normally three doors between my room and the port side mud pump room—two regular and one watertight. All three were gone, and I could see fire burning back in the #1 mud pump room, I could see just fine because the emergency lighting was on, and the third deck hadn't been damaged all that badly.

I remember we had a new welder onboard, Steve Davis, and he came out of his room and threw his hands out and said, "What are we gonna do?"

For me, instinct kicked in. "Follow me," I said, and we made our way down to the center passageway. My intent was to walk upstairs and make my way to the cinema room, as that was my inside muster station; however, the ceiling over the stairs had collapsed, and that way was blocked.

At the same time, Stumpy (Patrick Morgan), was trying to go out to the smoke deck and go up the stairs that way, but those stairs were blocked as well. I remember seeing him coming back through the door and saying, "You can't go that way. It's blocked!" So then, I went back down to the port forward column and walked up the spiral staircase to the second deck. When I walked out the door to the second deck, there was much more damage than what happened on the third deck. There was debris everywhere, and there was a lot of dust in the air, I assume from insulation and ceiling tiles. I don't remember really experiencing any gas effects at that time.

I made my way down to the cinema room, and the Medic, Bill Francis, was standing in the doorway. There were a lot of people about, but I was barely aware of them or what they were saying. I just remember looking into the cinema room and it was pitch black. I looked into the galley, and it was dark. But, I remember seeing the red and yellow paint of what appeared to be the pipe conveyor, normally on the top deck above.

I decided at that point that I did not want to stay inside and made my way out to the lifeboat deck. I ran out to the handrail and saw two people already in the water. I later found out that they were Brandon Bouillion (Weatherford) and Matt Hughes, (Roughneck). They had both decided to jump.

I remember then turning around and looking up in the derrick: The top drive was parked about halfway up, and there was a tornado of flames engulfing it coming up from the rotary. Flames were coming out of the draw-works shed, and there was a very powerful flame blowing from the starboard diverter line. It looked very much like a flare boom, flaring off gas. That's the point when everything came together in my head. From my studies of how well drilling works, I knew we had had a catastrophic blowout and there was nothing anyone could do except get off the rig. I remember my Chief Mechanic, Charles Cochrane, was standing next to me, and I said to him, "It's over boss. Time to get out of here."

He replied, "Yup, you're right."

By this time, a crowd had gathered on the lifeboat deck and people were starting to panic and flip-out. Darrin Rupinski (Assistant DPO) was trying to maintain order by ordering everyone behind the yellow line, but people ignored him and started to board the port lifeboat #1. In a situation like this, even someone as solid as me started to get a little anxious. So, I did what I know to do when I need help. I prayed. I prayed, "God, give me direction. Tell me what to do."

That voice that has guided me through so much of my life spoke, "Get on the lifeboat. You'll be alright." That was all I needed, and I boarded the lifeboat and never looked back. It seemed to fill up pretty quickly, and I remember our Bosun (Steve Richardson), getting in the seat, and asking everyone if they were ready. I remember Don Winslow standing up trying to take roll call and someone reaching up, grabbing him by the shoulder and forcing him back down in his seat. Steve pulled the cord, and away we went. Once in the water, they started the engine, two guys front and rear undid the D-rings, and away we went. Luckily, for us, the *Damon Bankston* was only a few thousand feet away, so we were there in no time. They moored us alongside, and we all climbed out onto the ship's main deck.

After getting out and walking around, and observing the scene, I was dumbfounded at first. I remember asking Randy Ezell, "What happened? I thought everything was going good."

He replied, "I don't know. I thought so, too."

And that was the most I talked for the rest of the night which was like a nightmare. Watching the rig burn, feeling the heat, smelling the burning paint, watching plumes of molten metal drop off into the Gulf just like a giant torch was burning through metal. I had no idea at that point who was alive or dead, injured or uninjured. I watched as the second lifeboat arrived, and then the life raft, and the fast rescue craft of the *Bankston* was out and about, I guess picking people out of the water.

I remember all the wounded being brought onboard. One in particular, Wyman Wheeler, was under a blanket in the triage. When I saw him, I knew the thing to do was talk to him, talk to him about anything other than what was happening. We talked about mud trucks, and the motor I was going to eventually build him someday. I told him he was going to be alright, that he was going to make it just fine.

By then, it was clear that the U.S. Coast Guard had taken over. There was one medevac chopper after another coming in to lift off the wounded and get them to shore. I can't remember if there were several choppers, or just one making repeated short trips.

Once all the wounded had been airlifted off, we settled in for what would be a very long night as we watched our home away from home being swallowed alive by the flames. It seems to me that the derrick only lasted about an hour before it buckled and fell over into the Gulf. And it was like that all night, watching one thing after another be destroyed on the rig. The fire was so hot that you could feel it. I have no idea how far away we were.

There was hardly any sleep that night, even though I was exhausted. At one point, I put in ear plugs and tried to lay down on the hard deck and rest my head on my life jacket, but I couldn't sleep right away. People were milling about the *Bankston*. There were tons of conversations going on everywhere, but I wasn't paying any attention. I was thinking about the fact that I left my computer, which had a picture of my newborn daughter on the screensaver. And how I left my wallet, and my phone behind, and that I had no real way to contact the outside world until we eventually got to shore. And then I thought, *How in the world am I going to get home without any ID?* Somehow, I fell asleep for a few hours. I remember looking down at the decks below, and seeing Jimmy Harrell, dressed in nothing but orange coveralls, standing up in his bare feet, propped up on some dunnage on the forward main deck of the boat, his head in his hands.

That morning, the *Bankston* pulled up to a Diamond Drilling Company semi-submersible. I am assuming it was a team of BP engineers. Our Subsea Engineers were loaded onto a Billy Pugh and taken up onto their rig, and transferred to an ROV intervention boat standing by. They also offloaded a medical treatment team onto the *Bankston*. As we pulled away, the ROV intervention boat started heading back toward the *Horizon*, I guess to do a hot stab intervention of the BOP, to try to shut the well in. I didn't know it at the time and not sure if anyone else did either, but Transocean's internal investigation determined that the BOP had already been functioned by drill crew during the initial well flow.

I recall it was somewhere around 8:00 a.m. of the 21st when we pulled out and started heading for shore. I remember having such a sad feeling in my gut as we passed by the *Horizon*, and I knew that would be the last time I would physically see her. I thought to myself, *What a waste of one hell of a fine drilling rig*.

The sail home seemed to take forever. There was nothing to do except reflect on what happened, trying to make sense of it all. We stopped by a Total E&P production platform in the afternoon at some point. While there, they offloaded a Coast Guard preliminary investigation team onboard the *Bankston*, and the hands from the Total rig sent us down a care package full of cigarettes, chew, coveralls, clothes, and other miscellaneous items. Then as we headed out again, the investigation team had us gather in the ship's galley to take down written witness statements from everyone. Some people were hostile, some indifferent, but we all went along with it.

It seems to me it was around midnight before we finally got into Fourchon. Once we were close to land and had cell service, Andrea (Fleytas) let me borrow her iPhone so could call home and let my wife—at home nursing our two-month-old daughter at the time—know I was alright. We both cried.

I didn't know it at the time, but she already knew I was alright because a family friend (who was privy to inside information), had called our church Pastor's wife to get hold of my wife to let her know I was okay. If I remember right, our pastor's wife had called to let her know.

I don't remember the exact timeline, but earlier on Wednesday, my wife received a call from someone at Transocean to let her know that there had been an accident onboard *Horizon*. Unfortunately, the Transocean person calling was also fielding several different phone calls in her office, and my wife overheard her say, "I don't really know what's going on. There was an accident, and I don't know who or how many survived." My wife said she collapsed and did the only thing she knew to do: She prayed. She was glad she had not turned on the news that morning because she was exhausted from night-feeding our daughter. Once I talked to her, and we were both relieved that I was okay, I hung up and told her I would call her once I got settled in on land and knew what was going to happen.

The *Bankston* backed into its stall in Fourchon, and we offloaded. I was so relieved to be on dry land, but was pretty shocked at what happened next, thinking it was over: The Coast Guard required everyone to provide them with a urine sample. I went along with it, but I was pretty annoyed.

Once that was done, we mingled with the various Transocean hierarchy walking around. I remember a Transocean higher-up who asked me, "What in the world happened?"

I replied, "If you want to know what happened, go grab you a handful of mud and concrete chunks off the ass end of that boat, that will tell you a lot!" I am sure he may not have liked my answer, but I have a brash way of just telling things like they are, which has gotten me in trouble, often.

Soon after, we boarded buses and headed for New Orleans. We had State Trooper escorts, and I remember the press all over outside the gates trying to get in and interview people. I don't know if they ever got in or not.

We made our way to Crown Plaza in New Orleans where we got off and unloaded. They had a reception ready for us, and there were a lot of families there and food and drinks available. We were ushered into a room where the rig manager addressed everyone. I will refrain from sharing my feelings about this. After the meeting, we mingled about and ate breakfast. I remember meeting family members, but one stands out in my memory: Roy Kemp's sister asked me if I had seen Wyatt [Roy]. I didn't know what to say. I just lost it and had to turn away and remove myself.

I retired to my room to call family and get some much-needed sleep. I woke up later that night, got dressed in my blue coveralls, and was escorted by Transocean and a DHS agent through the New Orleans airport all the way to the gate. Sitting at the gate, CNN was on TV, and of course, it was 24/7 coverage showing the *Horizon* burn. I felt awkward. I didn't really say anything or make eye contact with anyone. I just wanted to get home.

Once I landed in Houston at Hobby Airport, my father-in-law picked me up, shook my hand and said, "I'll bet you're glad that's over."

"Yes, I most certainly am," I replied. Little did I know that it was *far* from over.

There isn't a day that goes by that I don't think about that night, and about it all. I still see it vividly in my mind, and smell the burning paint, and hear the crunching steel, and see the plumes of molten metal falling off into the Gulf. I think about the 11 who are now gone. How one day you're here, the next day you're gone. I could write a lot about each one of them. I keep telling myself they're still here, just on another assignment somewhere, and that I will see them again someday...But, I know, just not here in this world. R.I.P. Jason, Dale, Roy, Don, Shane, Gordon, Karl, Dewey, Blair, Adam, and Steve. Y'all are the best! May you all never be forgotten.

Bill Francis (*Deepwater Horizon* Rig Medic)

I had only been part of the crew about a year when the incident happened. Prior to working here, I was on the *Discoverer Deepseas* and the *Cajun Express*.

My first year onboard the *Horizon*, there was very little to do because the crew worked so safely. I treated the occasional cough, dehydration, etc. The few injuries I treated were minor. I never once in that year felt uneasy, worried, or in danger. I had the utmost confidence in our supervisors and ultimately, in Jimmy Harrell, the OIM.

April 20th, 2010: It was the end of my hitch, and I was ready for some time off. I also liked wrapping up a drill site and moving, because you never know what's next. As end-of-hitch duties, I spent the day writing notes to my relief, Matt Keller. I wrapped up my inventory sheet, placed my orders, got all my signatures for the controlled substances handover, and tidied any other loose ends.

There were VIPs from Transocean and BP onboard to present the rig an award for seven years without a Lost Time Incident. All through the day, I heard some loud noises that I had not heard before. I inquired a couple of times and was told at one point it was the Bosun and crew needle-gunning and cleaning the deck. It seemed like the noises were different than what I was used to hearing.

It was about 9:00 p.m. I was packed, had everything done, and was enjoying a chat online when the lights went out. I thought we were doing a blackout drill to show off the system to the VIPs. I waited for the alarm to go off. It seemed like five minutes, but then came a boom, followed by the alarm. I walked out of my stateroom and into the hospital, opened the door into what used to be the hallway in front of the galley. The wall had been destroyed, and people were trying to go to the galley because that was one of the backup muster locations.

My initial thoughts were that the cooks or baker had blown up the kitchen. I did not know what happened, but I instinctively started sending everyone to their lifeboat. I assisted some people from laundry, and helped a few up the stairs to get outside. I decided to look outside, and it appeared that most everyone was on the lifeboat deck. I turned around to see the derrick in flames.

David Young (DPO) was putting on bunker gear and I gave him a hand. He told me that Dale Burkeen was on the deck after being thrown from the crane. He started up the stairs but the heat was so intense, he could not keep going.

Everyone was trying to decide if we were abandoning ship or not. I talked to Matt Hughes (Floorhand) who was trying to jump over the handrail, and was able to coax him back inside. But then there was another small explosion and he took a running start and hurdled over. Stan Carden had rescued someone and brought him from the back of the rig, and he was asking for someone to help him go back inside to look for other people. I couldn't force myself to go back inside a burning rig not knowing the extent of the damage. He disappeared and eventually reappeared with another person.

At this point, I realized that I had not brought out any of my emergency equipment. There did not seem to be any injuries being reported, so I wasn't too concerned at the time. The one thing I wish I could have done different was to have gone back in for some of my equipment. Little did I know there were three severe injuries I would be dealing with later, as well as Jimmy having chest pains.

Once the decision was made to abandon ship, everyone started getting in lifeboats. This was uncomfortable and crammed, but tolerable. I was okay, until one of the VIPs got in and Buddy Trahan had a huge gash on his neck that did not appear as though he should be alive. He also had a broken leg and was slid into the boat. I could not get to him and several people were a bit unsettled at his injuries. I was one of the last ones in and it seemed all except three or four seats were full when I got in.

The lifeboat was deployed and we went to the nearby *Damon Bankston*. I'm not small and it wasn't the easiest task getting out. But even harder was the approximate 250 deadweight pounds of Buddy with the gash in his neck and broken leg. I waited for last, and asked a couple of people to help get him out. We finally did. We all got on deck and immediately a roll-call was started. I asked Carl Taylor (Radio Operator) how many were missing. He replied, "Eleven missing." I knew some had jumped in the water and hoped they would show up.

Onboard the *Bankston*, I was given a small room to treat wounds for the four most severe injuries—Buddy, Jimmy, one of the ETs (Electronic Technicians) who didn't know who or where he was, and one of the toughest men I have ever encountered, Wymon Wheeler. We also had 18 others with minor injuries and scrapes who were given ice packs, and quick treatment. I was tending to the main four, making continual rounds with the help of Troy Hadaway (Rig Safety Training Coordinator), but felt helpless without equipment.

The first I sent off by Coast Guard Medivac was the Buddy Trahan due to the severity of his injuries—the most life-threatening. The second tagged to go would have been Jimmy, but he adamantly refused; he wasn't leaving his crew! Instead, I sent the ET, because of his head injury. Most of the minors were airlifted to a nearby rig, while the major injuries had to be flown to a New Orleans hospital. It took U.S. Coast Guard helicopters about 30-40 minutes, roundtrip, as best I remember. Then Wymon. He was the last to go, but probably had the most painful injuries of all. I could not believe how well he handled himself with two broken femurs, the hardest bones in the human body. He left about 0300, and was the last patient I had.

Everyone else onboard reported no injuries, and Jimmy promised me his pain was relieved. I had quit smoking, but wanted a cigarette badly. I found one, but everyone quickly ran out. Most of us sat on the back of the boat watching the *Horizon* burn. Our home away from home. Many memories in my short time as well as all my possessions.

Shortly, the sun was coming up and the *Bankston* crew did what they could to accommodate us with meals and sleeping quarters. Most of us did not get a bed and remained on the deck. No one was allowed to use the telephone.

The U.S. Coast Guard arrived and insisted that the boat be stopped and to not proceed any further until they retrieved individual statements from each of us. I am not sure how long this took, but it was not quick. Then, a helicopter arrived with water, cigarettes, snack foods, which improved morale . . . until the remaining VIPs boarded the helicopter and fled to shore. We finally made landfall about 0500 on April 22nd. At this point, I had been awake about 30 hours.

Transocean had a lot of people waiting on us with food and water, but they didn't seem to understand that we all wanted to talk to our families, and they were still hesitant to let us use the phone! I was then dropped at a hotel, had to interview with a psychologist and our company Doctor. I grabbed some breakfast and headed to the hotel's computer. I was for sure thinking everyone would be on them, but they were free. I was able to log on and post on Facebook that I was fine. Finally, I headed to the room and got some sleep. I awoke to a meeting with more Transocean representatives who told me my phone and laptop would be replaced and they got me on a plane home without an ID. I still had my lifejacket that said *MEDIC* on it, and told them I would be keeping it. I later found out I had my set of keys to the rig. I had one of two master keys for the whole rig and still have both of these items—the lifejacket and keys—today.

I was relieved to finally be home, but could not quit dwelling on what happened. I knew that God was watching me that day because the explosion stopped right outside my door where the oxygen bottles were stored. I am thankful to still be alive.

To this day, I often see faces that I think are someone I was with on the *Horizon*. This still happens occasionally. I knew all 11, but knew Wyatt, Karl, Shane and Adam the best as a result of training them for emergencies on Sundays. Dale also from our smoke breaks. Seems like I see their faces here and there. I am thankful that those in my care all survived. I hope and pray that the families that suffered the losses have been able to cope, somehow.

Carl Taylor (*Deepwater Horizon* Radio Operator)

I arrived on the rig Wednesday, April 14th, 2010. My crew change was with the Drill C-Crew. The first day on the rig for the Radio Operator is always hectic. I have a short time to generate the day's POB (personnel on board), plan the personnel for the next day's helicopter arrival and departure, assign bunks for the oncoming personnel that do not have permanent bunks, set-up payroll, check and arrange travel for incoming employees as well as employees needing travel arrangements for schools they may be attending on their days off.

Over the next few days, Schlumberger was scheduled to go in and the Tank Cleaners were scheduled to come out. Thursday and Friday, I had opportunity to speak with B-Crew and others that were already on the rig prior to my arrival.

Part of my responsibilities included requests from the OIM for things, such as filling out paperwork on promotions, demotions, transfers and terminations. Monday morning, Jimmy Harrell, OIM, came into my office and told me to fill out promotion paperwork for Stephen Curtis to Assistant Driller, and Brandon Burgess to Toolpusher. After doing the paperwork, I took it to Jimmy's office for his signature. Not sure if Jimmy returned the paperwork for me to send to Houston. Brandon was to be moved up to Toolpusher as Jason Anderson was going to a position on the *Discoverer Spirit*.

Tuesday morning, April 20, 2010, started out like most other weekdays, with the exception of having to get ready for several VIPs coming to the rig. This is always a headache for me because every one of them wants a private room. Luckily, the rig was fairly empty of extra personnel, and I was able to accommodate most of them. As usual, after dinner, I wandered around a little and ended up in my room around 7:30 p.m. I watched a little TV and was asleep by 8:30 p.m. That night started out no different than any other.

I was asleep for an hour or so when I was awakened by a jarring of the rig and an announcement of a fire on the rig floor and everyone to muster in the galley. Before I could get out of bed, the second explosion occurred. It literally blew me out of the bed and I ended up near my locker. As I pulled myself together, I was able to get my street clothes on. I exited my bedroom and looked down the hall toward the galley and immediately knew we would not muster there. The pipe conveyor that used to sit on the main deck [above] was now sitting in the middle of the galley. The atmosphere had already filled with the smell of gas and was thick with grit and sand particles that burned and scratched my throat and lungs as I tried to breathe. Vision was extremely limited and people were running, hollering, and praying.

I tried to get into my office to get my hands on the day's POB list. I knew we would need the POB on the bridge to take muster. My office was just next door to my bedroom, but I was unable to get into my office. So, I proceeded to the bridge to find the master POB.

There was a lot happening on the bridge and I saw some real heroes and leaders in action that may not tell their part of the story. There were people panicking and there were people with very cool heads. Andrea Fleytas was very calm. She helped me find the master POB, and afterwards, was the one making the Mayday calls. If it had not been for Nick Wilson, David Sims would have gone down with the rig, still on the bridge; he was not going to leave. Nick literally drug him off the bridge. David Sims was in worse shape than Mike Williams as far as being hysterical and panicked.

I made it to the *Bankston* workboat with the master POB. After taking at least four musters, I had nailed down the eleven people missing. This was known by 1:00 a.m.!

We sat on the cold, metal deck of the *Bankston*, watching the *Horizon* burn and begin sinking with our missing brothers still onboard until after daylight. As it was sinking, we began at idle speed towards New Orleans. A few people were able to grab their cell phones when we abandoned, but there was no service, and they would not let anyone use the boat telephones. I guess they did not want us talking to anyone. Still at idle speed we made at least three stops at different platforms. One to supposedly take on supplies, one to take the VIPs off, and one to let the Coast Guard board.

I was on the *Horizon* about four years and enjoyed it. I met a lot of good people. It's so hard for that to outweigh the negative parts of that night. I was the Radio Operator and didn't know crap about drilling, but I knew everyone that was on that rig.

Jerry Isaac (*Deepwater Horizon* Mechanical Supervisor)

I was over the Engineers, Welders, and Mechanics. At 5:00 p.m. that day, I was laying under the iron roughneck on the rig floor. All my mechanics were tied up and they knew the Drill Crew was having problems on the rig floor. At 5:00, I got finished changing out the hose in the belly pan. I gave Steve Curtis the thumbs-up and he saluted me. That was the last time I saw Steve, last time I saw him and Dewey because I had a Supervisors' meeting and had to leave the rig floor.

Me and Steve went to Ohio bow hunting every year. Steve and I were as close as two brothers could ever think about being. Him and his son, Trevor, came up and dove hunted with us every year. Thank God, I was able to come back and deal with my cows here, because this has been the only sanity I have been able to get out of this entire thing.

Micah Sandel (*Deepwater Horizon* Crane Operator)

I watched from gantry crane all the guys trying so hard to save our lives! I watched Don Clark run from the riser deck, where the bucking unit was, up to the rig floor and into the fire and try to help. I watched Dale put the crane down and run down toward the rig floor.

I watched Steve, Jason, and Dewey. I didn't see anyone else on the floor...and I watched everything that happened, and when it all blew up, that was it...I tried to get back to where Dale was, but the fire was so intense. I don't consider myself a hero at all. I was scared.

I will never forget what they—Jason, Don, Steve, Karl, Roy, Dale, Shane—did for me and family. Thank y'all.

Nick Wilson (*Deepwater Horizon* BP Logistics Coordinator)

I had been on-hitch 14 days. Bob (Kaluza) came out to relieve Ronnie (Sepulvado). Ronnie had to fly in for Well Control School. They spent a bit of time handing over that weekend, so it wasn't like Ronnie said, "Bob, here's the rig. By the way, your tower starts at 6:00 p.m." Some people would like to think that's the way it happened, but that's not the case.

My room onboard the rig was 243. After the first explosion, I got up from the floor, grabbed my flashlight, opened the safe and grabbed the Pelican case with the Iridium satellite phone in it, and headed up to the bridge. I could have gotten more of my personal effects, but they were not important at the time. I knew that if I could get outside and get that phone out, I could use it to get us help coming and that was my sole intent.

I had the only working phone on the entire vessel. We tested it each hitch during our fire drills and through our repetitive training each week, and I remembered to use it.

I got up to the bridge and told Curt [*Deepwater Horizon* Captain], "I'm going to step out and make a phone call." I stepped out onto the wing deck walkway that went around the bridge, next to where the Weatherford container was stored. I am looking up at the derrick and thought to myself, *there are 1,000 gallons of aviation fuel sitting just here next to me.*

I called the guys at the dock. Normally, they would answer and put you straight on hold. I said, "Hey, this is Nick on the rig. I cannot hold! This is important! I need to talk!" Because sometimes, the Logistics guy may answer or one of the other guys would. I said, "Hey look, the rig is on fire"

He said, "What?"

I said, "There are f***ing flames shooting out of the f***ing derrick, the f***ing rig is on fire!" He was stunned. I said, "Call who you need to call to get everything activated. What do we have in the area?" He started naming off the ones that were at NaKika and Thunderhorse. I said, "Good. You may as well call and get the S61, but let me go back in here and find some things out and I will call you back," and hung up.

We normally flew S92 helicopters to and from the rig out of PHI in Houma, Louisiana, but we also had an S61 Cougar always on standby for Search and Rescue.

After I hung up, I am standing there watching the fire shooting out of the derrick. I remember two people walking by. I could tell someone was hurt and the other guy was helping him walk. As they walked by me, I looked down on the deck and remembered thinking to myself, *God, I hope these guys don't fall down because I don't want to have to write a traction report for someone tripping and falling right now.* Your mind always goes back to the basics.

I went back into the bridge and told Curt, "Hey, I got in touch with the Shorebase. They are notified. We have help on the way and there are some boats in the field that will start moving this way as well as possibly the S61 may be getting in the air."

Curt asked, "Where are they going to land?"

"We can use NaKika," I said, "or Thunderhorse as a staging area if we need to."

He said, "We are evacuating."

"Okay," I replied, "I will get with Shorebase and let them know what is going on."

I went back outside and called the guys again. "It has gotten worse and we have started to evacuate the rig. I will call you back when I get on the boat when I know more information."

I happened to turn around and look down, and I saw stuff floating in the water. I said to myself, *That's people!* I was seeing the reflective tape on the life jackets. For the longest time, that image has haunted me. I have nightmares thinking that it was some of our guys floating in the water, dead. Every now and then, my dreams take me back to that point in time.

The bridge was completely blacked out due to the loss of power. Curt, Yancy, Andrea, Carl, David Sims, Pat O' Brian were on the bridge. Some conversations I was not privy to or didn't overhear, but I do remember all of them being on the bridge at the time of the incident. Yancy and Andrea were trying to do what they could with the station-keeping.

Curt said, "Y'all need to get to the lifeboats." There was some discussion, and I looked at David Sims and said, "You get in my ass pocket, right here behind me and Pat, you get behind David and we are going to go out and down this set of stairs and get to the lifeboat. We are not stopping until we get there!"

I headed out with David and Pat for the lifeboats. I opened the starboard-side door leading out of the bridge and stopped. I am looking at the fire coming out of the derrick. I recalled being a child and looking out the door at the hard rain, thinking that maybe it will subside and I can take off. My mind was wanting me to stay until the fire calmed down some and when it did, we would run. This thing wasn't dying down. *We have to go, now!* Hit the door, hugged the handrail with the guys following me and got down to the lifeboat deck.

t 1 had already launched, so we went to Lifeboat 2. We boarded the lifeboat, llowed with Buddy Trahan, and Jimmy Harrell came into the boat sed the door and launched. I was sitting on the inside next to

Patrick Morgan and just directly across from me was Jimmy Harrell and next to him was Buddy Trahan. When Buddy leaned over, there was a gash in his neck by his collar bone that you could have fit a coffee mug inside of.

Patrick said, "Mr. Buddy, why don't you lean back up some?"

He replied, "I'm halfway comfortable like this," as he leaned over propping himself up on his arms.

I remember Jimmy saying, "Somebody get me some water so I can get this shit out of my eyes." He said his eyes were burning.

Someone said, "Try not to rub your eyes. That's insulation in your eyes and it's going to burn."

"Someone get me some damn water so I can wash it out," he asked again.

I wasn't even supposed to be onboard. I was filling in for Mike Dunn that had been accepted into the Wellsite Leaders of the Future program. Ricky Dendy (BP Logistics Coordinator and Mike's replacement) and I had decided that we would work the schedule around when Mike departed. So, in essence, I wasn't supposed to be there.

Survivor's guilt does bother me a lot. What if I had been on the rig floor with Ronnie when it happened? It may have been 13 people instead of 11 with myself and Ronnie Sepulvado being the other two.

Mike Jones, *NaKika* Medic

I remember it like it was last night. After a full day of 16 hours, I went to bed about 2145 [9:45 p.m.]. I was just dozing off when the Barge Supervisor came in, told me the *Horizon* had blown up, was on fire, and to expect 126 people. I jumped up, dressed, and went to sickbay. In a few minutes, HSSE/Rob Doherty showed up and said I didn't have room in sickbay. I told him we would move to the TV room on the first floor and set up. Seemed like a couple minutes and the Dynamic deck crew walked in and asked, "What do you want moved?" We moved all my supplies down to the TV/Galley area, and pulled the divider making two rooms. Our TS Operator was also an LVN, and asked what he could do. I told him he would be triage. We set up the back of the TV room for red tags, the front for yellow tags, the helicopter waiting room for green or walking wounded and in case we had some expectants, an SCBA (self-contained breathing apparatus) room with a guard on each door.

Everything had been set up, checked and rechecked, and we just were waiting for word. At 0100, Rob came back saying a Cougar S92 chopper had two patients coming our way; one was confirmed burns, other not sure. At 0115, Buddy Trahan arrived in a Stokes basket. He had serious burns, an open fracture, and was in shock. After aggressive treatment, I had time to visit with him. He named all but two of the 11 guys, stating the they [the two] were Mud Company guys and on loan from *Thunderhorse*.

I had someone with each of the patients the whole time they were here. These people would talk to them, get phone numbers and call to let their loved ones know they were okay and safe on *NaKika*. I got embarrassed cause one Planner told Buddy, "Look, Mike is the best Medic in the Gulf. You are in great hands." Hard to be humble after that, don't you know.

So, as soon as we could get a bird free, we shipped Buddy and three others to the burn center in Mobile Bay. An hour later, we moved two more, then by 0430, all ten had been flown out, with the last six sent to West Jeff. Thankfully, we never did get the whole crew. We were set up just in case, and it took a team to receive the injured, provide the care we could, comfort them, call their families and yes, food and drink for those who were cleared for it. Then safe transport back to a bird for the ride to a hospital for definitive care. Several of us went 36 hours non-stop.

Once the patients were gone, I was up top with the rest of helideck crew, refueling birds about every 30 to 45 minutes. In 7 days, we refueled 48 helicopters, pumped 18,660 gallons of JP-4 fuel, we fed each crew snacks or meals through the whole thing. During this time, we could see the flames and smoke from Horizon, and I was on deck when she went down. It was a very somber time for the platform as we are all brothers in this line of work.

I have heard from different people about five of my patients: Buddy survived, had heart issues and retired. Many of the others recovered, and only one went back to work in the Gulf. I think of that night often and wonder if we could have done anything different. But, the same answer keeps coming back: We reacted to the situation, provided the best care and comfort we could, and moved them on safely to others to continue what we had started. The galley crew, crane crew, construction crew all played a big part. Even those who didn't get woken up for the initial response, when they got up the next morning, they stepped in to relieve those who had been up.

Injustice, the American Way

"...in BP. We care about the small people."
~~Carl-Henric Svanberg[28]

After the *Deepwater Horizon* sunk, as hours turned into days, the hopes of finding survivors began to sink also. For the eleven families of the men killed in action, losing their loved ones was becoming their new reality. The families of the injured survivors were just beginning to learn how to cope with a new world of pain, scars, and physical, mental, and emotional challenges.

I won't attempt to generalize this process for each family or every person. I think every reader can imagine—if not relate to—something of what it must have been like: To be a wife, a child, a father, a mother, a brother, a sister, a grandpa or grandma, grandchild, niece or nephew, a girlfriend, or even a close friend or neighbor—to hear that news was tough for all the "*Deepwater Horizon* Family", and most of us can *only* imagine. But for these grieving families, the anguish was just beginning.

It started with the maelstrom of 24/7 news. This channel turned ugly almost immediately, and there seemed little that any of these families could do to "change the channel" so to speak. It came in two forms of ugly: The media, via television, newspapers, or internet, and reporters for the same.

While everybody agrees that oil blowing uncontrollably into the Gulf of Mexico is a disaster, it appeared to many devastated families each grieving their lost or injured loved ones that they were all but forgotten in a matter of days.

"A lot of times we felt overshadowed by the actual oil spill instead of the death of those 11 men that we lost," Jason Anderson's widow, Shelley, told CNN.[29]

Another characteristic of our "news media" today—and one likely lost on most news consumers (unless it were to happen to you or someone you loved) is the media's rush to judgment. Even before funeral arrangements had been made, so-called "experts", people who had never set foot on a platform or had never worn a work glove, were laying blame: Blaming this device, this company, and even this person for failing to do this or that. Yes, families even had to hear their deceased's name used in the context of "mistakes" and "human error". News feeds were vying to outdo themselves in reporting "the cause of the accident".

---

[28] Gerhart, Ann. "BP Chairman Talks about the 'Small People,' Further Angering Gulf." <u>The Washington Post</u>. 17 June 2010. http://www.washingtonpost.com/wp-dyn/content/article/2010/06/16/AR2010061605528.html.

[29] Adams, Char. "Wife of Deepwater Horizon Victim Breaks Down as She Recalls Husband's Last Trip Home Before Death: 'Jason, Would Have Never Let Me Worry'", PeopleMovies.com. September 30, 2016. http://people.com/movies/wife-of-deepwater-horizon-victim-breaks-down-in-emotional-interview/

And then there were the reporters. Imagine, if you can, that you just realized that your spouse—scheduled to be in your arms today—was not coming home. Would never be coming home. That life as you knew it only a few hours ago would now be dramatically and forever changed. And out on your lawn appear news vans, setting up their antennae and heading your way. Those first weeks and even months were hell on all the bereaving families. But, their pain was only beginning.

Most people believe that when a loved one is maimed or killed as a result of gross negligence on the parts of the employer or owners or operators of a business, they are afforded some protection under the law. That they have legal recourse to sue for damages—not only for the financial losses of losing the breadwinner, but also for the loss of never having that loved one in your life again. That belief is valid for any business that is on-shore, or within three miles of the coast.

However, if that business is a ship or a platform operating in the open water three or more miles from the shore, the avenues for protection are governed by three specific Federal laws, one passed prior to the Civil War and two passed just after World War I! I'll discuss how these antiquated laws were used by the corporate legal teams to limit their liabilities later. But I wanted to explain how, for the 115 people who survived the *Deepwater Horizon*, that the nightmare continued to be unnecessarily prolonged.

The PSV *Damon B. Bankston*, a supply ship owned by Tidewater Marine, was on location to assist with loading and unloading for the temporary abandonment of the Macondo well. After the explosions and fires, the *Bankston* mustered all hands and sent their own rescue craft into the waters to search and retrieve survivors.

As survivors boarded the *Damon B. Bankston*, the roster was checked. Injured were triaged and treated as best as possible in the *Bankston* medical room. The most seriously injured were airlifted by U.S. Coast Guard helicopter. Now, one would think that rushing these brave survivors ashore to reunite them with families would be a top priority. It was not. In fact, they weren't even allowed to call their families, and it appeared that the trauma and duress these survivors had just experienced was ignored. It started with the *Damon B. Bankston* having to remain on-scene near the still burning *Horizon* until a vessel from the USCG arrived to take over crisis management. One survivor described the experience like being forced to watch your house burn, knowing that family members were still inside. It didn't stop there.

Many hours after the explosions, the *Damon B. Bankston* was ordered to shore. However, even that ride was a delayed, slow-boat trek, making at least two stops at rigs along the way—difficult for people who were completely exhausted and just wanted to be home and in the waiting arms of family.

USCG personnel then boarded the *Damon B. Bankston* and handed every person a report form and required each person to complete their account of everything that had transpired leading up to and during the accident. Every one of these people had been through hell, and were now being required to write detailed reports, in the eerie glow of the burning *Deepwater Horizon*.

Carl Taylor, *Deepwater Horizon* Radio Operator, wrote, "The Coast Guard interviewed every person that was on the rig, all before we got to Fourchon. During my interview, I asked why we had to stay and watch the *Horizon* burn and sink. My interviewer stated that was BP's call, and that with the fast boats and helicopters available, they could have had everyone on shore within two hours.

"We got closer to the Mississippi River and began getting cell service. I was able to borrow a cell phone and call my wife who had been waiting for eighteen hours to find out if I was dead or alive!"

Did you catch that Eighteen hours before finding out whether he was dead or alive! And recall Carl stated that he knew the names of the eleven missing by 1:00 a.m., and that information was relayed up the chain immediately. Still, the families had not been informed.

When the survivors finally arrived on-dock about 20 hours later, the Transocean team was ready with Port-O-Lets set up for each person to undergo a urinalysis test.

"We had been on the *Bankston* for almost twenty hours. There were people without shoes or clothes, and then we were lined up and made take a drug test once onshore. After the drug test, we were bussed to New Orleans, another two-and-a-half hours," Carl continued. "I honestly think our treatment on the *Bankston* was worse than how you would treat a herd of cattle."

They were given bags of sandwiches, a change of clothes, transported to a hotel room to shower, and eventually, a Transocean form—a waiver, of sorts that affirmed, in summary, they knew nothing of what caused the accident, and that they were not injured. They were told that they needed to sign the form before they could go home to their families.

"These men are told they have to sign these statements or they can't go home," said Houston Lawyer, Anthony Buzbee. "I think it's pretty callous, but I'm not surprised by it." Most signed. They were exhausted, physically and emotionally; many, including Steven Davis, had been awake 50 hours straight, or more. He signed just so he could go home.

Seventeen of the 115 rescued sustained injuries that were immediate and obvious. The most seriously injured were airlifted by medevac chopper to trauma centers. Several were released that night, while the more seriously injured required longer treatment. Others sustained injuries that manifested later. Treatment bills mounted; incomes stopped for many.

Matthew Jacobs told CNN, "You have to live your life now taking medicine every day to try to keep the nightmares from coming back. It's always in the back of your mind, and I think about it every day."

One would think that people who'd dedicated the better part of their lives to working hard and working safely for a company, but who had the misfortune of being wounded in the line of duty, would be fully cared for by their employer. Well, I'll let the following letter speak what those companies *really* did to care for their injured employees:

From Buddy J. Trahan, dated Jan. 15, 2013

The Honorable Sarah S. Vance
United States District Court Judge
Eastern District of Louisiana
500 Poydras Street, Room C-255
New Orleans, LA 70130

    Re: *United States v. BP Exploration and Production, Inc.*
             Case Number 2012R00459 and Court Docket Number: 12-CR-00292

Dear Judge Vance:

    I am writing to you in response to the recent letter from the Department of Justice notifying me of my right to submit a written impact statement as a victim of crimes committed by BP arising out of the Macondo well explosion. I write because I was on the rig at the time of the explosion and personally experienced the consequences of BP's criminal conduct on April 20, 2010, and every day thereafter.

    It is incomprehensible that BP will be permitted to settle its criminal liability when, after nearly 3 years of opportunity, it has failed and refused to satisfactorily address the claims of victims injured or killed as a result of its conduct. Simply put, individuals, like myself, and families of individuals who were killed still have claims outstanding against BP that remain unresolved. Indeed, after close to 3 years and countless BP advertisements publicizing its commitment to the victims of the Macondo well explosion, BP has failed and refused to adequately address victims whose lives were irreparably damaged as a result of its conduct. BP has gone so far as to effectively disclaim responsibility by repeatedly telling me to seek my relief from other parties.

[Omitted material]

> Although many people believe that the claims of those directly affected by the explosion would have been the first addressed, that did not happen with me. Instead, BP focused its attention on repairing its public image through billboards, commercials, large donations and publicity stunts. For example, I read that BP paid nearly $5 million dollars for Christmas lights on a boardwalk in Florida and was lauded in business journals for paying hundreds of millions to Gulf Coast luxury condo owners. Yet, I was on the rig at the time of the explosion and despite needing 4 units of blood to survive my injuries, BP told me to look elsewhere when presented with my claim. I am reported to be the most seriously injured survivor of the Macondo well explosion, and, to date, I have not received any restitution for my injuries from BP or any other responsible parties.

While Buddy Trahan is not the spokesperson for all the victims and families, his letter to Judge Vance speaks volumes. Jerry Isaac, *Deepwater Horizon* Mechanical Supervisor, wrote, "When the rig blew up and it blew me down that hallway, it blew out that L1 and S5 [spinal disc/vertebrae] that was already bulging."

He continued, "When Transocean called me and told me they were cutting my wages and cutting my insurance out, I said, 'Lady, the rig manager told me it might take me six months and it might take me a year to get my life back together. Then they called me a month and a half later and gave me the date I had to be back on the rig or I was terminated.' I said, 'Lady, I am having problems with my back right now, but you just made my mind up.' When you lose feeling from your waist down, and you can't pee right and you can't shit right, something's wrong. Then a person is going to cut my wages like I done this to myself? That is not right."

For months and even years, lawsuits were stymied by the three Congressional Acts I mentioned earlier. Specifically, these antiquated laws were:

- The Ship Owners' Liability Act of 1851

    > This Act was passed nearly 170 years ago to promote shipping during a time when the country needed increased shipping to grow the economy.
    > This Act limits a vessel owner's liability to the post-casualty value of the vessel and surviving freight.
    >> **Note:** The Act was used after the sinking of the *Titanic* to limit the ship owners' liability to the value of the handful of lifeboats that survived and the fraction of freight that was recovered.
    > On May 13, 2010, Transocean filed a petition in Admiralty to limit its total liability to $26,764,083 (~$26.8M) under this Act.

- The Death on the High Seas Act (DOHSA) of 1920

> This Act normally permits only a civil action in Admiralty where a death results from a wrongful act or negligence and allows fair compensation for pecuniary losses only.
>   - "Pecuniary losses" include loss of financial support, loss of services of the decedent, loss of inheritance, and funeral expenses.
>   - "Non-pecuniary damages" consist of compensation for loss of society, loss of consortium and punitive damages.
> "DOHSA has been the exclusive remedy for the family members of those killed in international waters, meaning neither state wrongful death statutes, nor maritime law may supplement the provided remedies."[30]

- The Jones Act of 1920

    > The Jones Act governs recoveries for wrongful death and survival actions against the employer of a seaman for pecuniary losses.
    > It is not the exclusive action and does not preclude other remedies.

None of the companies responsible for the accident could ever bring back the lost sons, husbands, brothers, fathers, or heal the wounds of the broken; however, by failing to reach out to the survivors and families, BP and Transocean continued perpetrating injury.

"The only communication we have had with British Petroleum are the two plants sent to my husband's memorial and two representatives that identified themselves as BP people," wrote Shelley Anderson, widow of Transocean drilling supervisor Jason Anderson. "We have seen the commercials on TV that say BP is going to 'make this right.' They are going to do 'whatever it takes.' If anything, they have made things worse and serve as a constant reminder that they are doing 'whatever it takes' to not 'make this right'."

Congress tried to right some of the wrong, and several bills were drafted. House Resolution (H.R.) 5503, "Securing Protections for the Injured from the Limitations on Liability (SPILL) Act" was submitted in June 2010 and passed by the House of Representatives.[31] The SPILL Act was given to the Senate; Senate Bill S3600-111 (Fairness in Admiralty and Maritime Law Act) was a drafted, introduced, and promptly referred to the Senate Committee on Commerce, Science, and Transportation. There it has essentially died. Enter in the lobbyists.

The offshore oil and gas companies had odd bedfellows in lobby efforts to thwart any reform to the three antiquated Acts of Congress: the cruise line industry. In

---

[30] Linser, Ryan. *Ensuring Adequate Compensation to the Victims of the Deepwater Horizon Explosion: Who Says You Can't Teach an Old Dog New Tricks?"* 45 J. Marshall L. Rev. 515 (2012) http://repository.jmls.edu/lawreview/vol45/iss2/12.
[31] Ibid.

fact, the "cruise industry spent $2.2 million fighting these changes. The Carnival cruise line company alone has donated more than $400,000 since 2007 to members of Congress from both parties, according to the Center for Responsive Politics."[32] Likely the results of effective lobbying efforts from the cruise line industry, perhaps other maritime interests, and most certainly, the offshore oil and gas industry—other than HR 5503 being passed by the House in July 2010—no legislative reform has come out of the Congress to rectify the blatant legal disparity of protections afforded workers (and travelers) on land versus those off-shore beyond three miles.

The pre-Civil War Act protecting maritime interests for the good of the fledgling U.S. economy, or the DOHSA and Jones Act passed in the 1920s to provide *something* to widows (i.e. pecuniary damages) need to be repealed or amended to reflect 20th century realities. This situation defies reason and logical explanation: That a person's status of protection from gross negligence and willful misconduct suddenly changes the instant the "magic line" of three miles into the water is crossed!

Fortunately, the *Deepwater Horizon's* injured survivors and the 11 families of those killed began to settle with BP, et al. Certainly, no amount of money will adequately replace the loss of their loved ones, or rectify the trauma and debilitating injuries sustained because of the accident. However, some fair measure of compensation for the pain and suffering is due. Hopefully, these settlements, along with other imposed damages, will sway all offshore companies to exercise all means practical to assure the safety of their crews.

---

[32] Walker, Jim. "Death On The High Seas Act Protects BP and Cruise Lines at the Grieving Family's Expense". Jim Walker's Cruise Law News. Posted June 16, 2010.
http://www.cruiselawnews.com/2010/06/articles/maritime-death/death-on-the-high-seas-act-protects-bp-and-cruise-lines-at-the-grieving-familys-expense/)

Chris

That motherf###er [Chris Munger] was one strong bastard! Having him around was like having a portable winch. And he had a college degree in Communications. Brains and Brawn. Don't get on this guy's bad side!

Peter Cyr

I remember when Chris broke that marine department 36-inch aluminum pipe wrench. I was holding back-up with a steel one and he just lifted up an POW! It snapped! He turned to Paul Vaughn and looked down at him, handed him the handle, and said, "Sorry I broke yer wrench." Paul didn't know what to say, so he said, "That's ok. I'll get you another one."

Priceless.

David Colson

Chris once held 100 feet of six-inch bulk hose over the side while we replaced the 50-foot section on deck. I wanted to tie it off, but he was like, "No, I got this." He must have been holding at least 400 pounds.

Peter Cyr

I remember him holding me upside down by my ankle straight arm and Allen Seraile the same way with the other arm. Change fell out of my pocket.

Pete French

The Aftermath

I get frustrated having to constantly defend the Horizon and her people...My people...Our people!
~~Delton E. Kennedy, Driller, *Deepwater Horizon*

The effects of the *Deepwater Horizon* accident rippled across the Gulf of Mexico and around the world, and are still being felt today in the offshore oil and gas exploration and production industry. Changes occurred in governmental organizations, company organizations, as well as the leadership of both. There were changes in regulations and governmental oversight, changes in insuring industry assets, legal and contractual changes, changes in technology, operational processes, and contingency plans. Lastly, there were attitudinal changes across the industry, in the halls of politics, and across the social landscape.

While many of these changes brought significant costs to exploration and production, many of them, at least according to the COS (Center for Offshore Safety), have made the industry arguably safer and even more robust.[33]

One of the first major changes was the six-month moratorium on drilling in the entire GoM. On May 30, 2010, U.S. Secretary of the Interior, Ken Salazar, issued a moratorium on all drilling of the OCS (Outer Continental Shelf), or water depths greater than 500 feet, in response to the Macondo well disaster.[34]

This moratorium was met with much alarm from the industry—based on the irreparable economic harm the moratorium would cause—and at least one lawsuit (Hornbeck Offshore Services v. Salazar). The U.S. MMS (Minerals Management Service) cited the legal framework first established by the OCSLA (Outer Continental Shelf Lands Act), granting federal jurisdiction over the OCS. They also cited Title 30, Mineral Resources of the CFR (Code of Federal Regulations) Part 250—Oil and Gas and Sulphur Operations in the Outer Continental Shelf—which granted the Secretary of Interior authority to issue any suspension of operation. The OCSLA also authorized "suspension or temporary prohibition of any operation or activity, including production, pursuant to any lease or permit...if there is a threat of serious, irreparable, or immediate harm or damage to life (including fish and other aquatic life), to property, to any mineral deposits (in areas leased or not leased), or to the marine, coastal, or human environment."[35]

The Hornbeck v. Salazar litigation was ruled in favor of the plaintiffs by a Federal Court, finding that the DOI's moratorium was too broad, arbitrary, and not

---

[33] "Establishing a Culture of Safety." Center for Offshore Safety. http://www.centerforoffshoresafety.org/
[34] Lagarde, Jesse. "Moratorium Following the BP Oil Spill." p. 3. http://www.dodsonhooks.com/wp-content/uploads/2014/12/Moratorium-Following-the-BP-Oil-Spill.pdf
[35] Lagarde. pp. 4-5

adequately justified. The Judge granted a temporary injunction to allow resumption of drilling in the GoM.[36] However, that reprieve was short-lived. The DOI rescinded the original moratorium and filed a second one to cover all drilling that utilized BOPs, effectively negating drilling in any waters deeper than 500 feet. This moratorium lasted until October 12, 2010.

The biggest concern in states with heavy offshore presence was that the moratorium threatened the livelihoods of many people directly and indirectly involved with oil and gas exploration and production. Estimates of job losses resulting from the moratorium varied wildly. The State of Louisiana estimated that as many as 318,000 Louisiana residents directly linked to the oil industry (seventeen percent of all jobs in the state) would be adversely affected by the moratorium. Even the Federal government's own estimates (which are arguably not objective) began with an initial estimated loss of 23,000 jobs in the Gulf coast region, but was downgraded later to only 8,000-12,000.[37] I've heard it suggested that having the government estimate the economic damage of its own actions is like having a burglar estimate the total value of the property he stole. Estimates from other studies ranged from 10,000-46,000 jobs lost.

Getting an accurate value of the number of jobs lost due to the moratorium was difficult. There are many people who are dependent upon robust offshore oil and gas exploration and production, directly and indirectly.

Take, for one example, people who produce, store, load, and transport drill pipe. When drilling operations are ongoing, drill pipe is a largescale consumable, and there is a string of people in the "food chain" to get drill pipe to drillships: pipe manufacturers, truckers, pipe yards, longshoremen, supply ship crews. In addition, there are entire businesses built on supporting and servicing the offshore drilling industry: food, water, clothing, and personal gear distributors, warehouses, logistics planners, repair parts and drilling tools distributors, longshoremen, supply ships, aviation transports, maintenance and technical specialists, fuel suppliers, etc. This list is by no means comprehensive, but it gives an idea of some of the people affected by a cessation of offshore drilling. And this doesn't include the businesses that support these workers and their families where they live and work, such as grocery stores, gas stations, restaurants, etc. Even these supporting businesses felt the loss of revenues from their clientele who were directly paid by the offshore industry.

However, even after the moratorium was lifted, getting permits granted proved arduous. As late as February 2011, there were only six permits pending, and none had received approval. A key issue was a drilling company's ability to demonstrate

---

[36] Lagarde. pp. 8-9
[37] Aldy, Joseph E., RFF DP 14-27, "The Labor Market Impacts of the 2010 Deepwater Horizon Oil Spill and Offshore Oil Drilling Moratorium", August 15, 2014 (Washington, DC) http://www.rff.org/research/publications/labor-market-impacts-2010-deepwater-horizon-oil-spill-and-offshore-oil

a viable means to respond to a deepwater well blowout and to effectively seal the well. Not only that, the government required redundant capabilities so that a second well blowout in GoM could also be effectively contained and capped without significant harm.

Largely in response to the needs to develop capabilities to contain more than one deepwater well blowout, various GoM operators formed two independent consortiums: Marine Well Containment Co. with 10 member companies,[38] and the Helix Well Containment Co. with 16 GoM deepwater operators.[39] These consortium companies represented an industry collaboration in response to the government's requirement to provide responsive well containment in the GoM's deep waters.

And while these responses appeared to satisfy the requirement for a well-containment solution, and seemed to satisfy the government's requirement and allow drilling permits, there were limitations to their "capping stack" solution, which I will discuss from a Driller's perspective later in this chapter.

Soon after the accident, between the first and second drilling moratoriums, the DOI MMS was reorganized into a leasing arm (the Bureau of Ocean Energy Management, or BOEM), and a regulatory management and enforcement arm (the Bureau of Safety and Environmental Enforcement, or BSEE). This was done largely in response to public criticism of the MMS being responsible for regulating the industry that produces huge revenues for the U.S. Treasury through offshore drilling leases granted by the very same MMS.

In early 2011, the API (American Petroleum Institute) approved the charter of an industry-sponsored group focused exclusively on offshore safety, the Center for Offshore Safety (COS). COS has 25 member companies, including owners, operators, leaseholders, drilling contractors, and service/equipment providers. All current members have successfully completed a COS SEMS (Safety and Environmental Management System) audit by an accredited, independent third-party audit organization to demonstrate they meet or exceed API Recommended Practice 75.[40] [41]

I mentioned earlier that there were technological effects, or technical changes and changes to the ways certain technology had been used. One of the biggest areas of focus was BOPs. The API revamped a recommended practice and issued the API Standard 53, "Blowout Prevention Equipment Systems for Drilling Wells," in November 2012. This new standard added procedures for mandatory testing and

---

[38] Marine Well Containment Co. <http://www.marinewellcontainment.com/>.
[39] Helix Well Containment Co. <htttp://www.hwcg.org/>.
[40] Center for Offshore Safety. <http://www.centerforoffshoresafety.org/>.
[41] Weeden, Scott. "Pressure Control Equipment Redesigned after Macondo Failures: Focus on BOPs." Oil and Gas Investor. <http://www.oilandgasinvestor.com/moving-forward-macondo-five-years-later-789176>.

maintenance of BOPs.[42] Additionally, there has been a reliability BOP database developed where all BOP component and subsystem failures worldwide are reported and tracked to provide industry-wide trending and reliability models for BOP systems. There are also proposed design, construction, maintenance, and inspection changes still being developed for adaptation.

One of the *Deepwater Horizon* crew members, Owen McWhorter, Subsea Engineer, helped retrieve the *Horizon* BOP for failure analyses. After the retrieval, he concluded the following about the BOP:

"Myself and Chris Pleasant were on the *Q4000* when they pulled the *Horizon's* BOP off-bottom after they finally got the well killed and the BOP unlatched.... Chris and I climbed into the work basket and went up to the top of the BOP stack, looked over inside of there, and we saw the shear rams closed. I said to Chris, 'That is one pretty sight.'"

"He said, 'You ain't joking, brother.'"

"'All this time,' I said, 'I have known damn well that those rams closed....'"

"All I will say is that a straight piece of pipe will get sheared every single time in a set of shear rams. But, a second set of shear rams that have been [suggested as] required by regulations now will be doing the same thing as the first set of shear rams—trying to shear a pipe that has been bent as was the situation on the *Horizon*."

Developing technical competencies has also been an area of renewed emphasis. State-of-the-art, onshore training facilities to develop competencies of drilling crews working together encountering a variety of offshore drilling scenarios have been developed. The IADC created a subsidiary, the WCI (Well Control Institute), which focuses on well control, including technologies for automating well kick detections and enabling early detection of well control events.[43] [44]

Owen McWhorter continued his opinion: "If the procedures would have been available and the guys trained on it, the LMRP should have been disconnected when they first saw mud coming out of the hole, going to the crown. But the procedures were not written that way. They were written to close the annular and not to disconnect the LMRP."

---

[42] ENERKNOL RESEARCH, "New Offshore Oil Regulations Respond To Key Failures Of Deepwater Horizon Spill." Breaking Energy.com. 27 April 2015. http://breakingenergy.com/2015/04/27/new-offshore-oil-regulations-respond-to-key-failures-of-deepwater-horizon-spill/. http://breakingenergy.com/2015/04/27/new-offshore-oil-regulations-respond-to-key-failures-of-deepwater-horizon-spill/
[43] "Well Control Institute™ (WCI™)." <http://www.iadc.org/well-control-institute/>.
[44] Ibid.

According to a BOP Technologies article, "A BSEE-sponsored study that looked at the history of blowouts found that, out of eleven deepwater well control incidents, the BOP stack failed to work five times. That does not include shallow water incidents like the 1979 IXTOC I blowout in Campeche Bay, Mexico, where the BOP shear rams failed."[45] Further, this article also recommends against the BSEE-proposed changes for double-shear rams because of the increased BOP weight and footprint, and the risks, such as fatigue-loading on the wellhead. These have been considered, but not adapted.

The total loss of the *Deepwater Horizon* had effects on the insurance rates for all drilling assets, not only in the GoM, but worldwide. Estimates for insurance premium increases resulting from the *Horizon* loss are difficult to quantify, partly because rates were already trending higher before 2010. Insurance rate increases are arguably impossible to tie *directly* to the accident because annual insurance premiums are adjusted based on industry claims over periods of time. Nonetheless, the *Deepwater Horizon* total loss (and the other insurance claims resulting from Macondo well disaster) were huge, and figured into a series of other significant losses across the global oil and gas industry and claims submitted to those who insure them. Some insurers backed out of the offshore business altogether, while others dropped their lines for insuring against third-party liabilities.

Still, some estimates put the average increase to insurance rates for deepwater drillships at $15,000 per day.[46] Many drilling contractors claimed they were paying 20 percent higher premiums, while others estimate 50 percent higher premiums for rigs operating in deepwater and 15 to 25 percent for shallow water rigs. While it may be difficult to evaluate the direct impact to insurance rates for offshore oil and gas exploration and production, the loss of the *Deepwater Horizon* and crew, the Macondo well disaster and ensuing clean-up costs and liabilities, all resulted in significant and long-lasting increases in insurance rates.

Finally, leadership changes also occurred. BP's beleaguered CEO, Tony Hayward, stepped down in July 2010. Transocean's CEO Steven Newman resigned in 2015 after guiding Transocean through five of the most challenging years of its history. On the government side, while not attributed to the U.S. Government's mishandling of the Macondo well disaster clean-up, DOI Secretary Ken Salazar resigned in 2013; this occurred after the DOI reorganization, the announcement and early phases of implementing the five-year plan for offshore oil exploration and production, and approval of GoM oil and gas exploration and production leases and resumption of drilling.

---

[45] "The Last Line of Defense on Oilfield Blowouts Needs to Really Work." BOP Technologies.com. <http://boptechnologies.com/the-last-line-of-defense-on-oilfield-blowouts-needs-to-really-work/>.
[46] Ingersoll, Christina, et al. BP and the Deepwater Horizon Disaster of 2010. MITSloan Management Report 10-110, Rev. 3 Apr 2010.

Certainly, the accident affected many, many people. Nonetheless, despite slumping market prices, the industry continues to recover. Many lessons learned are being taught around the world, not only in classrooms and simulators, but from one rig-hand to another. New technical solutions and processes to prevent an offshore blowout have been developed and continue to be refined. Methods continue to be developed to cap a deepwater well and to contain and capture a worst-case spill. While this tragedy at sea was one of the nation's costliest, there have been industry improvements worldwide that *should have* made the industry safer.

Even with procedural, training, regulatory, best practice, and equipment changes, an event like this could happen again. I have had opportunities to question the effectiveness of some of these solutions in private and public forums.

One specific time that sticks in my mind is the 2013 OTC (Offshore Technology Conference) in Houston, Texas. The OTC is *the* biggest Oil and Gas conference in the world. Every oilfield vendor from every part of the world is there selling everything from "rope and soap", to every conceivable oilfield service, any equipment imaginable, and unveiling all the newest technology. I went to attend the Dual Gradient Drilling Workshop.

But there was also a topical luncheon being held on the Deepwater GoM Capping Stack Demonstration. Marty Massey, CEO with MWCC, and Phillip Smith, GM with Shell Emergency Management and Deepwater, were the presenters. Marty discussed the case study information and tied it back to the techniques that were used to cap the Macondo well.

MWCC was proposing to create a conglomerate of most of the large oil and gas operators in the GoM. To do so, these operators and drilling contractors would pay to become members of MWCC. It was a "pay to play" consortium, the benefit being having a response team ready if a well experienced a need for it. However, there were limitations, namely time, equipment, and resources. This was three years after the Macondo well, remember.

All I saw and heard in MWCC's proposal would be a logistical nightmare. After the presentation, however, I patiently listened to the questions posed by engineers from all over the world. I could appreciate their perspectives because collective scrutiny and rigor "proves" concepts.

I waited for the questions to taper off, and stepped up to the line and waited patiently, hoping I could remember my questions because I hadn't written anything down. The gentlemen in front of me stepped away from the mic with a "Thank-you," and then it was my turn to speak.

"First, thank you for this presentation and information," I said. "It shows the true heart and innovation and how so many companies and people can come together in the middle of a crisis." I felt a bit nervous and my voice probably showed it. "But, I do have a question or two. First, I'm sorry if it was mentioned before as I may have missed it, but how big is the footprint of the entire system before it is deployed offshore?"

Marty explained that it would be placed onto multiple vessels in a central location and dispatched upon need. I don't remember the exact specifics, but whatever were the specific sizes mentioned made my jaw drop. In 2013, I had 19 years of hands-on experience—drilling, R&D, upgrade and repair—so I was used to "big stuff", but this looked like an impossible monster to deploy.

"Mr. Massey," I said, "just from deploying dual gradient equipment, I understand that the footprint that you just mentioned is most certainly not going to be achievable overnight, and while this system is being prepared for deployment, the well is flowing at whatever rate it would like." The room became immediately silent as Marty stated they had special teams developed and trained to minimize the reaction and deployment times.

"Okay. Thank you. Now for my second question. How many of these systems are in existence at the moment?"

"One 10K [10,000psi] system," Mr. Massey responded.

I stood there in complete amazement now. I knew that there had been developments and equipment on their way, but we were three years down the road now! And, as a human race of very smart people, have we not come up with a better idea than this? I am not knocking the industry for how slow we are to innovate. We are not the "Speedy Gonzalez" industry when it comes to new techniques. *But, after the largest oil and gas disaster in the history of drilling in the Gulf of Mexico, this was all we had?*

"That's all gentlemen," I said. "Thank you for your time." I turned and walked away from the mic, grabbed my bag next to the table, and exited the room. I felt as if we were no closer to having a viable solution to help in the event of a blowout than we were three years ago. I knew that my feelings were swayed because of my personal connection, but kind of felt short-changed.

Sometime later, I was involved in a well control simulation with a client in Kuala Lumpur. This client had paid for a consultant from Wild Well Control to sit in and advise during the exercise. My relief was still on-seat, so I quietly sat behind him to observe the scenario play out: First the well kicked, then the BOPs failed, then they couldn't unlatch. So, I slid my chair up next to my relief and told him to slack off the tensioners and fail the riser, then drive away with the ship.

He looked at me. I could tell it bothered him to go to that option, but he did it anyway. He failed the riser and moved the vessel off-location just enough to get everyone safely off the rig. Now it was Wild Well Control's turn to step in and tell us about the deployment of their capping system. I sat and listened to the mobilization plans, the logistical plans, and the overall way that it was going to be contained. I asked my relief to ask them, where the capping stack was located. They told us it was in Europe. Not even in Asia! To my amazement, this didn't seem to bother anyone in the room because this was just a drill, but understand that getting permits, flying equipment like that into country, getting it onto a boat and getting out to location takes more than just weeks.

We ended the scenario and I pulled the drilling manager to the side and said, "Look, if you're entertaining this capping stack method, you better have it in-country and it needs to be ready to be deployed overnight, not flown in from other countries. The logistical part of this is a killer and you need to be better prepared." He agreed.

Now this technique, albeit new-sounding, is not actually new. It's the same way we have been controlling wells since the '30s, and the invention of the first "ram type" preventer by Cameron. But now it was changing like a chameleon into something that was upwards of millions of dollars to deploy and hundreds of thousands of dollars to reserve as a contingency for an operation.

Time and again, I always come back to the same preventative solution: Good engineers design good wells that are not approved unless they are. The simple matter of fact is that when things are done properly, in a method where the engineering can be proven, drilling operations can and will be performed safely. If not, then the kneejerk reaction is to engineer the life out of it. Like I said before, I appreciate the technology, but in wells that are even the least bit complicated, this capping stack system needs to be developed and installed onboard vessels, the crews need to be trained and able to use it right that minute. Doing the right thing right the first time on every well, while following the proper process, is the *tried and true* solution.

Blue Eyes

Jason would often say on his last little bit of tour before he was getting ready to leave, "Yeah, getting packed-up to head home to see Blue Eyes." I never knew how close those words would hit home with me until I met his wife, Shelley, for the first time in Jackson, Mississippi. It was during the Transocean memorial held for the guys that were lost, May 25, 2010.

I had flown in from Newfoundland, met one of my colleagues, Katy Holst, from Deer Lodge, Montana. She used to work with us on the Horizon as a rig engineer. We rode over to together to the Jackson Convention Complex. I had been gone from the rig for just over two years, but I had kept in contact with everyone that I used to work with. As we were walking through the breezeway, I looked at Katy. She asked, "You okay?"

I took a deep breath. "This is going to be one of the hardest things in my life, Katy girl."

She grabbed my shoulder with one hand and said, "I know, but we will do it together, with the rig and everyone else." She smiled.

We went inside and the temperature in the building was super cool, but my skin was warm from nerves. I hadn't seen the team in a long time and never had met some of their families. It was like going to a family reunion for the first time and only knowing my side of the family. The other side of the family were the family members of the crew mates I had worked with for so long and never met.

As we went through the doors, we were handed the blue ribbons with the Deepwater Horizon and 11 gold stars. I pinned it to my shirt thinking, "This is what's left of my crew?" I broke down crying, but kept walking.

There were many people already inside, but the crew members and families began to take seats as I moved up closer. I sat in front of James Musgrove (51) from Kountze, Texas, one of our Roustabouts. I lowered my head as the prayers started; so did the tears. All I could see were their faces, on the rig, the memories flashing back over and over. Mr. James knew I was in a bind. He took a red bandana from his pocket and touched me on the shoulder. "Hey boss man, looks like you need this." I took it from him as he gently squeezed my shoulder and sat down.

There was so much emotion in that room, you could hear tears falling everywhere. With the loss of my mother in January and now losing eight of my rig brothers, I was brought to my knees with despair and so many questions. I knew that the team that I left wouldn't have gotten themselves into this position on their own. I knew there had to be other players involved. And I just knew in my heart that Jason would have done everything in his power to save those guys.

I was sobbing profusely and finally had to get up and walk out into the hallway. I saw a lady with blonde-looking hair holding a tissue, patting her eyes. I walked over to her and she turned around. It was Shelley. Her blue eyes cut right through me, and immediately I recalled Jason's words—"Blue Eyes". All I could do was reach out to her. We embraced with a hug and cried a little.

I finally said, "I'm Greg."

"I know who you are," she said. "Jason thought a lot of you."

"I am so sorry, Shelley."

She was crying softly into my chest, "Why, why did this have to happen?"

"I don't know, Shelly. I wish I knew. Wish I had the answers. Wish they were still here."

Once the service was over, all of the family and crew mates walked upstairs to sit down for dinner. I remember Steve Newman, President of Transocean at the time, led the prayer and spoke a few words. You could still hear the tears falling. I had known Steve for many years. He was a good guy—compassionate about people—and this was hurting him just as much as it was hurting everyone else.

I kissed my kids goodbye the next morning, and boarded a plane back to Newfoundland, gripped with sadness and resentment, a roller coaster of different emotions. Still to this day, my eyes blur up whenever I speak about it.

Greg Williams

Memorials: Our *Horizon*!

"I wish to God I could go back to that rig and do what I used to do."
~~Patrick Morgan, Assistant Driller, *Deepwater Horizon*

Wonderful displays, acts of kindness bestowed on the families, and tributes dedicated to honoring the 11 were amazing. There were candles lit and statues commemorating those lost, crosses placed on the sea floor, crosses placed on beaches, memorial tributes, such as the Annual Jason Anderson Memorial Golf Tournament, wood carvings, and metal etchings. Even people on cruises paused so that flowers could be tossed into the ocean. Rig crews passing the *Horizon's* final location held memorials on their bows and tossed roses into the sea. Each year, rigs all over the world still pause for a moment of silence to respect the anniversary of the accident, then blow their ship's whistle 11 times in memory of the 11 men who perished aboard the *Deepwater Horizon*. This tradition will always continue, at least on any vessel or operation that I manage.

Memorial statues were erected in Fourchon and New Orleans, Louisiana. Transocean commissioned an artist create a statue to honor the fallen 11. Taking photos of each of the men, the artist created an amalgam of them for the statue's head. Before the official unveiling, as the masterpiece was being examined, someone discovered a curious raised circular pattern on the upper right breast pocket. Apparently, so many of the photos of the men had snuff can rings on the pockets and the artist just assumed that ring was part of the coverall design! Today, if you look closely at the statue, you can see the very faint etchings from where he removed the raised ring when it was pointed out to him that wasn't an *actual feature* of the coveralls.[47] Most of us agree that the snuff can ring should have remained since was a more authentic representation.

When Katie Sellers (Williams), *Deepwater Horizon* 2nd Mate and DPO was attending memorials for Dale Burkeen and Dewy Revette, she was inspired to create quilts for surviving family members. Katie wrote, "I had never sewn a day in my life, but am pretty strong-willed, and went out and bought a sewing machine the moment I got home. It took me awhile, but I made that quilt for Andrea Fleytas and gave it to her the night before Jason Anderson's memorial." Katie made it her personal mission to make a quilt for each of the families who had lost someone on the *Horizon*.

When *Horizon's* one-year anniversary loomed closer, Katie and I were working for Anadarko on Transocean's *Discoverer Spirit* with eleven other former *Horizon* crew off the coast of Tonga. It was a day that we were all dreading. Katy wrote the following from that day:

---

[47] Ron Guidry credits the Transocean Headquarters Office facilities manager for sharing the story about the statue.

Wednesday April 20, 2011

1 Year
(Hand Drawn)
Flags Flown Onboard
Discoverer Spirit
In
Honor And Remembrance
Forward Mast On Monkey Island
27° 13.4' N 090° 50.2' W
W. Tonga Green Canyon 726/770 #1
Many Heavy Hearts Today. So Many In My Thoughts And Prayers.
Glances, From My *Horizon* Family, We Know, Nothing Is Said
Our Eyes Say All We Need
Small Talk And Side Glances From The Other Crew Of The *Spirit*
Statue Unveiling In Houston, Tribute Videos, Wreaths
Laid On The Site, News Reports. I Try To Block It All Out And
Focus On Something Else, Anything Else, Pray
Moment of Silence @ 21:49
I Feel Anxious Watching The Clock
Chest Feels Heavy
Met Greg Williams, Toolpusher, Under The Helideck And Sit On
The Old Wooden Porch Swing. Cool Breeze, Calm Night.
We Talk And Reminisce About Our Time, Our *Horizon* Crew, Old Times
Memories, Funny Stories To Drown Out The Internal Ticking Of The Clock...
Waiting For The "Dee Doo" And Moment
Of Silence To Be Announced. We Both Get Quiet. I Start To Feel Nauseous
And Then The Moment
11 Blasts Of The Ship's Whistle
I Count Them As They Sound And With The Last
Blast...Silence, And Then I Break Down. We Both Sit and Sob In Silence. Greg
Scoots Over And Puts
His Arm Around Me. That Was His Drill Crew Before
He Left.
All I Can Say Is "I Miss Them" And Stare Out Over
The Water. "Me, Too," Said Greg.
Mike Dow Came Down From Monkey Island Where
He Recorded The Flags Flying Over The *Spirit*. He Had
Been Crying. We Made Room For Him On The Swing
And All Just Swayed And Sat In Silence.
You Are Missed.

It was strange that I had been assigned to the *Discoverer Spirit* as the Senior Toolpusher, the position Jason Anderson was scheduled to assume just one year earlier. Did I find it hard not to think that I could be here working for Jason? Or, that I could have been sitting where Dewey Revette had been on April 20th, 2010? Most certainly, I did, and not a day goes by that I don't think, "what if?"

In October 2011, Transocean held a contest to name its newest rig in memory of *The 11*. An employee from Egypt, Gihan Awward, won the company-wide contest. The name she submitted? *Honor*.

Perhaps some of the most profoundly honoring words came from Patrick Morgan, *Deepwater Horizon* Assistant Driller. Simply, "I wish to God I could go back to that rig and do what I used to do."

Amen, brother. Amen.

Mike

My best story about Mike Dow was when the drain on the bridge water cooler was clogged. He went and got some of that Liquid Fire drain cleaner from the warehouse. I was sitting at my desk and he was about to pour the drain cleaner into the water fountain. I was like, "Woah! You read the label on that thing? That stuff can violently react with the clog and come back up at you. You need proper PPE to use that!"

I had him go get a chemical apron and some elbow-length chemical gloves. When he got back I told him he needed face protection also and handed him a welding hood from out of my desk. (Why did I have a welding helmet in my desk? Well, you never know when a situation like this will arise when you can use one of these, and this was one of those situations.) So, I had him all decked out, on the bridge, with a rubber apron, rubber gloves that go all the way to your elbows and a welding mask and I've convinced him that this Liquid Fire was the most powerful drain cleaner made. So, he's standing in front of the water cooler all decked out like an armored knight going into battle, or ready to handle nuclear waste, and holding the bottle of drain cleaner at arm's length. I couldn't believe he actually bought all my bullshit, and I was thinking, "Oh man, this needs a picture!"

As soon as he started pouring I took a picture. The flash went off, and he jumped like six feet, back-pedaling so fast he almost fell over. He thought the water fountain had exploded!

I've still got that picture.

Peter Cyr

Deepwater Horizon, The "Movie"

"In the real story of Deepwater Horizon and her crew, truth truly was, and is, more powerful than fiction."
~~Greg Williams

In 2016, a movie was released by both Summit Entertainment and Lionsgate Entertainment, entitled *Deepwater Horizon*. Quite a number of people have seen it, in the U.S. and abroad, so perhaps you've heard of it, or have even seen it. While I'm glad that this tragedy got the national and international recognition in a major motion picture it deserved, I and the rest of the *Horizon* family are highly disappointed that it did not tell the real story. That the script was so far removed from the truth, it just added further injustice to the survivors and families of the *Deepwater Horizon*.

The movie was based, at least in part, on a *New York Times* article that ran December 25, 2010, entitled *Deepwater Horizon's Final Hours.* The survivors and the families of those lost gave little input into the film, if at all. So, if movie producers want to assert they are making a film "based on a true story," it would follow that they should do some due diligence and get the real story, from "jam up" hands, and not a newbie trying to cash in on the heroism of others. The real shame is that those who produced this movie not only missed the *real* story, but they missed a really, really great story!

This is why I have undertaken this effort make the *real* story known: the real story of offshore drilling, the real story of the *Deepwater Horizon*, and the *real* story of the *real* people who crewed that rig, Our Horizon! I am also producing a documentary dedicated to telling the truth about the rig and her crew, about how so many fought to save their fellow crewmates and their rig the night of the blowout. I am blessed to have shared air with some of those very heroes.

Jerry Isaac, *Deepwater Horizon* Mechanical Supervisor on the night of the incident, echoes this sentiment: "None of us wants any recognition. It's about knowing the *true* story."

Micah Sandel, *Deepwater Horizon* Crane Operator, adds, "I just want the truth to be told. Some of the things the movie portrays, like, they are not even close to what happened. What aggravates me the most is that the real heroes—the ones that mean the most—aren't even noted."

All of us from the *Horizon* are family. And, all of us lost something that day. We all lost brothers, brothers with whom we shared six months of our lives out of every year, brothers we watched grow up and mature into respectable hands and people. We all lost family that night. Anyone who works in this business knows exactly what I am talking about.

The words of Andrea Roberts, a Transocean "Green Team" member who supported her *Deepwater Horizon* crew from onshore, has summed it up the most succinctly: "The *Deepwater Horizon* <u>will</u> be remembered, and not just as an oil spill."

Adam

When I saw too many people getting behind the Driller, I would leave. They are trying to push a crew in the back of their mind and they have an AD out there physically doing it and the other one next to them in the AD chair, six screens going at once, and talking on the radio to a Shakerhand. All they need is one more guy in the Drillers' cabin making coffee. So, I interacted more with the Roustabouts and that's where Adam Weise and I became friends.

When I heard Noel Sanchez was from San Antonio, Texas, I thought, "Man now I got another one from the same city." So, we soon became friends. One day, Noel calls me and says, "Hey man meet me down here by the knuckle boom crane." I go over to meet him and there's this guy with him. Noel says, "This is Adam, and he's from San Antonio, too."

I said, "You got to be kidding me. Hey Adam." And I introduced myself. Adams said he was from Yorktown. I said, "Ah yeah, that's cool, man." We all stood there and kept talking a while, 'cuz now we got us a group going. Kinda like those Louisiana boys. Finally got a group of us from the heart of Texas. I finally got me some people!

I tried to make sure I ate lunch with Adam so we could visit. One time, I came in the galley and there was a Happy Birthday cake. I said, "Man, that's nice of you guys to make me a birthday cake." And before I could get to it, Adam cut a big piece out of it. So, I just said, "You're welcome. And yes, you can have that corner piece of my cake."

He said in the calmest voice, "Screw you dude. That's my cake."

I said, "No, today's my birthday.

"No shit? Today's my birthday, also."

I said, "You got to be kidding me."

So here we are from the same area, same birthday. From that day on, it was always Adam and I checking on each other, and making sure the other was doing okay.

Mitch Gill

Conclusion

"One time I was making my rounds and came upon Shane (Roshto). He said 'Man, how do you stay so clean? Every time you come around, you're so clean.' I said, 'Shane, if you ever find me dirty, you better call the Medic because one of two things happened: I have either fallen down, or someone has pushed me off something.' He said, 'Man, I need a job like yours.' I said, 'You do, son, you really do...I won't lie to you.'"
~~Mitch Gill, BP HSE (Bumped from being on the *Deepwater Horizon*, April 20, 2010)

After reading this book, it is my greatest hope that you walk away with a realization that the men and women who worked the decks of the *Deepwater Horizon*, from its design and build in Ulsan to the 2010 tragedy in the Gulf of Mexico, were *real* people. It is also my hope that you will come away with an appreciation and a respect for *Our Horizon* family.

I hope that you can appreciate the perspective from one who learned his way up to that "Driller's chair", as well as from the stories of those who worked together to make amazing finds and to break records.

I hope that I have shown what could have prevented the accident, and how, if it had been implemented or used, could have averted this tragedy. And, most of all, from those who contributed their first-hand accounts of that fateful night, what they lived and saw; and then, the exposure of another tragedy of just how pathetically the *Deepwater Horizon* survivors were treated after the explosions.

To all *Our Horizon* family, I pray I've told the story that you have been deprived of reading for far too long—the *true* story. I hope that this book has brought some of the characters and personalities to life of the true heroes of that wonderful, wonderful rig, the *Deepwater Horizon*!

Appreciation

A heartfelt thank you to content contributors:

Andrea Roberts	Micah Sandel
Bill Francis	Michael Cook
Carl Taylor	Mike Glendenning
Cyndi Johnston	Mike Jones
Daniel Hobson	Mitch Gill
Dave Young	Nick Wilson
David Colson	Owen McWhorter
Delton Kennedy	Patrick Morgan
Dennis Martinez	Pete Cyr
Dustin Brown	Pete French
Greg Meche	Randy Harris
Jaime Rene Serna	Richard Kennedy
Jerry Isaac	Ron Guidry
Katie Sellers (Williams)	Russ Cummings
Mark Whittle	Tracy Kleppinger Melton
Matt Hughes	Tyson Cullum
All the current and past members of the *Deepwater Horizon* Alumni Group for their memories and stories.	

Another huge thank you to the financial contributors:

Mike Glendenning	James and Heather McGee
Carl Taylor	Donnie Williams
Nick and Julia Wilson	Bonnie and Stan Carden
Patrick Morgan	Mike Dow
Mitch Gill	Thomas and Robin Field
Owen Mcwhorter	John O'Malley
Jordan Michalov	Henning Hansen
John Litwinowicz	Hurley Padgett
Amanda Smith	Mustapha Bouaici
Darren Etherington	Joe Welsh
Jimmy Delval	Ronnie and Linda Sepulvado

Thanks to personal mentors and friends who've passed on:

I owe a large amount of credit to all of you for the friendship and the conversations, and for just being good people. Some, I didn't know as personally as others, but all will be dearly missed.

Audy LaRay "Jed" Williamson – Driller	Scott Bruce – Service Operator
James Votaw – Senior Toolpusher	Luther McRaney – Mechanic
Karl Rhodes – Floorhand	Joyce Hollis- Radio operator
Matt Jacobs – Roustabout	Pete Cyr- Chief Mate
Jim Harrell – Bosun	

Glossary of Terms

TERM	DEFINITION
APV	Air Pressure Vessel
Backreaming	An intentional pause in drilling to clean the hole by circulating drilling fluids
Billy Pugh	A basket designed to transfer personnel using a rig crane designed and built by the Billy Pugh Co.
BHA	Bottom Hole Assembly
BOP	Blowout Preventer
Bust-out	Get started, career-wise, in the oilfield
Drilling connection	Connection of drillpipe made to continue drilling deeper
ET	Electronics Technician
Fingerboard	A rack of vertical "pins" that tubulars are stacked vertically for more expeditious connections
Galley	Ship's mess hall, cafeteria, dining hall, etc.
Hitch	Rig hands' work period, such as 20 days on (followed by 10 off) or 14 on and 14 off
HSE	Health, Safety, and Environmental
IADC	International Association of Drilling Contractors
Jam-up	Very good and hard-working; tops
LMRP	Lower Marine Riser Package
Marine Riser	A large-diameter pipe between the bottom of a drilling rig and the BOP through which all well-drilling equipment is passed
Moonpool	An area of the deck open to the water below
MWD	Measurement While Drilling
OIM	Offshore Installation Manager
PLC	Programmable logic controller
PMs	Preventive Maintenance Tasks
POB	Personnel On-Board
Pre-Tour	[Pronounce like "pre-tower"] A meeting of the crew going on tour (i.e. starting their shift) where key elements of the planned activities are discussed
RBS	Raised backup system

TERM	DEFINITION
Roughneck	A member of a rig-floor drilling crew
ROV	Remotely-Operated Vehicle
Stateroom	Small bunk room on a ship
TD	(noun) Total Depth; (verb) Reach the total depth of a drilling section
Tour	[Pronounced like "tower"] A work-shift, usually 12 hours
Tripping pipe	(Or "Making a round trip" or simply "Making a trip") is the physical act of pulling the drill string out of the wellbore and then running it back in
Tubulars	Another term for pipe

Manufactured by Amazon.ca
Bolton, ON